Complex Inequality and 'Working Mothers'

Complex Inequality
and 'Working Mothers'

CLARE O'HAGAN

First published in 2015 by
Cork University Press
Youngline Industrial Estate
Pouladuff Road, Togher
Cork, Ireland

British Library Cataloguing in Publication Data
A CIP catalogue record for this book is available from the British Library.

ISBN 978-1-78205-124-4

Typeset by Tower Books, Ballincollig, County Cork
Printed in Malta by Gutenberg Press

www.corkuniversitypress.com

Contents

Introduction

The aim of this book is to reveal the experiences and practices of Irish women who combine motherhood with paid work, demonstrating the ways 'mother', 'worker' and 'working mother' are normatively constructed in Irish society, and the difficulties, challenges and conflicts women experience by being middle-class 'working mothers'[1] in Ireland. This book reveals a complex system of inequality occurring when women combine motherhood with paid work outside the home in Ireland. These inequalities occur at individual, discursive, social and structural levels and their combination makes it difficult for women to balance working and mothering lives. This complex inequality further reveals a gender system operating in public and private spheres to maintain 'working mothers' in a subordinate position in both.

Until relatively recently the most common division of labour within Irish couples was based on the male breadwinner and female homemaker. However, as a result of the rapid number of women entering the Irish workforce and the professions, dual-earning couples now make up a majority of working-age couples.[2] While societal expectations of women have changed considerably over the past number of decades, an equivalent shift has not occurred with the perceived roles of men. Thus, women often maintain jobs and careers outside the home while retaining primary responsibility for housework and childcare. Meanwhile, parenting (mothering) and paid work have both intensified, so there is less leisure time and a greater expectation of mothers' involvement in children's care and education. Motherhood discourses continue to promote women's role as primary carers, which reveals the persistence of gendered notions of motherhood and caring and a backlash against women's move to a more public role.

There is little Irish scholarship on the ways women combine motherhood with paid work. However, Asher, Di Quinzio and

Badinter[3] have concluded that combining motherhood with paid work is impossible given the way motherhood is constructed in the UK and the US, while other scholars urge women to celebrate their maternity.[4] In the US, Blair-Loy and Stone, and in Europe Jones and McKie, Biese and Jyrkinen have considered the situation of middle-class professional women who have 'opted out'[5] and found that women are really being pushed out by work environments that are hostile to women and the demands of family caregiving. Feminist writers have also considered the social construction of motherhood and the difficulties of conforming to 'ideal mother' roles[6] and the pressure on women to engage in intensive mothering in the US.[7] However, there is little scholarship exploring the ways in which women combine motherhood with paid work as an ongoing way of life.

In the UK, Gatrell explores women's and men's relationships to paid employment following parenthood,[8] as well as the ways newly maternal women negotiate parenting and employment.[9] Miller found that gendered moral rationalities shape women's motherhood behaviours,[10] while Reay exposes the way social inequality is reproduced in women's involvement in their children's schooling.[11] In a recent comparative study of mothers in Northern Ireland and the US, Smyth reveals the ways women negotiate their motherhood roles in both societies and she argues that women exercise agency as normatively committed subjects as well as members of reconsititutive communities. Her analysis explores the ordinary reasoned actions of mothers as they reflect on their routines, interactions and emotional reactions, and demonstrates the dynamic relationship between individual agency and normative complexity. (However, many women in Smyth's study were full-time mothers in the home.[12])

In Ireland, motherhood is contested. Kennedy celebrates many aspects of Irish motherhood,[13] but does not include employment, while White argues that mothers who work outside the home are better treated by the state in taxation and welfare systems than women who mother full-time in the home.[14] However, there is an abundance of media commentary on motherhood and women recognise, negotiate and position themselves in relation to the dominant and competing discourses of traditional and new capitalist motherhood, individualism, feminism and neo-liberalism in constructing themselves as 'working mothers' in Ireland. This book addresses the gap in the literature by exploring how women combine motherhood with paid work in Ireland from a sociological perspective and feminist standpoint, revealing the way middle-class mothers negotiate normative constructions of 'mother', 'worker' and 'working mother'. This work locates women's actions within an intersectional framework which acknowledges women's agency and locates women's choices within the dominant discourses women draw on and within the social structural systems of gender, family, the labour market and the state.

The absence of scholarly literature on women who combine motherhood with paid work in Ireland reflects that 'working mothers' are a relatively recent phenomenon. While significant numbers of married women in the US and UK have been participating in paid work since the 1950s, the legislation that prohibited married women working outside the home in Ireland was only removed as a pre-condition to Ireland's membership of the EU in 1973,[15] resulting in a dramatic increase in the proportion of married women, and specifically mothers, in the labour force thereafter. In 1971 only eight per cent of married women were in the labour force, however, by 2008, sixty-nine per cent of all married women aged between twenty-five and sixty-four were in the labour force.[16] Entering paid employment did not relieve women of their maternal responsibilities, however, and many feminist writers found that women entered the paid labour force only at the expense of taking on a second shift, because they still retained responsibility for childcare and domestic duties.[17] Consequently, forty per cent of Irish women are prevented from achieving a desired balance between employment and care responsibilities.[18] Women who had completed formal education and who worked full-time were over three times more likely than men working full-time to feel that their caring responsibilities did not allow them to do the kind of paid work they wished to do.[19] The European Community Household Panel found that even women who were in full-time employment felt constrained by their care responsibilities in a way men did not.[20]

Perhaps one of the most significant aspects of the interface between family and work is the fact that the values and rationalities of each are diametrically opposed: 'the assumption underlying all highly paid careers is that work will take priority over everything else'.[21] The push for productivity at almost any cost is clearly at odds with the affective priorities of family life.[22] Commitment in the workplace is often judged by the number of hours employees are available to work, and sometimes by the availability of workers for out-of-work socialising. However, caring time is more fluid and responsive and there are very different gendered values attached to productive/work time and caring/process time.[23] Given the realities of limited time, it is difficult to see how family and career commitments cannot come into conflict for women who continue to carry the major responsibility for family functioning. It has also been noted that caring time is gendered[24] and the impact of care work on women's employment is reflected in the fact that women work on average fewer hours than men, and in lower-grade occupations.

When women become mothers, they experience inequalities in families because of their gender, undertaking the greater proportion of housework, childcare and household labour.[25] Where women participate in paid work, they experience inequalities in the workplace because of their gender, earning less and experiencing occupational segregation.[26] Where women with children engage in paid work, these inequalities are not added together, they mutate into new and complex forms of inequality. Women's increased participation in paid work has not guaranteed pay parity with men, and motherhood negatively impacts women's employment while fatherhood has little effect on men's. Whether in paid work or not, women still specialise in family work while men still specialise in market work, because market work continues to be framed around the neo-liberal assumption that ideal workers are unencumbered by care responsibilities.[27] O'Sullivan claims the economy's need for the extra capacity offered by women workers, including mothers, is the macro-level driver behind women's participation, rather than any restructuring of gender roles: 'It remains a workforce designed for a worker with no family responsibilities and good behind-the-scenes support (a male worker in short)'.[28]

Irish society is in a state of flux, with traditional and new capitalist motherhood discourses circulating simultaneously with discourses of neo-liberalism, individualism and feminism. On the surface, these discourses appear to conflict and women are encouraged to both devote copious amounts of time and effort to developing their children, while also to commit themselves to productive paid work. These discourses emanate from, circulate in and shape the institutions of family, workplace and society, while women themselves are positioned differently by these discourses which is reflected in the ways women take up, refuse, contest or reproduce them in their daily lives as 'mothers', 'workers' and 'working mothers'.

Changes in orders of discourse are a precondition for wider processes of social change, which originate from a change in discourse.[29] Fairclough argues that the process of 'changing the subject' can be thought of in terms of the inculcation of new discourses, as people come to 'own' discourses, to position themselves inside them, to act and think and talk and see themselves in terms of new discourses.[30] Discourses which have been effective in wider processes of social change in Ireland, and in changing the subject of women in Irish society, are the discourses of motherhood, neo-liberalism, individualism and feminism.

Women take up discursive positions, subject positions and social positions deriving from these dominant discourses. Subject positions are different from social positions. Social positions are based on structural organisation such as class, race and gender, which circumscribe and access movement into certain subject positions.[31] Motherhood is a discursive position which informs the take up and content of the subject position mother. The particular shape subject positions take depends not only upon their position within wider discourses and institutions but also how they are taken up. Power operates through dominant discourses and shapes women's 'choices' regarding combining motherhood with paid work, and in terms of the explanations and meanings they give to 'mother', 'worker' and 'working mother' and to their experiences. Women

> [U]se aspects of them, reject some, and play a part in framing them, thus assisting in the development and change of discourse. Women are both within and outside discourse at the same time.[32]

Subject positions are the effects of discourse and organisational structures. In this research the discourses of neo-liberalism, motherhood, feminism and individualism are available for distribution and women construct themselves as mothers and workers with reference to these dominant discourses and within the organisational structures of family, workplace and society. Women's everyday practices are examined to explore the ways power operates through discourses and institutions to reproduce the norms of 'ideal worker' and 'ideal mother' as well as the ways women act discursively to position themselves as subjects of discourse. Patriarchy is seen as a hegemonic gender order imposed through individual, collective and institutional behaviours and discourse is the political process through which patriarchal power is exercised.

A considerable challenge in approaching this research was identifying a theoretical framework which would reveal all the complexities of inequality and privilege that women experience at an individual level, identify the causes of these inequalities with reference to the structural social system and demonstrate the way these inequalities are created and maintained. I found the concept of intersectionality a useful analytical tool to examine and theorise the complexity of women's experiences of being 'working mothers'. As Crenshaw originally articulated, intersectionality explained the ways black women workers experienced new and complex forms of inequality because they were invisible to race- or gender-only concepts of discrimination; hence, 'all the blacks are men and all the women are white'.[33] Crenshaw demonstrated that systems of oppression converge to create new and complex forms of inequality which differ from any one form of oppression viewed in isolation. Intersectionality theory emerged from feminist studies of gender inequality and demonstrated that when gender is combined with other grounds, such as race or class, it creates new complex forms of inequality.

Feminist intersectional scholarship highlights the ways in which mainstream ideologies uphold multiple systems of inequality and deny the variation in individuals' life experiences. It is therefore important to dissect nuances in the imagery and the discourses of mainstream paid work and parenting.[34] Women in employment experience inequalities; mothers in the home experience inequalities; when women in employment are also mothers, they experience a new and complex form of inequality, and the purpose of this book is to reveal the extent of this complex inequality and the ways it is created and sustained. This book is based on focus groups and interviews with thirty employed women in a middle-class suburb of a regional city in Ireland. This research explores the situation of women with children of all ages, who are currently employed, some of whom work full-time, some part-time or reduced hours, in a variety of occupations across the public and private sectors, and takes an intersectional approach to reveal the complex inequalities women experience by combining motherhood with paid work.

Women with children who engage in paid work are an under-researched group and are located at the intersection of the categories 'mother' and 'worker'. I apply McCall's concept of intracategorical complexity[35] to explore inequalities and privileges at the level of individual women at the neglected social location of 'working mother' to reveal how the inequalities and privileges experienced at an individual level are created by the variations between women, dependent on their occupation, marital status and class. This approach uncovers the differences and complexities of experience embodied in the social location of 'working mother' as well as revealing the range of diversity and difference within the group of women. This research revealed that women drew on the dominant discourses of neo-liberalism, feminism, motherhood and individualism in explaining and justifying their individual ways of combining motherhood with paid work in Ireland, and their accounts reveal the ways women normatively construct 'mother', 'worker' and 'working mother'.

Inequality, Gender and Class

Equality is a contested concept. According to Lorber, feminists have stressed that gender inequality is not an individual matter, but is deeply ingrained in the structure of societies.[36] Liberal feminists argue that women and men are equal, and should be entitled to equal treatment. The measure of equal as 'the same' takes men's lives as the normative standard and liberal feminism has had some success in breaking down many barriers to women's entry into the labour force, particularly formerly male-dominated jobs and professions.

Radical and cultural feminists claim that women are 'equal but different' from men, sought to valorise women's difference, particularly motherhood, and sought to have an equal value placed on women's difference and had some success in drawing attention to women's reproductive ability as a site of their oppression. Multi-ethnic, post-modern feminism and queer theorists attack the dominant social order through questioning the clarity of the categories that comprise its hierarchies. These feminists argue women are 'equal and different' and deconstruct the interlocking structures of power and privilege that make one group of men dominant, and range everyone else in a complex ladder of increasing disadvantage, thus making no single aspect of inequality more important than any other.[37] Feminist scholars have shown that gender, ethnicity, religion and social class are structurally intertwined relationships.[38] 'Ethnicity, religion, social class and gender comprise a complex hierarchical stratification system in which upper-class, heterosexual, white men and women oppress lower-class women and men of disadvantaged ethnicities and religions'.[39] While multi-ethnic feminism focuses on the effects of location in a system of advantage and disadvantage, social construction feminism looks at the structure of the gendered social order as a whole. It sees gender as a society-wide institution that is built into all the major social organisations of society. As a social institution, gender determines the distribution of power, privileges, and economic resources. In social construction feminist theory, inequality is the core of gender itself: women and men are socially differentiated in order to justify treating them unequally. Lorber claims, 'Ethnicity, religion, social class and gender are the walls and windows of our lives – they structure what we experience, do, feel, see, and ultimately believe about ourselves and others'.[40] The subordinate group is not marked just by gender or by ethnicity or religion, but is in a social location in multiple systems of domination. Men are as oppressed as women, but men and women of disadvantaged groups are often oppressed in different ways. A recognition of multiple categories disturbs that neat polarity of familiar opposites and undercuts the assumption that one category is dominant and one subordinate, one normal and one deviant, one valued and one 'other'.

McCall contends that no single form of inequality can represent the rest, but that some forms of inequality seem to arise from the same conditions that might reduce other forms, including, potentially, a conflict between reducing gender inequality and reducing inequality among women.[41] Allowing women into positions of power in the world of paid work potentially reduces inequality between women and men. However, as not all women have equal access to positions of power in the work-world, this has the potential to create inequalities between women who can and women who cannot access these positions. This research demonstrates the ways in which the same conditions (paid employment and motherhood) privilege and regulate women at the same time, and identifies the social locations and institutional domains in which women are regulated. Following Ferree, I conceptualise gender equality as a concept that takes its meaning from the discursive and institutional contexts in which it appears.[42] This reveals the gender system and gender order operating in Ireland and the ways gender equality is conceptualised by women who normatively construct themselves as mother, worker and 'working mother' in their everyday practices and interactions.

I operationalise the category class in this study through Bourdieu's concept of class stratification.[43] Bourdieu employed the concept of capitals to illustrate how the knowledge and use of economic, cultural and social capitals constitute the markers between dominant and subordinate classes. A capital is the resource, the command of which enables one to exercise and resist domination and to maintain a position in the hierarchy of society. Economic capital, which is access to wealth and purchasing power, is the most important principle of domination in capitalist society; however, economic capital on its own is not sufficient to guarantee social position. Cultural capital is an individual's consumption patterns, taste, manners and aesthetic disposition, which are the result of social origin. Social capital is the network of connections needed to make use of educational achievements and economic capital. Bourdieu asserts the primacy of cultural capital by claiming that social capital and economic capital, though acquired cumulatively over time, are dependent on cultural capital. Capitals moderate the myriad of struggles between classes and class fractions in modern capitalist society and teach people to tailor their expectations and their view of themselves to their appropriate place in the social and economic hierarchy. At the same time, capitals provide people with vehicles to contest the place of a class in the social hierarchy, or to claim a place in a given class.

Bourdieu's concept of social class contributes to understanding how other relations of subordination, especially age and gender, merge with economic and cultural relations of subordination in sublimated forms.[44] Thus, Bourdieu illuminates how multiple forms of subordination articulate with one another. Following Bourdieu, in this study social class is also understood as a series of interconnected processes, rather than as an abstract construct to be analysed or examined within predefined boundaries of enquiry. Women's access to and aspirations with regard to economic, social and cultural capital are markers of their class position. This concept of class stratification is helpful in exposing how 'working mothers' experience intersecting inequalities and privileges in Irish society on the basis of gender and social class.

My interest in this topic initially arose from personal experience. I have twenty years' experience of working in industry, and for eight of those years I was a mother, at the time in my career when I was moving into positions of increasing responsibility. My experience during these years was of being an 'outsider', and having a definite sense of discomfort because no matter how much commitment I demonstrated to my career, I perceived that I was regarded by employers and colleagues as having conflicting priorities, because I was a mother. The experience of being an outsider and knowing at a deep level, no matter how I played the man's game by the man's rules, I would always be 'other' and 'different' because I was a woman and a mother, was frustrating and exhausting. On the other hand, the sense that I was failing as a mother because I was working outside the home contributed to my frustration. In addition to my own personal experience, my observation of friends and colleagues, and their efforts in juggling employment and family responsibilities, generated interest in researching this topic. The absence of literature on the issue of 'working mothers' in Ireland intrigued me, as did women's mostly uncomplaining acceptance of the efforts required of them in order to reconcile motherhood with paid work.

This research is conducted in Ireland, which has a specific, arguably stronger, motherhood ideology, given the historical influence of the Catholic church and that the legal barrier to married women's employment in the Civil Service was only removed in the 1970s. In Chapter 1, the political, legal and policy landscape in which women combine motherhood with paid work in Ireland is outlined. The effects of the dominant discourses of neo-liberalism, individualism, motherhood and feminism on social policy, tax and welfare systems are examined, demonstrating that Irish society is in a state of flux with different discursive strains exerting contradictory pressures on women both to commit themselves to productive paid work and to devote themselves to their families and to rear their children. Within these contradictory pressures, women combine motherhood with paid work with little social support. While there is no universal and generalisable female experience of the workforce, motherhood clearly has a negative effect on women's employment in Ireland. This is not unique to Ireland, but the impact of having children is greater in Ireland than in almost any Organisation for Economic Cooperation and Development (OECD) country.[45] Ireland is indeed no country for 'working mothers'.

Taking an intersectional approach, this research reveals that women experience inequalities and privileges at the neglected social location of 'working mother'. However, identifying and revealing inequalities and privileges does not explain them, and I apply Walby's concept of complexity theory to demonstrate how these inequalities and privileges are anchored in social systems and the ways the social relations of gender, class, motherhood and employment intersect with the institutions of family, workplace and society.[46] My aim in this research is to reveal the operation of power and its effects on women with children who engage in paid work outside the home. Ferree argues that discourse is the political process which promotes and maintains inequalities[47] and I use Foucault's concept of discursive power to demonstrate this.[48] This intersectional analysis was developed and emerged from the complexities of women's experiences as both individuals and as members of the group. This intersectional approach is outlined in Chapter 2.

One of the difficulties of researching women with children who engage in paid work outside the home is that the experiences of women vary significantly from each other, even while there are similarities among women because they are all mothers and all participate in paid work. No more than any other group of women occupying a similar social location, there are similarities deriving from their common positions; however, there are many differences depending on women's employment, family status, occupation and class. In Chapter 3, the thirty women who participated in this study are introduced, as well as the case study, research methodology and research methods. There are particular middle-class values evident in the narratives of these women and the discourses they draw on to explain and justify their individual ways of combining motherhood with paid work. In focus groups, the women were invited to discuss the practical issues that concerned them about being a 'working mother'. Analysis of these discussions revealed that the women drew on motherhood, feminism, neo-liberalism and individualism discourses and this provided the context for individual interviews which were conducted a year later with the same women. This methodology revealed the ways discourses circulate in and shape Irish society, and the ways in which power operates through the discourses of neo-liberalism, individualism, feminism and motherhood, even while there are tensions and contradictions between these discourses, which women refuse, engage with, resist, embrace and accommodate in the ways they combine motherhood and paid work in Ireland.

The process of making the 'right' choice to combine motherhood with paid work is examined in Chapter 4, which reveals the pressures women experience and the difficulties women encounter when choosing to combine motherhood with paid work. The rhetoric of choice is examined, as well as the constraints women experience when they attempt to make choices within conditions not of their own choosing. Women experience contradictory and conflicting pressures in workplaces, in the home and in society. Women take personal responsibility for their choices, which are made with little social support, and blame themselves when their choices result in negative outcomes. Many women's choices amount to no more than a series of unsatisfactory trade-offs, masquerading as individual choice.

Morality and choice are linked, and how women see morality in their choices to combine motherhood with paid work is explored in Chapter 5. Women in this study are the first generation with the 'choice' to combine motherhood with paid work. In the absence of established patterns of mothers' employment, women engage in reflexive moral reasoning and make gendered moral choices when making decisions regarding the ways they will combine motherhood with paid work. Women consider their children, their employers and colleagues, their economic contribution to their families, their partners and societal expectations of mothers, in making decisions and rationalising and justifying their choices.

Dominant motherhood discourses and expectations are examined in Chapter 6, using Oakley's[49] concept of the myth of motherhood. According to this myth, children need mothers, mothers need children and motherhood represents the greatest achievement of a woman's life. Even though Oakley coined 'the myth' in the 1970s, women's accounts in twenty-first-century Ireland demonstrate the extent to which the myth is still promoted in new-capitalist, new-familialism and traditional discourses of motherhood, and women demonstrate the extent to which they have internalised the myth and their efforts in meeting its demands. The women in this research do not challenge any of the three assertions of the myth, but demonstrate that the myth of motherhood persists.

Childcare is central to women's participation in paid work and in Chapter 7, the childcare landscape in Ireland is outlined, revealing the difficulties women experience in sourcing, retaining and paying for childcare. The lack of regulation and support in childcare provision causes problems for 'working mothers' and there are also concerns for the welfare of children in the care of untrained, unregulated childminders, which adds to the pressure 'working mothers' experience. The Irish state's approach to child-care provision reflects the extent to which neo-liberalism is dominant in social policy. The conflict between discourses of neo-liberalism and discourses of motherhood is evident in the childcare landscape which reflects contradictions between women's place in the home and women's participation in paid work.

The relationships of 'working mothers' with their childmin-ders is explored in Chapter 8, which demonstrates that these relationships are complex, occasionally exploitative and some-times emotionally competitive. The different valuations of care when undertaken by mothers and by paid care workers reveals the complexity of the relationship between mothers and care workers and reveals significant differences among and between 'working mothers' and the women they engage to care for their children. Professional and childminding women are produced in relation to each other, and the relationship between 'working mothers' and care workers is hierarchically ordered, with women who provide childcare experiencing greater inequalities than the women whose children they mind. The different treatment of crèche workers and private childminders is explored. Private childminders are outside the remit of the market and some private childminders are also in receipt of welfare payments, which demonstrates the symbiotic relationship between poor childminding women and 'working mothers' and the gendered order of caring in Ireland.

Bourdieu[50] argued that capitals are markers of class position, and women demonstrate their efforts to ensure their children's acquisition of educational, social and cultural capital in Chapter 9. Acquisition of capital is a particular neo-liberal phenomenon, because as Warner argues, 'children appear to face an insecure economic future unless intensively trained to be exemplary capitalist "winners"'.[51] Due to neo-liberal policies and the government's reduction in spending and services, families, mostly mothers, are increasingly responsible for their children's education and acquisition of social and cultural capital in order to ensure their success in competitive Irish society. This responsibility leads 'working mothers' to make considerable efforts to develop their children's capitals, to a level commensurate with women in the area who do not engage in paid work outside the home.

Chapter 10 looks at the time poverty of 'working mothers', who are stretched in terms of demands on them to spend time at work and time at home, under systems governed by different values. Women devote time to their employment, their children, partners, housework and elderly parents. Women have made choices to combine motherhood with paid work and to realise these choices, women who engage in paid work outside the home are stretched to their limits; in the words of one woman, 'time for me is time for everybody'. Women's coping strategies include better management, cutting back on employment demands through reduced working hours, multitasking and outsourcing housework. Even still, many women found it impossible to reconcile gendered expectations both at work and at home and many women failed to combine motherhood with paid work in a satisfying way.

In the final chapter, an argument is made for a new discourse of equality that values caring equally with paid work and regards children as a social good. Pascall and Lewis argue that real equality will only be achieved when there is a new gender regime which delivers equality between women and men in the domains of paid work, care work, time, income and voice.[52] I suggest ways to deliver this new gender regime across these five domains, which include structural as well as social changes. These changes are necessary to facilitate the better reconciliation of working and caring for men as well as women, in order to create a more just and equal society for all.

CHAPTER 1

No country for 'working mothers'

Women are tempted by the promise of 'having it all', yet when they become mothers, they find that having anything at all in terms of work/life balance is very difficult indeed. This chapter presents the landscape in Ireland in which women combine motherhood with paid work. The influence of the dominant and conflicting discourses of neo-liberalism, individualism, feminism and motherhood on Irish social policy, and their central tenets are examined. Irish society is in a state of flux. Discourses of individualism and feminism have contributed to a liberalising of attitudes towards traditional gender roles, but women's roles have changed little in the private sphere, despite women's increased participation in the public sphere. Motherhood discourses continue to be promoted in the media and popular culture and shape the institutions of family, workplace and society, while neo-liberal and individualism discourses, operating in workplace and society, are evident in social inequalities and the widespread adoption of liberal-individualist attitudes.

Neo-Liberalism

The term 'neo-liberal' refers to a macro-economic doctrine which valorises private enterprise so that individuals are regarded as entrepreneurs and states are run like businesses. Neo-liberalism is based on the belief that freely adopted market mechanisms are the optimal way of organising all exchanges of goods and services. Free markets and free trade will unleash creative potential and entrepreneurial spirit, thereby leading to more individual liberty and a more efficient allocation of resources.[1] Neo-liberalism thus supports a regime of national practices and policies claiming fealty to the doctrine of enterprise.[2] Neo liberalism dedicates the state to championing private property rights, free markets and free trade,

1

while deregulating business and privatising collective assets. Harvey claims that neo-liberalism has become hegemonic world-wide as it has had the support of large debt restructuring organisations such as the World Bank, the International Monetary Fund, the European Monetary Fund and the European Central Bank, which were encouraged to promote neo-liberalism in order to revitalise capital accumulation.[3] However, as Ferguson argues,[4] neo-liberalism is deployed in many diverse ways, as increasingly nation states and social policies are de-coupled.

According to Treanor, neo-liberalism is a philosophy that sees the world in terms of market metaphors.[5] Referring to nations as companies is typically neo-liberal and 'Ireland Inc.' was traded in the global marketplace as a location for entrepreneurs because competition for inward investment is the core doctrine of neo-liberalism. According to the then Tánaiste,[6] 'Geographically we are closer to Berlin than Boston. Spiritually we are probably a lot closer to Boston than Berlin', citing Ireland's identification with 'the American way . . . rugged individualism . . . an economic model that is heavily based on enterprise and incentive, on individual effort and with limited government intervention.'[7]

The Irish government's adoption of neo-liberal policy caused considerable social and cultural change, which emanated from a change in the order of discourse. Prior to 1980, dominant political-economic discourse in Ireland was 'Catholic Corporatist'.[8] This changed to neo-liberalism following Ireland's joining the European Union (EU) in 1973, and since the 1980s, Ireland has pursued neo-liberal economic policies. The negotiation of centralised wage-bargaining agreements through social partnership from 1987 created a climate of stability and certainty that helped provide the context for increased overseas investment, industrial co-operation and job growth, combined with low inflation.[9] The partnership process reflects the interdependence between the economic and the political and the importance of a shared understanding of key economic and social mechanisms.[10] Boucher and Collins claim the partnership processes in Ireland are operating primarily in the service of neo-liberalism,[11] as through the partnership process, the state effectively co-opted social groups to neo-liberalism. The partnership process reformed the industrial relations legal and institutional framework and introduced a tax structure favourable to private enterprise. It can be argued that neo-liberalism has been a corrective to policies that favoured the working class over capitalist interests and the partnership process demonstrates that the state promotes and protects capitalist interests in Ireland, while limiting the power of the trades unions.[12]

One of the differences between classical liberalism and neo-liberalism is that liberalism sought to find a balance between state and market, public and private, while neo-liberalism puts mechanisms developed in the private sphere to work within the state itself.[13] While liberalism sought to reduce the role of the state to a minimum and replace it by private capital, neo-liberalism seeks to expand the role of private capital through the state by tax cuts, decreases in social spending, deregulation, and privatisation, making the state authoritarian and a dedicated facilitator of capitalist interests. Inglis claims the development of a global habitus is closely allied to the spread and development of the world capitalist system and the spiral of ever-increasing production and consumption.[14] However, globalisation and capitalism are linked in other ways. Ireland's movement towards a low tax/low spend economy, reliance on cheap credit, an inflated property boom, and an unregulated banking system meant that once the global economic crisis hit in 2007, Ireland was disproportionately and rapidly affected.[15] In 2008, Ireland transferred responsibility for the country's enormous private banking debts to the state and gave financial management of the state over to the Troika (representatives of the European Union, International Monetary Fund and European Central Bank) as part of Ireland's bailout mechanism. Consequently a new form of social partnership emerged, which introduced swingeing reductions in welfare, public services and public pay, with increased taxation in order to service the debt burden.

According to Moran, a very divisive ideological battle has been waged in Ireland, which has successfully pitted workers in the private sector against those in the public sector and distracted from the huge inequalities between the wealthy and the poor/working poor, which exists across the public/private sector divide.

> Media channels are dominated by the pragmatists of neo-liberalism (economists and politicians), who insistently and authoritatively tell us that our public and welfare services cost too much, that our pension bill is too high, that our public sector is inefficient, that our taxation is too high and stifling growth, and that we must 'pay the price for having partied too hard'. They ultimately tell us that we must accept the power

and authority of the markets – and this claim has been accepted as a basic truth even by trade unions and social justice organisations, who fight for some modicum of social justice or 'fairness' within a greater acceptance of an illegitimate debt burden and a society subordinated to market demands.[16]

Harvey claims that neo-liberalism is a global capitalist class power restoration project.[17] Neo-liberalism became dominant in countries where the national tax structure was progressive, where industrial policy was adversarial to business and where welfare was associated with the poor.[18] In countries which have a more liberal political structure, the pressures of neo-liberalism lead to reductions in the welfare state, favouring the interests of capital over those of labour.[19]

Discourses of neo-liberalism suggest all people of working age should participate in paid work to contribute to the economy; furthermore, participation in employment is necessary to fit with dominant social values, to achieve the social and cultural capital[20] required to ensure economic self-sufficiency and an end to poverty and social exclusion. Harvey suggests that neo-liberals promote entrepreneurialism as the normative source of human happiness.[21] Ferguson claims that neo-liberalism promotes new constructions of 'active and responsible' citizens, who operate as a miniature firm, responding to incentives, rationally assessing risks and prudently choosing from among different courses of action.[22]

Esping-Andersen developed a typology of national approaches to the organisation of employment, social support and care, allocating different responsibilities to the state, the market and the family.[23] These approaches have been adapted by others to encompass the gender dimensions of social policy configurations.[24] It has been noted that these welfare regimes create different incentives for women, particularly married women and mothers, to participate in the workforce. Ireland has a market-centred welfare regime which includes a reliance on means-tested assistance, modest universal transfers, a preference for market provided welfare and an emphasis on self-reliance mainly through paid labour.[25]

The government's neo-liberal economic policies encourage women's employment and their economic contribution to the state. In Budget 2000 the then Minister for Finance introduced tax individualisation, which was achieved over the course of three budgets.[26] The individualisation of the tax system was regarded as the state's adoption of neo-liberal economic policy by encouraging and supporting mothers' employment. By 2002, when the individualisation programme was completed, a double-income married couple had double the tax allowances that a single-income married couple received. The single-income couple continues to pay the higher tax rate while the two-income household can have double the income before paying the higher rate of tax. The individualisation proposals were seen as a reward to women in the workforce vis-à-vis women in the home.[27] At the Family Fora[28] many people reported that the individualisation of the tax system signified to them that the government values economic activity more highly than family-related forms of activity such as caring for children and other family members. Individualisation of the tax system has been particularly divisive. Women 'at home' resent tax allowances for women at work, and those at work resent their taxes facilitating other women to stay at home full-time.[29]

Mothers are increasingly being commoditised by the state in terms of employment and welfare systems, and welfare and tax policy promotes alternative kinds of motherhood based on marital status.[30] In welfare policy, women who are married to unemployed men are classified as 'qualified adults' and treated as dependants, while women who are lone parents are supported by the state, on condition that they do not cohabit, which effectively means the state replaces the male breadwinner. If married women work full-time in the home, their work is not recognised in welfare policy, or for pension purposes. In tax policy, women who are married and choose to work full-time in the home are penalised because individualisation of the tax system means only those working in the formal economy are entitled to any tax relief.

The recent recession notwithstanding, orthodox accounts of social and cultural change provide a generalised correlation between economic success and a climate of national self-confidence and creativity. However, Ireland's adoption of neo-liberal policies, combined with the rise of individualism has resulted in Ireland being among the developed world's most unequal societies and Ireland is first in the EU-15 in terms of income inequality.[31] CORI[32] claims that Ireland is characterised by a widening gap between rich and poor and that absolute inequality has increased. Cantillon et al[33] argue the state has 'consistently prioritised the needs of the economy over social objectives', while Kirby[34] claims the state has favoured market forces to the detriment of social well-being, arguing that 'economic success correlates with social failure'. Murray[35] claims Irish society has embraced the modern soul of Europe in which 'only that which is profitable is good, what is legal is moral, what is bigger is better'.

The central tenets of neo-liberalism discourse are that market forces, including the labour market, will self-regulate without interference from the state. Humans exist to participate in the labour market and those who do not have failed in some way.[36] A strong discursive strain is that women, like men, must invest in and manage their careers, and make good choices which lead to economic success and material comfort. To be successful in neo-liberalism discourse is to be a productive and responsible citizen, without any dependence on the state.

Individualism

Closely linked to discourses of neo-liberalism, is the concept of individualism. The rise of individualism is linked to global capitalism, in which individuals are positioned entirely as producers and consumers. Global capitalism encourages the primacy of the individual in terms of identity, work, consumption, politics and culture,[37] where 'socio-economic relations place the emphasis on an individualised sense of responsibility for personal achievement'.[38] Discourses of individualism suggest that people are free to choose their identities and lifestyles and indeed, must do so in order to demonstrate their success as people. The cry of the liberal is that the more opportunity individuals have to make their own rational choices within open markets, the better for them, the better for their society, and the better for the common global good.[39] The growth of globalisation is intrinsically tied into the growth of individualism. The penetration of the market into everyday life has created a new individualism revolving around personal identities and lifestyles.[40] When individualism discourses are widely adopted by individuals in neo-liberal democracies, individualisation of that society occurs.

O'Connor claims that individualisation is one of the most fundamental long-term processes transforming Irish society,[41] while Inglis regards the increasing individualisation of Irish society as a crucially important process to which he attributes the decline of Catholicism and the rise of globalisation.[42] In Ireland, the traditional social relationships, bonds and belief systems that used to determine Irish people's lives in the narrowest detail have been losing some of their meaning. New space and options have opened up as well as new regulations emanating from the institutions of the labour market, welfare state and education system.[43] A cultural change happened from the 1960s onwards, in which 'a new philosophy of liberal individualism and self-indulgence' began to emerge with 'a new ethic of self-realisation'.[44] However, the influence of Catholicism on normative constructions of motherhood in Ireland is nevertheless considerable. The Catholic church has influenced the legal framework, with the Irish Constitution endorsing the male breadwinner role and relegating women to a life 'within the home'.[45] Its influence was particularly forceful and successful in its efforts to resist social reform in the domain where it saw itself as holding the moral monopoly, namely, on issues such as contraception, divorce and abortion.[46] Contraception was illegal until 1979,[47] divorce was introduced in 1996,[48] and abortion in very limited circumstances introduced in 2013.[49] The Catholic church currently controls eighty-nine per cent of primary schools in Ireland, therefore strongly influencing cultural ideals and norms. According to Inglis, 'The State may have decided in its economic policies to pursue unashamedly economic growth and success. But the residues of Catholic culture lingered for longer in the Irish collective unconscious'.[50] This demonstrates a change in the order of discourse from traditional Catholic conservatism to liberal individualism, from 'a Catholic culture of self-denial to a consumer culture of self-indulgence'.[51]

In individualism discourses, the worker is an individual in search of meaning, achievement and self-actualisation. Work is not simply a source of income, but also a source of personal growth and fulfillment; thus the individual is not to be emancipated from work (perceived as merely a job or economic necessity), but the individual is to be fulfilled in work which will provide meaning, identity and personal satisfaction.[52] The myriad of choices that confront us in modern society lead to the self becoming a 'reflexive product'[53] with individuals choosing and planning their lifestyles and biographies. In this perspective the individual becomes responsible for the creation of the self. However, Lash[54] insists on the need to be conscious of how structures may constrain the choices available to individuals, while Anthias[55] and Adkins[56] highlight the significance of social or structural divisions such as class, race and gender. Irish women are constituted by the promise of 'freedom' to invent themselves, but as Franklin, Lury and Stacey[57] argue, 'it is the requirement of the exercise of the will which is the decisive means by which the global citizen is established', and it is important to examine the ways in which globalisation and individualism 'identify "choice" as its origin and produce new regulatory effects'.[58]

Hilliard[59] argues that an excessive belief in individual autonomy can have dangerous social and personal consequences: individuals whose biographies are seen to be out of line with the priorities of 'success' in their society, such as remaining poor in a rich world, will be blamed not only for their individual 'failure', but for woes afflicting the wider society, as single mothers were in Britain in the last few decades of the twentieth century.[60] The structural problems of a society can then be explained by the shortcomings of individuals or groups. The emphasis on individual autonomy and agency raises important issues for 'working mothers'. Autonomous beings are self-governing, having the freedom and discretion to make decisions about the way they live their lives, following their own individual guiding principles. Autonomy thus establishes the descriptive standard for what is assumed distinctive of human beings. But autonomy serves as a prescriptive standard as well: one who is able to decide the direction of her life is to be respected for this ability.[61] Consequently, women who have dependent children and cannot exercise autonomy struggle with individualism discourses, because, as Di Quinzio[62] notes, motherhood and individualism are incompatible.

The choice and autonomy which is assumed in discourses of individualism raises conflicts for feminists between the drive to overcome the historical subjugation that has deprived women of autonomy and choice in public life on the one hand, and the conviction, on the other, that the institutions of the workplace and society offer predominantly impoverished and ultimately degrading opportunities for choice by women trapped in patriarchy.[63] McKinnon[64] claims women today are the bearers of a new self, a neo-liberal subjectivity, one based on individualism and self-invention from the perspective of individualisation theory, which has led to the popular feminism of 'having it all'. A consequence of individualism in contemporary Ireland is that women are charged with active steering of their own lives. However, women are also charged with devoting their lives to family and community. The result of combining motherhood with paid work, while retaining responsibility for home and family, has negative consequences for women's self-esteem and well-being, and as Oakley[65] argues, there is a risk that these will become progressively more pronounced as society goes further in the direction of greedy individualism.

In the domain of primary relationships, individualism puts increasing pressure on traditional role patterns and on work relationships between men and women. Pascall and Lewis claim that individualisation challenges the structures that supported care in state and family.[66] They claim the links that joined men to women, cash to care and incomes to carers have all been fractured, and the social, political and economic changes that brought about individualisation have not been matched by the development of new gender models. Beck-Gernsheim[67] argues that processes of individualisation generate an obligation to achieve a life of one's own, and a longing for ties, closeness and community. Where the dynamic of individualism imposes itself, more effort than before must be expended to keep the various individual biographies within the ordinary compass of the family.[68] This effort falls to women, particularly mothers.

In contemporary societies, individualism is maintained by women and men's realistic expectations of the choices available to them. As Williams asks 'why change a system in which women often describe economic marginalisation as their own choice?'[69] It does not matter if the free choice is more illusory than real, if people are trampled on in the marketplace, or if the consequences of unrestricted freedom of choice are socially and personally disastrous.[70] However, individualism is also maintained by individual or group attempts to achieve what Bourdieu[71] calls social and cultural capital, which effectively perpetuates a structure where different groups are rewarded unequally and leads to intimidation, oppression and exclusion of other individuals and groups.

The central tenets of individualism are that people can and should, may and must, actively steer their own lives by exercising autonomous choice. Adults exercise free will and voluntarily choose to engage in paid work because employment is the route to economic self-sufficiency and promotes self-esteem.[72] Individuals are entirely responsible for the choices they make and the outcomes of their choices are their own responsibility. Success or failure is an entirely personal affair, regardless of the choices, opportunities or resources available to individuals. A strong discursive strain in individualism discourses is that having a career and contributing to the formal economy is necessary in order to be considered successful.

Feminism

Feminism is an intellectual, philosophical and political movement which demonstrates the many ways in which the world is gendered and the implications for women's lives. Feminist activism and scholarship emanated from a change in the order of discourse and has had significant positive effects on Irish women's lives. Drawing on individualist principles, liberal feminists have made some progress in advancing the 'equality agenda' in relation to women's participation in public life and in the workforce, and in Ireland over the last fifty years, women's lives have changed dramatically as a result of feminist activism and scholarship. Feminist discourses challenged conservative Catholic discourse, particularly in relation to gender roles. However, the Irish state has been reluctant to facilitate role change for women. Gender equality in Ireland started from a lower base than other countries, because of the powerful political influence of the Catholic church on social policy, and Irish feminist campaigns met with considerable opposition. Strategic feminist campaigns to compel the state to honour the conditions of membership of the then EEC were essential to ensure key legislative and political changes were introduced. In addition to compelling the state to improve the legal situation of women, the women's movement also encouraged Irish women to embrace these new structural improvements in women's lives by reducing their childbearing by using contraception, to participate in the professions in greater numbers and to assert their economic independence in marriage.[73]

In the 1960s a woman could expect to retire from work on marriage and devote herself thereafter to caring for her husband and the four or more children which would follow. In the twenty-first century, a woman can expect to continue in employment beyond marriage, to postpone or delay having children until she is thirty, to cohabit before marriage (if indeed she marries at all) and she is likely to have one or two children.[74] In Ireland today the legacy of radical feminists is evident in relation to women's reproductive rights, including the legalisation of contraception and the establishment of state-sponsored family planning clinics and non-directive crisis pregnancy services.

Liberal feminism advocates equality for women in the public and private spheres, campaigns for women's rights and interests and aims to achieve equal rights and legal protection for women. Liberal feminists suggest women should be economically independent, exercise their right to work outside the home and engage in public life. The focus of much liberal feminist thought and action has been on women's access to the public sphere as a means of individual and collective liberation. In 1973, the ban on married women working in the civil service, local authorities and health boards was removed as a pre-condition to Ireland's membership of the then EEC.[75] In 1974, the Anti-Discrimination (Pay) Act established the right of men and women to equal pay if they are employed in like work by the same or an associated employer.[76] The provision of allowances for deserted wives, unmarried mothers and prisoners' wives was implemented in the Social Welfare Act 1974.[77] Other progress included the elimination of discrimination against single women in relation to social welfare payments, the establishment of the state's duty to provide free legal aid in family law cases, and the removal of the differential treatment of 'illegitimate children' in Irish law and protection for the rights of children born outside marriage. These were significant developments for the increasing numbers of women with children living in non-marital circumstances in Irish social policy, which demonstrates a liberalising of attitudes towards marriage, marital breakdown and single parenthood, as well as a change in order of discourse from Catholic corporatism and its influence on social policy.

However, the leverage offered by the EU was also significant in reducing the Irish state's opposition to women's equality. The EU forced Ireland to introduce equal pay[78] and since then several EU measures have been introduced to facilitate women's participation in employment including maternity, adoptive, parental, carers and force majeure leave, as well as outlawing discrimination on the grounds of gender, marital status and family responsibilities (Appendix 1). These measures aimed to provide women with equal legal rights to those of men in the employment arena.

Some of the successes of Irish feminism have had a general, but uneven, impact on all women across class divides. Concrete gains since the 1970s reflect general societal acceptance of the more moderate demands of liberal feminism, mainly in the areas of paid employment and property rights. Furthermore, it is argued that the form taken by equality legislation may have benefited middle-class women far more than their working-class sisters.[79] The legacy for many women who were prevented from engaging in paid work because of the marriage bar is that they may spend their old age in poverty. The implications of pension changes and cutbacks in recent budgets mean many more women will have insufficient employment contributions to be entitled to a state old-age pension. Bacik[80] claims many of the legal changes brought about have not been really effective. The forms of inequality may have changed, and some individual women may have achieved positions of power, but substantive inequalities remain. Legislation alone is insufficient to tackle the many gender inequalities that persist.

Feminist and individualist discourses have contributed to women's changing role in Irish society, but resistance is evident in an anti-feminist backlash. In a society that has experienced such recent and radical change in both family life and in the institutional framework governing women's lives, such resistance is not surprising. Neither is it surprising that the now established feminist challenge to traditional male authority and power in family life is perceived as a threat by some sections of society. A key myth promoted by organised advocates of traditional values is that 'feminists' in Ireland prioritised the promotion of women in the workforce to the complete neglect of women's rights in the home. This myth has been effective and in consequence women in the workforce are pitted against women working in the home, for which both groups blame feminism. A significant issue for many women is that men's role in the home has not adapted to women's participation in employment. Hence women experience the double burden, leading many women to believe their participation in paid work, without relinquishing their responsibilities in the home, has created a double bind for which feminism is also responsible.

In fact, Irish feminists right across both radical and liberal ideological strands of the women's movement united on the question of women's employment rights and challenged traditional stereotypes regarding the male breadwinning father/homemaking mother.[81] Those on the left and in the trade unions, in particular, aimed to develop the conditions in which a majority of women in

Ireland could at least choose to combine motherhood and employment, regardless of their social class and marital status.[82] Feminist
advocacy of 'working mothers' has at base, been about dismantling
an automatic equation of women with caregiving, family and
home.[83] As more 'working mothers' participated in the public
sphere, liberal feminists expected that eventually the public sphere
would introduce such practices as flexible hours and on-site childcare, so that women could combine the roles of mother and paid
worker with ease. This would, it was hoped, lead to 'working
mothers' and 'women in the home' at least paralleling each other in
acceptance. However, these feminist hopes have not become a
reality. Although access to the public sphere has indeed increased
for many women, Gray argues it has brought with it new practices
of gender/sexual regulation and subordination often in and
through discourses of women's liberation.[84] An ongoing issue for
feminist activism and scholarship in Ireland is to successfully challenge the entrenched and deeply gendered patterns of unpaid,
caring work while securing government resources to enhance and
encourage more flexible and inclusive working patterns for both
women and men.[85] The central tenets of feminist discourse are that
women are as entitled as men to have rights and entitlements to
freedom of choice, to participate in the public sphere, and to pursue
careers and families if they wish. This has led to the discursive
strain of 'having it all'. However, another strain of feminist discourse sees caring, for children and other dependent persons, as
work that should be recognised and valued, and as the responsibility of families, society and the state.

Motherhood

As DiQuinzio[86] notes, it is very difficult to challenge motherhood
on individualist terms, and it is on the grounds of their maternity
that women experience most resistance to their changing role.
Kaplan[87] argues the backlash against women's changing role is
evident in a plethora of contradictory discourses of motherhood
which all have anxiety in common because childbirth and childcare
are no longer viewed as automatically natural parts of the woman's
lifecycle. These contradictory discourses include intensive mothering, new-familialism, and new-capitalist motherhood which
promote mothers' full-time care, development and economic provision for children. Mothers are also regarded as being responsible

for family functioning, thus women are charged with preservation of the family, which is the central unit of society.

Dominant motherhood discourses make combining motherhood with paid work difficult. Buxton argues this has resulted in 'the mother war',[88] which is a war between those who believe that mothers should work and those who insist they should not. 'It is a war between the politically correct Superwoman and the maternally correct Earthmother', the most public manifestations of which are media debates engaged in by journalists and fuelled by politicians, academics and ordinary citizens eager to share their ideas. In Ireland, White's thesis that the state recognises and rewards mothers' paid employment and does not recognise nor value the contribution women make when full-time in the home, contributes to the 'mother war'.[89] These debates about the desirability and effectiveness of 'working mothers' heighten the expectation of maternal perfection through selflessness; if a mother is doing a paid job, whether or not she actually has the choice to do so, she can be judged to be failing in her primary childrearing duties.[90]

The new focus on the child, together with a backlash against women's progress in the public sphere, has led to the emergence of new-capitalist mother discourses which contribute to the pressures 'working mothers' experience. As Warner notes

> It wouldn't be enough for a woman to give her 'soul' to motherhood. She'd have to give her body, mind and marriage, too. She'd be expected to lose herself within motherhood, first in a fusion-like bonding with her baby and later in the rounds of kid activities that would devour her life.[91]

Many writers have taken issue with new-familialism and intensive mothering discourses, claiming they represent a backlash against feminism's progress.[92] These discourses blame feminism and 'working mothers' for all manner of social ills from childhood diabetes to underage sex and juvenile crime, in an attempt to appeal to women to reduce their participation in public life and return to private roles in the patriarchal, nuclear family, for the sake of their children.

Miller argues that motherhood is lived out in a 'moral minefield',[93] while Duncan and Edwards claim gendered moral rationalities shape social negotiations around mothering and paid work.[94] The taken-for-granted nature of mothering and care work presents problems for women who try to combine motherhood with paid work in Ireland. Women's political, cultural and economic designation as carers is constructed as 'free choice', yet there is a moral imperative on women to do care work that does not apply equally to men; a highly gendered moral code impels women to do the greater part of primary caring, with most believing they have no choice in the matter.[95] The way women are exploited in relation to care work is particularly acute for mothers, because of the way it is morally inscripted in Ireland.[96]

The reluctance to recognise unpaid caring as a form of work arises from the widespread global allegiance to the feminine, as opposed to feminist, ethic of care which defines care as a moral obligation for women, governed by the rules of selflessness and self-sacrifice.[97] As Nussbaum,[98] Kittay,[99] Tronto[100] and Lynch[101] have pointed out, 'caring' has a dual meaning; caring is active and passive, incorporating both 'caring for' in the physical sense as well as 'caring about' in the emotional sense.[102] Caring, therefore conflates labour and love. Lynch developed the term 'love labour' to describe all the work that is involved in caring.[103] 'Love labour' involves emotional and other work orientated towards the enrichment and enablement of others. It involves both emotional work (thinking of and planning for others, attentiveness, listening, managing relations and conflict), as well as material tasks (cleaning, cooking, washing, lifting and attending). It has been argued that these unique and particular emotional aspects of caring work mean it is impossible to commodify them in any usually economically understood sense of the term.[104]

Relations of care, love and solidarity matter because the development of care, love and solidarity relations involves effort, time and energy. Those aspects of relationships that boost confidence, inspire strength and encouragement, give people a sense of belonging, and a sense of being wanted and needed and of being free (e.g. what mothers want for their children), cannot be commoditised as they can only exist in a context where there is some choice or decision to care and commit oneself for the sake of the relationship (to the child) and not for payment. The 'love labour' women do in caring for their children is often experienced both as a burden and a pleasure. This is not to deny the reality of the 'compulsory altruism' which has been a feature of so many Irish women's lives.[105] Lynch and Lyons and Baker et al argue that care work, and in particular the emotional work involved in care, is a field of social action within and through which inequalities and exploitations can occur, just as they can occur in the economic, political or cultural sphere.[106] High status for both men and women is inversely related to the doing of love, care and solidarity work, as idealised workers are 'zero loaded' workers: these are without care, be it by being detached from dependency relations or by ignoring them, delegating dependency work to others (paying others to do it) or by commanding others to do their dependency work.[107]

As most care labour is unpaid – especially maternal love-labouring, given its intimate and inalienable quality – those who perform it incur a material net burden due to loss of earnings and pensions.[108] Simultaneously, women enable others, mostly men, to pursue more materially beneficial activities, notably paid work and leisure.[109] More than half-a-million women in 2011 were looking after home/family compared with only 9,600 men.[110] The impact of care work, especially maternal care, on women's employment is reflected in the fact that women work on average fewer hours than men, and in lower grade occupations. Part-time work is a clearly delineated coping strategy to enable women to deal with home and childcare duties in addition to formal employment.[111] Of those who worked less than twenty-nine hours per week in 2011, seventy-five per cent were women.[112] Men worked an average of forty hours a week in 2011 compared with thirty-one hours for women and married men worked longer hours than married women, with forty-five per cent of married men working for forty hours or more a week compared with only fifteen per cent of married women.[113] 'The position of women . . . who combine the role of worker and carer [is] not adequately recognised in social provision'[114] and there is no valuing, or acknowledgement that care remains primarily women's responsibility and is maintained as each woman's private issue. Moran notes that many carers do not have the time to engage in the labour market and suffer material deprivation as a consequence,[115] while Adam[116] and Davies[117] have also noted that caring time is gendered.

However, caring does not take place in a vacuum; it takes place in a nested set of power, class and gender relations and the moral imperative to undertake care work in all forms is much stronger for women than for men.[118] The division of care labour is gendered and classed locally and globally and women continue to bear disproportionate responsibility for care work, in the informal world of the family and in the formal world of the care economy.[119] According to

Lynch,[120] in general, men are more likely to be 'care commanders' and women 'care's foot soldiers'. Even where gender and power are identified in care arrangements, there is limited discussion of the gendered obligations to care.[121]

McKay asserts that 'present political and social systems and value structures obscure the central importance of care; and the means by which certain powerful groups and actors benefit from, whilst simultaneously, devaluing care'.[122] There are deep gender inequalities in the doing of care and love work that operate to the advantage of men. Feminist scholarship[123] has drawn attention to the salience of care and love as public goods and exposed the limitations of conceptualisations of citizenship devoid of a concept of care. It has also highlighted the importance of caring as work, work that needs to be rewarded and distributed equally between women and men. Furthermore, the complex way in which power relations and exploitation are embedded in all manner of care relations is the subject of a large body of feminist research, which demonstrates the ways care workers are open to exploitation as informal family 'carers' and as paid care workers.[124]

There are a number of conflicting discursive strains evident in motherhood discourses: women are charged with providing intensive care for their children, materially providing for their children, and raising productive and independent citizens. Intensive mothering and new-familialism discourses promote women's full-time care of their children in the home and suggest that children's needs can only be met by the child's mother. There is also a discursive strain that suggests that women are the custodians of the family, the central unit of society.

Women's and mothers' employment

The role of mothers is far from settled in Irish society. In the context of a society that values both achievement and independence for the individual and submission and altruism in the family, women combine motherhood with paid work. Women are participating in the workforce in greater numbers, may choose how many, if any, children to have, may or may not marry and can achieve high levels of education and compete for opportunities in the public world of work. Women who mother and engage in paid work experience difficulties combining the two. Women's lives are structured by the tensions between the promise of participation in the labour force on equal terms, their actual experience of the workplace, and their continual positioning as the guardians of family life.[125] The division among women regarding mothers' employment can lead to guilt among employed mothers and heightens ambivalence about taking up a job among others who are not employed.[126] The current thrust of government policy, to encourage if not push mothers into employment, can create a lot of difficulties for mothers. These are not just material or logistical in nature, especially in the sense of managing childcare, they are also emotional. 'Ambivalence, it seems, is the lot of many mothers. Many women feel torn between children and work'.[127]

Although the proportion of all women in the Irish labour force remained fairly stable for sixty years, being thirty-two per cent in 1926 and thirty-one per cent in 1986, in the thirty years between 1971 and 2001, the number of all women in paid employment rose by 140 per cent, compared to a rise of twenty-seven per cent in the number of men.[128] The Stockholm Council set an EU employment target of fifty-seven per cent for women aged fifteen to sixty-four by 2005. The EU did not quite reach this target, but Ireland did. The Lisbon Council, back in 2000, set an EU target of sixty per cent by 2010. In 1999, the female employment rate in Ireland, at fifty-one per cent, was below the EU average of fifty-three per cent. However, since then the employment rate for women has increased more rapidly in Ireland than in the EU as a whole, and in 2008 it was sixty-one per cent, which was above the EU average of fifty-nine per cent.[129] These figures can lead one to argue that women's employment, especially mothers' employment, facilitated the economic boom, popularly known as the Celtic Tiger.[130] (The term 'Celtic Tiger' refers to remarkable growth during the 1990s and 2000s in economic output, employment and incomes.[131])

The rise in married women's employment is even more dramatic. In 1971 only eight per cent of married women were in the labour force; in 1981 this had more than doubled to seventeen per cent and by 1991 it was twenty-seven per cent.[132] It was thirty-seven per cent in 1996; however, by 2008, sixty-nine per cent of all married women aged between twenty-five and sixty-four years of age were in the labour force.[133] Following the economic crisis in 2008, participation rates have fallen for both men and women. The EU employment target of sixty per cent was met by Ireland in 2007 and 2008, but not in 2009, 2010 or 2011, when the rate had fallen to fifty-six per cent. In 2012, forty-seven per cent of those in employment were women.[134]

However, for women, the highest participation rates occur in the childbearing years, with seventy-eight per cent of women aged between twenty-five and thirty-four years in the labour force.[135]

Despite the significant increases in women's employment, having children clearly has a negative effect on mothers' employment. This is evident in the participation rates of childless women relative to mothers, with eighty-six per cent of women without children in employment compared to fifty-seven per cent of women whose youngest child is aged nought to three years; fifty-two per cent of women whose youngest child is aged four to five years and fifty-eight per cent of women whose youngest child is aged six or over. Fatherhood does not have the same effect on male employment; eighty-five per cent of childless men are employed; seventy-nine per cent of fathers whose youngest child is aged nought to three years; seventy-four per cent of fathers whose youngest child is aged four to five years, and seventy-seven per cent of fathers whose youngest child is aged six or over.[136]

The unemployment rate for men in Ireland increased dramatically from five to fifteen per cent in 2009 and increased to seventeen per cent in 2011. The unemployment rate for women, increased from four per cent to eight per cent in 2009 and rose to ten per cent in 2011. These figures tend to suggest that many women are the sole earners in many households since 2009.

From a gender equality perspective, the dramatic influx of women into the labour market has had less of an impact on the quality of women's employment than might have been anticipated. In 1997, women's hourly earnings were eighty-one per cent of men's gross hourly earnings in Ireland, compared to eighty-four per cent in the EU as a whole. By 2006 women's earnings in Ireland had increased to ninety-one per cent of men's, and by 2012 had increased to ninety-four per cent; however, persons working fifteen hours or fewer are excluded from this indicator and these persons are more likely to be female and on lower incomes.[137] The difference between male and female incomes for persons aged fifteen to sixty-four years increased with age. The average income of women aged fifteen to twenty-four years was ninety-five per cent that of men in the same age group, while for the fifty-five to sixty-four years age group, women's average income was sixty-one per cent of men's.[138]

Following the recession in 2008, the government introduced a number of substantial cuts in successive budgets. Tax increases, income levies and pay cuts in the public sector were introduced, with tax bands widened to capture those earning more than €18,000 per year.[139] As the public sector is largely feminised and women are predominantly low earners, these cuts have disproportionately affected women. Furthermore, child benefit, carer's allowances, one parent family payments and maternity benefit have all been cut or taxed, moves which have also disproportionately affected women, who maintain primary responsibility for caring.[140]

In 2012, the government launched a new labour activation policy[141] in line with its neo-liberal agenda, which, in tandem with cuts to welfare payments, aimed to reduce the number of unemployed. Pathways to Work[142] included regular and ongoing engagement with the unemployed; greater targeting of activation places and opportunities; incentivising the take-up of opportunities; incentivising employers to provide more jobs for people who are unemployed and reforming institutions to deliver better services. Specific programmes included Job Bridge, and Work Placement Programmes which provide an additional €50 per week top-up payment to job seekers benefit or allowance, available for eighteen months for a job seeker to gain work experience. In 2013, the government launched Jobpath, a programme which allocates long-term unemployed people to private contractors who will be paid on the basis of results, i.e. a bounty will be paid for each person they place into sustained employment.[143]

Government employment policy is straightforward; its aim is to increase overall participation in the labour market. However, this is not unproblematic. Increased participation is premised on the neo-liberal understanding that increased employment is desirable, that it reduces poverty, provides economic and social citizenship and is a public good. The increase in women's employment has been stimulated by an increase in the services sector, with flexible forms of employment that are low paid and allow organisations to access skills without the costs of providing secure employment. This type of employment is not necessarily going to benefit the economy and, as Wickham warns, 'there is no inherent link between employment level and reduction of poverty'.[144]

In 2012, 700,000 people in Ireland were at risk of poverty, with 200,000 of these being children. Of the 700,000 people at risk of poverty, 120,000 are associated with the labour market; these are known as the 'working poor'[145] and the OECD[146] reported that in

Ireland, twenty-three per cent of women have incomes that put them at risk of poverty.[147] The Combat Poverty Agency reports that in 2009, 90,484 people were in receipt of the one-parent family payment. One-parent families, ninety-eight per cent of whom are headed by women, continue to live at poverty levels. Of one-parent families sixteen per cent live in consistent poverty, compared to seven per cent of the rest of the population as a whole. Furthermore fifty-six per cent suffer material deprivation, compared to the twenty-four per cent average for the country as a whole.[148] Almost sixty per cent of those receiving the payment are in employment; of these, most women work part-time, while most male lone parents work full-time.[149] Women tend to have more precarious forms of employment, providing flexible forms of employment as the market dictates. Those in precarious forms of employment, outside regular tax and social security networks have been called 'the precariat',[150] which is dominated by women, who tend to have little or no job security, access to sick pay or pension entitlements and receive lower rates of pay than the regular workforce. Lone parents often experience difficulty in accessing work, education and training opportunities because of a lack of good quality affordable childcare and after-school care. This means that job choices are often limited and low-paid. Many of these women are employed in the service sector and private households as reproductive or caring workers.

Between 2003 and time of writing, the government has been making concerted labour activation measures targeted at lone parents. In launching the 'Babies and Bosses' report, the OECD director stated 'single parents on social welfare who reject job offers should be forced to work'[151] and, while the then Minister for Social and Family Affairs, rejected this call for coercion, she supported the government working with lone parents to get them off welfare and into work. In 2006, the Family Support Unit at the Department of Social and Family Affairs proposed far-reaching measures and supports to work with lone parents to facilitate their transition to employment.[152] These measures included childcare supports, relaxation of the cohabitation restrictions and individual support in terms of training and education. However, following the recession in 2008, only those measures which represented cost savings to the exchequer have been implemented, i.e. cuts in payment rates, which have been aligned to the job seekers rate of €188 per adult and €29.30 per child per week. In addition, income disregard has been

reduced to €110 per week. Further reductions are planned: to €90 in 2014, €75 in 2015 and €60 in 2016.[153] Since 2011, eligibility for and restrictions to the one-parent family payment have included reducing the age limit of the child from eighteen years to seven years on a phased basis in a clear move to force lone parents, mainly women, to enter the labour market. It was reduced to age twelve in 2012, age ten in 2013 and to age seven in 2014.[154] According to Barnardos, 'This move is unacceptable given the absence of afford-able, quality afterschool care and the lack of availability of jobs. The reliance of lone parents on part time work as a result of their caring responsibilities leaves them particularly vulnerable to poverty if they do not have access to adequate supports'.[155]

McGinnity, Russell and Smyth claim that between 1990 to 2005, there were significant changes in the labour market behaviour of women and men in Ireland, which have been particularly dramatic for women, with rapidly growing labour force participation and employment rates.[156] Such changes have raised living standards and increased financial independence for many women. They have also transformed the way in which employment is distributed across households. Dual-earner arrangements are now the predominant model for working-age couples, even those with dependant children. Inglis[157] and O'Sullivan[158] claim a large new middle-class has emerged which has embraced the rise of consumer culture leading to the triumph of the idea that couples 'need' two incomes to service their mortgage and other consumption. In this analysis, the dual-income family is economically rational and the economic rationality of the dual-income family obscures the gender inequalities associated with it.[159] However, the changing profile of these couples also pres-ents a challenge to the concept of the male breadwinner. In a study of Irish couples aged twenty-six to forty years, Lunn and Fahey found that women have higher educational qualifications in thirty-four per cent of couples and in forty-two per cent of couples the woman has the higher occupational classification.[160] These figures might present a challenge to the male-breadwinner concept. If households make economically rational decisions to preserve household income after the arrival of children, then the parent who takes leave to provide care in thirty-four and forty-two per cent of these cases, will be the lower earner, or the one with lower occupational status, i.e. the man.

Nevertheless, traditional gender roles remain strong and underpin the gendered division of labour. Irish women currently do it all, and still do not have the same access to power, money and prestige as their male counterparts.[161] Women traditionally were providers of care and the 'love labour'[162] that supported and nurtured relationships in family and community. When women engage in paid work in pursuit of independence and autonomy they experience conflict, time pressure and the 'double burden'. Women in different class positions are more or less able to deal with the difficulties associated with women's participation in the labour force.[163] Those with the resources have access to a far greater range of support options; for example they may subcontract some of their domestic responsibilities by using formal childcare, or employing a housekeeper, nanny or au pair; they may also buy in domestic supports. High workloads (of paid and unpaid work) are also linked to lower life satisfaction; however, these do not cancel out the positive impact of employment on well-being.[164] In reality, combining motherhood with paid work is very difficult. There are some stress points; a significant proportion of the population reports feeling rushed and stressed, particularly those with high volumes of paid and unpaid work, who are predominantly 'working mothers'.[165]

No country for 'working mothers'

In the past twenty years Ireland has changed dramatically: socially, economically and culturally. 'Working mothers' in Ireland craft their working and mothering lives in the context of a society in flux. Women are positioned by discourses of neo-liberalism to be economically self-sufficient, contribute to the formal economy and paid work is seen as a public good. However, neo-liberal economic policies also enable the state to reduce its role in providing care, health and welfare supports. This means women who attempt to combine motherhood with paid employment experience difficulties because of the lack of state support for childcare and elder-care.

Individualism discourses suggest women, like men, are responsible for reflexively creating their own biographies and are free to make choices about their lifestyles and identities in order to maximise their success and happiness. Individualism requires autonomy; however mothers' autonomy is limited by having dependant children and gendered structural constraints in family and society which limit the choices available to them.

Discourses of liberal feminism encourage women to exercise independence both in and outside the home and liberal feminists in Ireland, as elsewhere, have had some success in supporting women's participation in the public sphere. However, this progress was not achieved by feminist activism alone; Ireland's membership of the EU was necessary to ensure Irish women's limited progress. Nevertheless, gender inequalities remain; the largest proportion of low-paid workers are women, and there are ongoing problems with occupational gender segregation. After nearly forty years of equal pay legislation, a gender pay differential remains and proper childcare remains unaffordable for most. Feminism advocates gender equality both in and outside the home. However, the anti-feminist backlash and intensive mothering discourses make it difficult for women who attempt to combine motherhood with paid work in Ireland.

Women are positioned by discourses of motherhood to be responsible for the physical, emotional, psychological and educational well-being of their children. Mothers are responsible for their children's care and development whether or not they engage in paid work outside the home. There are considerable anxieties surrounding motherhood in contemporary Irish society reflected in dominant motherhood discourses. Traditional appeals to a unified notion of the 'Irish mother' via the category 'women in the home', point to the continued valorisation of this figure in the reproduction of Irish femininities, while new-capitalist motherhood discourses have become the focus of acute anxieties about (re)productivity in the context of advanced global capitalism. The socio-economic contradictions between the demands and rewards of the labour market and the needs and rewards of the personal and familial are projected onto women.[166] According to Gray, women became the focus of struggles between neo-traditional and neo-liberal discourses of citizenship but in ways that identify 'the problem' as the choices that individual women make.[167] The resultant difficulties and tensions are defined as individual problems at both the micro and macro level. Despite feminist campaigns and legislative changes, many difficulties remain for Irish women in the workforce, including low pay, unequal pay, horizontal segregation, vertical segregation and discrimination on the grounds of gender. In Ireland, women are limited in their ability to be self-sufficient rational actors because women are charged with most caring work, which makes combining motherhood with paid work particularly difficult.

Whether in boom or bust situations, Irish governments have taken a laissez-faire policy approach to infrastructure to support mothers' employment, arguing the market will self-regulate. A neo-liberal fixation on low state intervention partially explains those policy choices. However, policy inaction is not just about ideology or cost avoidance. Policy paralysis is also due to politicians' fear of introducing reforms in the absence of policy consensus. It has been politically difficult in Ireland to mediate between political coalitions advocating conflicting policy options. Policy is limited by the strong veto power of employers who resist parental leave policies as well as a deeply rooted ideological ambivalence about mothers' labour market participation in a conservative, patriarchal, political culture.[168]

Irish women have had to adapt to the world of paid work, a world which developed based on patriarchal assumptions that care needs were looked after elsewhere, by women, in the unpaid private world of families, households and communities. Although the world of paid employment has taken on women workers in huge numbers, it has hardly changed its shape or organisation and hegemonic power relations persist in traditionally 'masculine' organisation cultures.[169] There has also been little response in the world of paid work to the dual roles that most women now occupy of carer-earner and the world of work has changed little because of the number of women participating in employment. Thus, women's increased labour force participation has been in traditionally 'female' sectors and at lower organisational levels. The world of work in Ireland 'continues to make little to no allowance for care needs and care provision'.[170] The Irish situation, therefore, can be characterised as a 'stalled revolution',[171] which effectively means that despite liberal beliefs about equality, women continue to perform the majority of 'family work'. Women are addressed as 'free' to construct themselves through paid work, work in the home, consumption, or activism so that these become equivalent 'lifestyle' options. Yet they have different public valences and are appropriated in a variety of ways to advance conservative agendas through gendered notions of motherhood and the family. Even though gender discourses have changed, in reality, both in public and private spheres, the structural changes necessary to support these changes in the order of discourse, and women's changing role, have not materialised.

'Real equality for women remains an aspiration; the feminist struggle is far from over'.[172]

Traditional gendered cultural values clash with feminist narratives of choice on the fault-line of motherhood. As long as caring, particularly for their own children, is maintained as the gendered responsibility of women only, Ireland is no country for women and no country for 'working mothers'.

CHAPTER 2

Complex inequality

In the context of women's increased participation in the labour force and higher levels of education, the patterns of inequality have changed between women and men, but in complex ways, not simply for better or worse.[1] For every inequality there is a privilege and the relationships of the 'working mothers' in this study to the labour market, the family and society demonstrate the ways in which inequalities sometimes privilege and some-times regulate women, depending on their class, education and marital status, and always regulate women because of their gender and their maternity. All of these relationships are dynamic and changing and interact to mutually promote, sustain, contest and reproduce privileges and inequalities.

Both Walby[2] and McCall[3] argue there is a disconnect between theory and social reality, with current theories unable to fully grasp the context of complex inequality. However, as Hayles[4] argues, reality is complexly patterned, but patterned nonetheless. We can determine the source of the complexity, we can describe it and we can theorise it. In this view, changes in patterns of inequality and in the underlying structural conditions of society are dynamic, complex and contingent, but also amenable to explanation.[5] Hawkesworth[6] claims that feminist scholars have contributed three major methodological innovations: the concept of intersectionality as a guiding research principle; standpoint theory as an analytical tool; and gender as an analytical category, all of which are employed to explain the complex inequality women experience at the intersection of mother and worker in this research.

Intersectionality

Intersectionality is a relatively new term to describe an old ques-tion in the theorisation of the relationship between different forms

27

of social inequality. Inequalities are social constructions that often give us power and options in some arenas while restricting our power and options in others.

> Intersectionality means that privilege and oppression . . . are not in fact singular. No one has a gender but not a race, a nationality but not a gender, an education but not an age. The location of people and groups within relations of production, reproduction and representation (relations that are organized worldwide in terms of gender inequality) is inherently multiple. These multiple social locations are often – not, as is often assumed, atypically – contradictory. Organizations as well as individuals hold multiple positions in regard to social relations of power and injustice, and typically enjoy privilege on some dimensions even while they struggle with oppression on another.[7]

Recognising multiple oppressions forces us to consider that most individuals occupy both dominant and subordinate positions at the same time. Thus white, professional men are privileged in relation to white professional women on the gender dimension. While a white working-class man will still experience privilege on the gender dimension he may experience inequality on the grounds of social class. Thus, it is possible to experience race and class privilege, and experience gender inequality, as many women in this research do. All the women in this research are white, heterosexual and able-bodied, thus are privileged on these dimensions, even while they experience inequality on the grounds of their gender and maternity.

The specific concept of intersectionality is attributed to critical race theorists, who, rejecting the notion of race, gender, ethnicity and class as separate and essentialist categories, developed the term 'intersectionality' to describe the interconnections and interdependence of race with other categories. Crenshaw[8] developed the term 'axes of oppression' to describe the complex inequality which arose at the intersection of race and gender, arguing that those at the intersection experienced a substantially different form of inequality than racial or gender inequalities viewed in isolation. Thus when researching black women workers, Crenshaw revealed that black women experienced inequalities relative to black men; however racial concepts of discrimination only considered race, not gender. Furthermore gender concepts of discrimination considered only white women as the archetype, therefore black women workers did not experience double inequality at the intersection of race and gender, but experienced a new more complex form of inequality, created at the intersection of both. Collins[9] argued that cultural patterns of oppression are not only interrelated, but are bound together and influenced by the intersectional systems of society, such as race, gender, class and ethnicity in a 'matrix of domination'. Similarly Brah and Phoenix[10] regard the concept of intersectionality as 'signifying the complex, irreducible, varied and variable effects which ensue when multiple axes of differentiation – economic, political, cultural, psychic, subjective and experiential – intersect in historically specific contexts', emphasising that different dimensions of social life cannot be separately extracted and presented as discrete and pure strands.

McCall[11] contends that no single form of inequality can represent the rest, but that some forms of inequality seem to arise from the same conditions that might reduce other forms, including, potentially, a conflict between reducing gender inequality and increasing inequality among women. Allowing women into positions of power in the world of work potentially reduces inequality between women and men; however, as not all women have equal access to positions of power in the world of paid work, this has the potential to create inequalities between women who can and cannot access these positions.

Women who mother and engage in paid work in Ireland are women who everyday are at a neglected social location. Many US and UK scholars have explored the difficulties professional and managerial women experience combining motherhood with paid work, managing the 'private world . . . of reproduction'[12] in the more public context of the organisation. Buzzanell and Liu[13] discuss the negotiations women make in relation to maternity leave, which they regard as a conflict management process. Similarly, in outlining the tensions and pressures imposed on newly maternal professionally employed women, Gattrell exposes employer antipathy toward the maternal body,[14] and she also outlines the efforts women make in performing 'maternal body work' in order to fit within the 'prevailing masculine symbolic order of professionalism' in workplaces.[15] Other writers have interviewed high-achieving professional women who 'opted out', and found that women reluctantly gave up their careers because they found themselves marginalised and stigmatised, negatively reinforced for trying to hold on to their careers after becoming mothers.[16] With the exception of these accounts of high achieving professional women in the US and UK, and 'celebrity moms' in popular press, including Madonna, Victoria Beckham and Angelina Jolie and the 'yummy mummy' phenomenon which promotes glamorous motherhood and presumes a certain wealth and lifestyle, most women who mother and engage in paid work on a day to day basis in Ireland, are under-researched and invisible.

However, one of the complications of focusing on specific groups in specific locations is that it leads to a problematic form of identity politics. Martinez[17] has likened the concentration on specific groups to the 'oppression olympics', criticising the notion that oppressions of specific groups can be quantified and that some oppressions are worse than others. With this perspective, the most oppressed group would take first place on top of the 'hierarchy of oppressions'. This perspective forecloses any resistance to power and ignores the multiplicity and contradictions in the relationships among different hierarchical systems.[18] Another complication with theorising simultaneously multiple complex inequalities is that at the point of intersection, it is insufficient to treat them merely as if they are to be added up.[19] It is not possible to add women's motherhood in the family to women's participation in employment and say that women who are 'working mothers' experience twice as many inequalities as a woman who only does one or the other. Furthermore, women may also experience raced, classed or other inequalities and these cannot be overlooked. Adding up the disadvantages, as in the notion of double or triple disadvantage does not fully account for the intersection; they may often, at least partially, mutually constitute each other.[20]

Attempts to study intersecting inequalities have introduced new methodological problems and have limited the range of approaches used to study intersectionality. McCall[21] contends that these developments can be traced to the complexity that arises when the subject of analysis expands to include multiple dimensions of social life and categories of analysis. She outlines three approaches to the study of intersectionality, based both on the demand to manage complexity and their stance toward categories. These three perspectives are defined primarily by the way they 'use analytical categories to explore the complexity of intersectionality in social life'.[22] Anticategorical complexity rejects categories altogether, intercategorical complexity takes a comparative approach between different groups being researched, and intracategorical complexity provisionally uses categories to account for the lived experience of a single group at neglected points of intersection. This approach begins with a unified intersectional core and works its way outward to unravel the influences of gender, class and other social relations.

Intracategorical complexity is the approach adopted in this research, to expose the intersecting inequalities experienced by this group at the social location of 'working mother'. This facilitated uncovering the differences and complexities of experience embodied at that location as well as revealing the range of diversity and difference within the group. Walby[23] argues the intracategorical approach has become a strategy for seeking out ever finer units for analysis, in pursuit of a pure intersecting category. There are no pure groups and there will always be more forms of difference and there will still be some differences within the group being researched; therefore it is also necessary to examine the social structural conditions that contribute to different forms of inequality. This overcomes the 'oppression olympics' perspective and facilitates our understanding of the complexity of inequality.

Intersectionality and the social system

Exploring the multiple intersecting inequalities women experience at the level of the individual does not adequately account for the social structural systems which interact with women's social positions to create intersecting inequalities. Researchers face a trade-off between intersecting inequalities at the level of the individual and at the level of the society. Phoenix asks if intersectionality fails to address structural inequalities because it focuses on agency on the one hand and fails to address agency if it produces fixed conceptualisations of structure on the other.[24]

The problem with analysing multiple complex inequalities is the absence of a concept of system in contemporary sociology, even though some concept of system is often found to be needed to address the conceptualisation of social interconnections.[25] Walby argues complexity theory is appropriate to studies of intersectionality, precisely because it has the conceptual tools to locate inequalities at the level of the individual and explain these with reference to the social structure, to locate the inequalities and social structures in an overall social system, theorising the nature and form of intersectionality and its impact on social systems, globally and locally.[26]

In complexity theory systems are self-reproducing and may be self-organising and self-defining. The system has autopoietic features, thus each component participates in the production or transformation of other components in the system. The system is produced by its components and in turn produces those components. In such a complex system, gender is not a dimension limited to the organisation of reproduction or family, class is not a dimension equated with the economy, and race is not a category reduced to the primacy of ethnicities, nations and borders, but all of the processes that systematically organise families, economies and nations are co-constructed along with the meanings of gender, race and class that are presented in and reinforced by these institutions, separately and together.

The system is an open system and takes all other systems as its environment. These are complex adaptive systems rather than hierarchically related elements and as one system changes, the others with whom it is interacting also change and they co-evolve. Not only are gender relations constituted in the economy, polity, violence and civil society, but so also are ethnic relations and class relations. These systems of social relations are constituted at different levels of abstraction; one level is emergent from another. An individual will participate in a number of different sets of social relations and systems that co-evolve in a changing fitness landscape, thus gender relations co-evolve in an environment that includes both class and ethnic relations.

Furthermore, the environment or landscape that each system faces is changed as a result of changes in the systems that constitute that landscape. So as one system evolves, it changes the landscape for others. The concept of path dependency facilitates the inclusion of temporality and sequencing within social theory. Path dependency means that events that occur at one moment in time have consequences at later times and that the order in which events and developments occur has consequences. Therefore, complexity theory considers each set of social relations – class, gender and ethnicity – as a social system. Each of these sets of social relations is not reduced to a cultural concept of identity, or economic concept of class. Instead, each set of social relations of inequality is understood as a social system with full ontological depth, being constituted in the institutional domains of economy, polity, violence and civil society.

Within each domain (economy, polity, violence, civil society), there are multiple sets of social relations, e.g. gender, class, ethnicity.[27] Each institutional domain and each set of social relations are conceptualised as systems, not parts of systems. Each system interacts and overlaps with the others. This avoids the rigidity of the notion of a system as made up of its parts. Conceptualising and exploring the separate systems of inequality in this way demonstrates the ways these systems mutually constitute each other, and reveals the multiple intersecting inequalities experienced by the group being researched.[28]

The social relations of gender, motherhood, class and the institutional domains of family, workplace and society in which they operate are dynamic and ongoing and evident in shifting times and spaces; therefore, gender relations are not fixed either for individual women or for the gender order. The inequalities women experience as workers contribute to the inequalities women experience as mothers and vice versa. The processes and institutions which create these inequalities are mutually dependent, therefore the inequalities may partially constitute and reinforce one another. Walby's conceptualisation of complexity theory facilitates locating the inequalities and privileges women experience at an individual level in the structural social system. This is not to focus on structure at the expense of agency or vice versa but considers both.

Ferree[29] builds on Walby's work with complexity theory and adopts a more dynamic and institutional understanding of intersectionality, which she calls interactive intersectionality;[30] this views the dimensions of inequality themselves as dynamic and in changing, mutually constituted relationships with each other, from which they cannot be disentangled. Ferree calls it interactive intersectionality to emphasise its structuration[31] as an ongoing multi-level process from which agency cannot be erased. The inequalities women experience because of their motherhood may also partially constitute the inequalities women experience as workers, while these inequalities may privilege as well as regulate. The concepts of 'structuration', and in particular 'agency', are necessary and important dimensions of the study of the inequalities experienced at the intersections of worker and mother, as women are making choices and exercising agency, even if not always in conditions of their own choosing. Furthermore, Ferree[32] argues that intersectionality cannot be located at any one level of analysis, whether that is individual or institutional. The 'intersection of gender and race' is not any number of specific locations occupied by individuals or groups, but a process through which race or gender take on different meanings depending on whether, how and by whom, race or gender is seen as relevant to an individual's employment, economic status or desirability. Women's motherhood may be regarded as a positive attribute in the family, but the same motherhood can be regarded negatively in the world of work, demonstrating the way in which the same characteristic takes on a different meaning in different settings.

Discourse and Power

To her concept of interactive intersectionality, Ferree[33] adds an emphasis on discourse as the political process by which the co-creation of inequality between processes (race, class, gender) and domains (family, society, work) occurs. Her approach rests on understanding the co-formation of knowledge and power, stresses the historical development of institutions that shape consciousness and practice, and identifies discourse as a crucial arena of political activity.[34] Ferree's concept of discourse as the political process which gives meaning to gender, mother, worker in different institutions and social locations is a necessary part of conceptualising intersectionality. In this research, women's narratives reveal how they draw on the broad discourses of neo-liberalism, feminism, motherhood and individualism. These discourses reveal the operation of power, because as Foucault[35] claims, power is exercised through discourse and he demonstrates that discourses are an organisation of power. In modern society the behaviour of individuals and groups is increasingly pervasively controlled through standards of normality which are disseminated by a range of assessing, diagnostic, prognostic and normative knowledges. Foucault writes of regimes of 'power/knowledge' or 'discourses' – structured ways of knowing and exercising power – and he exposes discourse as a decentred form of power, distributed over a complex of discursive sites. Foucault argues, since modern power operates in a capillary fashion throughout the social body, it is best grasped in its concrete and local effects and in the everyday practices which sustain and reproduce power relations. Modern disciplinary society can dispense with direct forms of repression and constraint because social control is achieved by means of subtler strategies of normalisation, strategies which produce self-regulating 'normalised' individuals.[36] Modern regimes of power operate to produce us as subjects who are both the objects and vehicles of power and it is necessary to recognise that there is not a simple divide between accepted and excluded discourse nor between a dominant and dominated discourse. However, there are 'a multiplicity of discursive elements that come into play in various strategies', that can transmit, produce and reinforce power, but also expose power, which makes resistance to power possible.[37] In this research it is the meanings that women give to 'mother', 'worker' and 'working mother' that reveal the operation of power through the discourses of neo-liberalism, feminism, individualism and motherhood, which create and sustain gender relations and the gender order in Irish society. There are competing strains within and between these discourses which are dominant in different contexts. Thus women must decide which strain or discourse to recognise or reject. One of the problematic features of any notion of discourse is that it is difficult to assess where the discourse begins and ends, because discourses become part of our daily lives. Dominant discourses are those which have gained sufficient status to be put beyond question or critique. While such discourses frequently have institutional power, they may also be appropriated into individuals lives and explanatory and descriptive schemas as ways to explain events and experiences.[38]

Subjectivity is used to mean the conditions of being subjected to frameworks of regulation, knowledge and discourse and constructing subjectivity in the process. Women, mothers and workers are subject positions constituted through discourse, rather than pre-existing discourse. In claiming discourse is the political process in interactive intersectionality, Ferree draws attention away from 'different' identities and bodies to the contextual processes and conditions in which representations of identity and difference are produced, governed and socially organised. Such a shift is analytically important because it exposes the myth that identities naturally pre-exist and the fallacy that subjects have identities and bodies. This, in turn, draws attention to the doing or making of difference, and serves to show that subjects are produced as identities through discursive processes.[39]

Intersectionality can reveal the 'scattered hegemonies' that differentially structure our everyday lives by tying discourses of gender to global economic structures, patriarchal nationalisms, contending traditions and local issues of domination.[40] 'There is no Patriarch Headquarters with flags and limousines, where all the strategies are worked out';[41] instead there is 'a multiplicity of discourses produced by a whole series of mechanisms operating in different institutions'.[42] The interplay of gender with other structures, such as class, creates further (unequal) relationships.[43] Power operates through the broad dominant discourses of neo-liberalism, individualism, feminism and motherhood, to place women in an inferior hierarchical position to men in the gender order.

Both discourse and intersectionality can be more productively approached through the study of configurations, a term McCall uses to describe attention to patterns, interactions among elements that have paradoxical and conflicting meanings depending on the specific context as a whole. Such configurations – both of discourses and of intersectionality in this and other aspects of the social order – have stability, but also change. Women's motherhood in the family interacts with women's employment in the workplace to create patterns of inequalities or privileges which are only experienced by members of the group of 'working mothers'.

While no concept is perfectly able to capture all the complexities of inequality, this intersectional approach reveals complex inequality at the intersection of mother and worker. This framework examines inequalities at the level of the individual, locates these inequalities in the social structural system, recognises discourse as the political process which creates and sustains inequalities and identifies patterns between discourse and intersectionality. This approach exposes the ways women's paid work and motherhood interacts with family, workplace and society to create multiple intersecting inequalities and privileges, even while patterns are dynamic and changing. There are symbiotic relationships between discourse and intersectionality at individual and structural levels which reveal the ways new and complex inequalities are created and maintained for 'working mothers' in Ireland.

Feminist Standpoint

Experience has been seen as *the* basis of feminism,[44] in that feminism as a social movement and as a personal politics began the moment women began to talk to each other and make sense of their experiences as women.[45] A feminist standpoint is one major strand of theorising experience that has contributed to the development of feminist epistemologies. The principal claim regarding feminist standpoint theories is that certain socio-political positions occupied by women (and by extension other groups who lack social and economic privilege) can become sites of epistemic privilege and thus productive starting points for enquiry about those who are socially and politically marginalised, and can also reveal the way power operates to maintain those who are socially and political privileged. Thus researching subordinated locations and the knowledge they foster not only provides insight into the lives of members of subordinated groups, but also casts light on dominant group practices, especially those that create and reproduce inequality. A standpoint makes visible aspects of social relations that are unavailable from dominant perspectives, and in so doing generates the kinds of questions that will lead to a more complete and true account of those relations.[46]

Using a feminist materialist approach, Hartsock claims that women's experiences of their daily lives give them privileged knowledge of social reality.[47] Hartsock suggests that the experience of motherhood as an institution, rather than simply just through individual and personal experience, creates the relational self. Thus,

> Motherhood in the large sense, i.e. motherhood as an institution rather than experience, including pregnancy and the preparation for motherhood almost all female children receive as socialization, results in the construction of female existence as centred on a complex relational nexus.[48]

Critically, this has an epistemological consequence, with women's lives providing the basis for a privileged, yet mediated view of gendered power structures in society.

'A standpoint is *not* how folks in a particular social location think.'[49] This point has been reaffirmed by many, if not all, of the major standpoint theorists since Hartsock distinguished a standpoint from the spontaneous consciousness of social actors. A crucial element of standpoint theory is the distinction between experience and knowledge. However, in researching an aspect of women's lives, it is possible only to achieve partial truth or partial knowledge. One of the most important criticisms of standpoint theory has been a focus on the relationship between reality and experiences that in turn invokes notions of truth.[50] The notion of lived experience, if taken to an extreme, can privilege individual experience and knowledge to the exclusion of a collective standpoint. All women are different from each other and each woman has multiple identities, any one of which might arguably provide a standpoint for knowledge.[51] There is no reality out there waiting to be discovered, but there are many subjective experiences, even though women, and other groups of people, share a commonality of experience and oppression.[52] Stanley and Wise assert that there are multiple realities and that individuals understand social reality through lived experience, which is 'daily constructed by us in routine and mundane ways, as we go about the ordinary and everyday business of living', and argue social realities are constructed through human perceptions.[53] The belief that the social world is interpreted and constructed does not deny the importance or validity of agency and lived experience. It is important to 'take other people's truths seriously' and accord respect to people's everyday lives, for whom experiences are 'valid and true'.[54] In fact, as Temple argues, 'it is by listening and learning from other people's experiences that the researcher can learn "the truth" is not the same for everyone'.[55] However, 'experience is not something which language reflects. In so far as it is meaningful, experience is constituted in language'.[56] If experience is a phenomenon of language, then our focus should change from looking at experiences themselves as evidence of reality and toward looking at how discourse and representation constitute experiences.[57]

Discourses become effective to the extent that they attach themselves to a technology for their realisation. Technologies are collections of forms of knowledge which operate via particular techniques which are 'oriented to produce certain political outcomes'.[58] There is no preconstituted inner self to be communicated in the world; it comes into being through discourse and the recognition of others. Therefore, the self is not knowable outside of discourse and recognition. Discourses of 'motherhood' can operate as a 'metalanguage' which produce the subject position 'mother' and which mask the operation of other axes of difference and power.[59]

Experience conflates the 'lived' with those discursive 'regimes of truth' that govern the transmission of the 'lived' into discourse. The ontological level of 'lived' experience can be understood as discursive categories working through embodied living subjects who perceive them as 'realities'.[60] The experiences articulated by women cannot be seen as 'a pre-given ontology that precedes its expression'.[61] Women's experiences are constructed through the institutional and discursive technologies of motherhood, neo-liberalism, individualism and feminism, as well as class and gender and the relative abilities of these technologies, in different contexts, to produce certain kinds of selves.[62]

This research explores how discourse and representation constitute women's experience and identifies the politics of class, gender, mother and worker and the power dynamics that constitute and normalise particular categories of difference that then get produced as women's 'experience'. The focus is on how discourses and the politics of class, gender, mother, worker, family and 'working mother' are disciplinary in the sense of ordering and classifying, but are simultaneously productive and creative and are understood relationally by participants in relation to social and economic institutions and practices.

Developing a 'working mothers' standpoint, while providing a view of institutional and discursive power structures, does not assume homogeneity of experience among the group of women. This is intersectional research, and 'working mothers' are not a pure group[63] and in this research, in addition to developing a shared standpoint, I reveal the intersecting inequalities and privileges which in turn reveal the diversity and difference within the group of women. As Stanley and Wise argue, 'the experience of "women" is ontologically fractured and complex because we do not all share one single and unseamed reality'.[64] The claim that women's lives provide a better starting point for thought is not about arguing for *one* position. Starting from the thoughts of different people with different experiences from our own, helps to increase our ability to understand the perspectives of the powerful and the less powerful.[65] This standpoint and the experiences of 'working mothers' thus provides a privileged, yet mediated view of gendered institutional and discursive power structures in society.

Collins aims to work with both the notion of a shared standpoint and the notion of intersectionality to develop a highly nuanced and specific model.

> Intersectionality . . . highlights how . . . social groups are positioned within unjust power relations, but it does so in a way

that introduces added complexity to formerly race-, class-, and gender-only approaches to social phenomena.[66]

Collins is careful to state that while it is easier to apply intersectionality to individual analyses of experience, it is important not to elevate individual analyses over structural analyses. In this context, intersectionality 'provides an interpretive framework for thinking through how intersections of race and class, or race and gender, or sexuality and class, for example, shape any group's experience across specific social contexts'.[67]

In this research, women's experiences as outlined in their narratives reveal the inequalities and privileges women encounter every day by combining motherhood with paid work in Ireland. Following Collins, my intention is to place 'women's experiences in the center of analysis without privileging those experiences',[68] by analysing the experiences of women to reveal the power operating through discourses and institutions which create inequalities and privileges for these women. Their experience is the starting point for analysis, but it is what these experiences reveal about power and its effects that is the focus of this research. Treating people's everyday lives as a sociological problematic means exploring interactions between women and wider social structures and relations.[69] This research reaches out from the experience of women to explore gendered power relations in Irish society. By revealing the range of experiences and complexities within and between the group of 'working mothers', I develop a 'working mothers' standpoint, which reveals the operation of power at individual and societal levels and the operation of power through discourses, which reveals the symbiotic relationship between categories and intersections, and which creates and maintains inequalities and privileges for 'working mothers' in one middle-class Irish suburb.

Intersectional analysis

Intersectionality is an analytical tool for studying, understanding and responding to the ways in which gender intersects with other identities and categories, and how these intersections contribute to unique experiences of oppression and privilege. The point is not to deny the importance of categories but to focus on the process by which they are created.[70] Moreover, the point of the analysis is not to isolate different 'identities', within one 'identity'; such an approach would simply reinscribe the additive model.[71] Following McCall and Skeggs[72] I treat dominant categories as constructs, but misleading constructs, which will allow the representation of the diversity and heterogeneity of experience.

> To say that a category such as race or gender is socially con-
> structed is not to say that that category has no significance in
> our world. On the contrary, a large and continuing project for
> subordinated people – and indeed, one of the projects for
> which postmodern theories have been very helpful – is
> thinking about the way in which power has clustered around
> certain categories and is exercised against others.[73]

The categories of mother, worker and 'working mother', are not only categories of identification but are also hierarchically organised. As Crenshaw originally articulated, intersectionality is an alternative to the essentialism in 'identity' politics. Crenshaw specifies, however, that the problem is not the existence of categories but rather the values of hierarchy that fill up and inform categories.

According to Cole, translating the theoretical insights of intersectionality into empirical research does not require the adoption of a new set of methods, but rather, a reconceptualisation of the meaning and consequences of social categories. She suggests three questions that can guide researchers wishing to use this type of reconceptualisation in their research: 'Who is included within this category? What role does inequality play? And where are the similarities?'[74] Cole's reconceptualisation of the meaning and consequences of social categories by interrogating membership, inequality and similarities within categories, facilitated applying an intersectional standpoint to this empirical research.

Analyses that presume to focus on gender, say, in the absence of other category memberships, implicitly assume a host of other social statuses that usually go unnamed: middle-class standing, hetero-sexuality, able-bodiedness and white race.[75] Scholars who attend to which groups are represented and which tend to be excluded – either by focusing their work on members of subordinate groups[76] or conversely, by explicitly identifying and investigating the multiple identities that define privilege[77] – disrupt these assumptions by identifying the ways that race, class or other identities shape the meaning of gender. Such attention is critical because failure to attend to how social categories depend on one another for meaning renders our knowledge of any one category both incomplete and biased. Spelman[78] noted that Chodorow considered only the specific practices of western families with race and class privilege when making universal claims about the characteristics of mothering[79] in her landmark book *The Reproduction of Mothering*. Spelman concluded, 'it is theoretically significant . . . if statements that appear true about "men and women" clearly aren't true when we specify that we are talking about men and women of different classes or races'.[80] Attending to who is included within a category can lead to a more nuanced understanding of how social categories of identity, difference and disadvantage shape experience and improves our ability to theorise and empirically investigate the ways social categories structure individual and social life. Constructs like race and gender affect beliefs about what is possible or desirable, and define the contours of an individual's opportunities and life chances through social and institutional practices.[81]

In this research, participants in the category being studied are white, women, mothers, employees, middle-class, able-bodied, heterosexual, some of whom have partners, most of whom are Irish. As wives, mothers and daughters of white men, white women derive social and economic benefits from existing inequities; thus, even those who are feminists may participate in a form of complicity with the status quo. Therefore, rather than merely calling for attention to the ways that these categories of identity, difference and disadvantage intersect, we can identify specific mechanisms through which they do.[82]

Weber and Parra-Medina have made a useful distinction between looking 'downstream' for causes (i.e. in individual behaviour that might be associated with social category membership) and 'upstream' at 'the group processes that define systems of social inequality' such as laws, institutional practices and public policies.[83] Considering the role of inequality enables looking 'upstream' by drawing attention to how 'working mothers' stand in relation to each other and to public and private institutions including families, workplaces and society, and correspondingly how political, material and social inequality leads to class and gender differences in outcomes.[84]

Gender and motherhood are marking mechanisms for all women in this research, which leads to inequalities experienced at an individual level, in families, workplaces and society, but it is important to recognise that while oppression is common, the forms it takes are conditioned by class, age, sexuality and other structural, historical and geographical differences between women. Differences in women's class, marital status, occupation and employment reveal inequalities between women and the ways these inequalities are the product of political, material and social inequality in the structural social system, leading to different individual outcomes in terms of inequality or privilege.

MacLean suggests the workings of privilege are often invisible to the privileged and in one sense, it is a commonplace observation that positions of social group privilege tend to shield privileged people from the actualities of other people's oppression.[85] Having privileges due to membership of dominant groups can insulate agents from opportunities to acquire knowledge about a given form of oppression, whereas having experienced a given form of oppression provides opportunities for understanding its contours. As hooks argues, 'organizing around your oppression' may provide an excuse for many privileged women to ignore their own status and the oppression of others.[86] MacLean[87] argues that agents with multiple social group privileges are often positioned so that the intersections of structures of disadvantage are less readily visible to them, which means that oppression can appear less 'intersectional' from the standpoint of privilege. However, she also suggests that a form of oppression appears separable or isolatable when the agent who is being oppressed is not simultaneously experiencing other types of oppression, but is in the presence of his/her own privileges. It may be obvious to these middle-class 'working mothers' that they are oppressed because of their gender, both in the family and in the workplace. However, it may be less obvious to them that they are privileged by being, white, middle-class, able bodied, partnered and heterosexual. It is also critically important from an intersectional standpoint that in recognising similarities, researchers remain sensitive to nuanced differences across groups even where similarities are found; for example, although middle-class, white, partnered 'working mothers' and working-class, white, single 'working mothers' might experience some of the same stressors in similar ways, their experiences are not equivalent or identical.

Intersectionality makes plain that gender, race, class and sexuality simultaneously affect the perceptions, experiences and opportunities of everyone living in a society stratified along these dimensions. To understand any one of these dimensions, we must address them in combination. As Hancock has argued, intersectionality does not simply describe a content specialisation addressing issues germane to specific populations; it is also a paradigm for theory and research offering new ways of understanding the complex causality that characterises social phenomena.[88] This reconceptualisation of social categories can help identify the inequalities and privileges women experience 'downstream' as a result of their behaviour, deriving from their positioning within dominant discourses, and locate the causes of these inequalities and privileges 'upstream' in the structural social system, and reveal the ways that intersecting inequalities depend upon and mutually construct each other and work together to shape outcomes for women in the composite category 'working mother'.

CHAPTER 3

'Working mothers' research

This case study examines the intersecting inequalities and privileges experienced by women who combine motherhood with paid work. I selected a middle-class suburb in a provincial city familiar to me and which I believed would facilitate access to many middle-class 'working mothers'. The area is long-established but has undergone a major population boom in the last two decades. This local area is identified as predominantly middle-class and suburban. Women were recruited through four primary schools in the area, two boys' schools and two girls' schools, allowing for the possibility that women might have older and younger children. Letters were sent home in the school bags of those children living with their mothers, inviting women who were engaged in paid work of any kind to participate in this study.

McCall[1] asserts that case study approaches, which are compatible with the intracategorical complexity approach, represent the most effective way of empirically researching the meanings of social categories in light of their intersections. Case studies are an effective way of managing intersections because one can start with an individual, group, event, or context, then work outward to unravel how categories are lived and experienced.[2] Case studies strive to portray 'the close-up reality and thick description of participants' lived experiences'.[3] This approach considers what identities are being lived, by whom and when and also considers when and how some categories might unsettle, undo or cancel out other categories as they intersect.[4] The qualitative methods of focus groups and semi-structured interviews were employed, because we can enhance our understanding both by adding layers of information and by using one type of data to validate or refine another.[5]

'Working mothers'

Thirty women participated in this research; half of the women worked full-time, and half worked reduced hours, part-time or were job sharing. The participants are almost evenly employed in public- and private-sector organisations.

In Ireland, the eleven-category Socio Economic Grouping (SEG) classification system brings together people with broadly similar economic and social status and people are assigned to a particular SEG on the basis of their occupational and employment status.[6] The seven category Social Class Groups classification aims to bring together persons with similar social and economic statuses on the basis of the level of skill or educational attainment required. The Social Class Group was first used in the 1996 Census and is based on the UK Standard Occupational Classification[7] with modifications to reflect Irish labour market conditions. In determining social class, occupations are ranked by the level of skill required on a social-class scale ranging from 1 (highest) to 7 (lowest).

TABLE 1: IRISH CLASSIFICATION SYSTEM

Socio-economic groups		Social class groups	
A	Employers and managers	1	Professional workers
B	Higher professional	2	Managerial and technical
C	Lower professional		
D	Non-manual	3	Non-manual
E	Manual skilled	4	Skilled manual
F	Semi-skilled	5	Semi-skilled
G	Unskilled	6	Unskilled
H	Own account workers		
I	Farmers		
J	Agricultural workers		
Z	All others gainfully occupied and unknown	7	All others gainfully occupied and unknown

Socio Economic Groupings, *Census of Population 1996* (Cork: Central Statistics Office, 1996).

All participants in the study, according to the Irish Classification System are ranked in the top five socio-economic groupings (A–E) and the top five social-class groups (1–5).

TABLE 2: PARTICIPANTS' SOCIO-ECONOMIC GROUPING
AND SOCIAL CLASS

Participant	Socio-economic group	Social class groups
Faye	A	I
Jasmine	A	2
Jane	A	2
Collette	A	2
Amanda	A	2
Audrey	A	2
Gina	A	3
Jean	B	I
Freya	B	I
Grace	B	I
Kate	B	I
Eithne	B	2
Ameila	C	2
Anita	C	2
June	C	2
Amy	C	2
Florence	C	2
Avril	C	2
Aisling	C	2
Agatha	C	3
Tamsin	C	3
Joy	D	3
Angela	D	3
Sabine	D	3
Anna	D	3
Cindy	D	3
Colleen	D	3
Yolanda	D	3
Anastasia	D	5
Brona	E	4

(All names are pseudonyms)

This study was conducted in a middle-class suburb of a provincial city, and in the 2006 Census[8] the year in which the research was conducted, data on this city reveals the professional and middle-class profile of women in this research, relative to the city of which the suburb is a part.

TABLE 3: PROFILES OF PARTICIPANTS IN RELATION
TO THE PROVINCIAL CITY

Socio-economic group	Description	% of women in the study in each group	% of women in the city in each group
A	Employers and managers	23	9.74
B	Higher professionals	17	5.48
C	Lower professionals	30	10.25
D	Non-manual	27	24.34
E	Manual skilled	3	5.77
F	Semi-skilled	0	8.88
G	Unskilled	0	4.60
H	Own account workers	0	2.20
I	Farmers	0	0.08
J	Agricultural workers	0	0.07
Z	All others gainfully occupied and unknown	0	28.59
		100%	100%

Limitations to the classification system are that the code to which a person's occupation is linked is determined by the kind of work he or she performs in earning a living; therefore, the socio-economic group may not be an accurate reflection of social class, for instance, if a person is employed at a lower or higher occupation than their qualification level. Given the predominance of women who work full-time in the home in the local suburb, this may also distort these findings. In contrast to socio-economic group, the social class of family dependants is derived from the social class of the parent having the highest social class.

At the focus groups, participants completed biographical questionnaires which provided details of their family, childcare and employment situations. These details were provided at the time of the focus group discussions, but changes in circumstances revealed at interview one year later, are outlined in their biographies (Appendix 2).

TABLE 4: PARTICIPANTS' BIOGRAPHICAL DETAILS
(FOCUS GROUP)

Pseudonym	Working pattern	Hours per week	Occupation and sector	Childcare arrangement	No. children	Partnership status
Agatha	Full-time	32	Travel consultant private sector	Husband and sister	2	Married
Aisling	Full-time	30	Teacher 3rd level public sector	Childminder's home	4	Married
Amanda	Full-time	39	Clinic nurse manager public sector	Childminder own home	2	Married
Ameila	Part-time	15	Nurse public sector	Childminder own home	3	Married
Amy	Part-time	19	Midwife public sector	Childminder own home	2	Married
Anastasia	Part-time	29	Personal carer private sector	Husband and sister	2	Married
Angela	Part-time	14	Respite carer public sector	Neighbour [irregular hours]	3	Married
Anita	Part-time	15	Nurse public sector	None	2	Married
Anna	Part-time	18	Civil servant public sector	Childminder's home	3	Married
Audrey	Full-time	39	Director of nursing public sector	Childminder own home	3	Married
Avril	Full-time	28	Physiotherapist public sector	Childminder own home	5	Married
Brona	Full-time	36 (3 x 12)	General operator private sector	Childminder own home	3	Married
Cindy	Part-time	20	Retail sales assistant private sector	Grandparents	2	Married
Colleen	Reduced hours	32	Quality specialist private sector	Childminder's home	1	Separated
Collette	Full-time	38	Software manager private sector	Childminder's home	2	Married

TABLE 4: PARTICIPANTS' BIOGRAPHICAL DETAILS
(FOCUS GROUP) *(cont.)*

Pseudonym	Working pattern	Hours per week	Occupation and sector	Childcare arrangement	No. children	Partnership status
Eithne	Full-time	35	Product development executive private sector	Crèche and husband	2	Married
Faye	Full-time	45	Company director private sector	Childminder 4 days husband 1 day	2	Married
Florence	Part-time	24	Nurse public sector	Childminder own home	3	Married
Freya	Full-time	38	Accountant private sector	Crèche 1 child au pair 2 children	3	Married
Gina	Job sharing	19	Bank official private sector	Childminder own home	2	Married
Grace	Reduced hours	28	Inspector public sector	Childminder's home	2	Married
Jane	Full-time	36	Advertising manager private sector	Grandparents 2 days Childminder's home 3 days	1	Divorced
Jasmine	Full-time	30+	School principal public sector	Husband and after school club	2	Married
Jean	Reduced hours	30	Accountant private sector	Parents 1 child Childminder 2 childlren	3	Married
Joy	Part-time	8-16	Market researcher private sector	Husband	3	Married
June	Part-time	18	Midwife public sector	Childminder's home	3	Married
Kate	Full-time	40+	Lecturer public sector	Sister	4	Married
Sabine	Part-time	17.5	Accounts assistant public sector	Parents-in-law	2	Married
Tamsin	Full-time	39	Shipping clerk private sector	Childminder's home	1	Divorced; remarried
Yolanda	Full-time (parental leave 1 day/week	32 (4×8)	Accounts assistant public sector	Parents 2 days childminder 2 days	2	Married

Focus Groups

I employed the qualitative method of focus groups to initially explore with the women the ways in which they combined motherhood with paid work, to establish how discourses of motherhood were accepted, challenged, reinforced or resisted and to examine women's experience of inequalities at the level of the individual, as well as to reveal the range of diversity and difference within the group of women.

Key features of a focus group such as providing access to participants' own language, encouraging the production of more fully articulated accounts and observing the process of collective-sense-making are particularly appropriate where primary qualitative data is required. Wilkinson argues that 'focus groups are a particularly *good* choice of method when the purpose of the research is to elicit people's understandings, opinions and views, or to explore how these are advanced, elaborated and negotiated in a social context.[9] The reduced influence of the researcher makes focus groups suited to intersectional feminist research[10] because there is greater scope for participants to set the research agenda and to develop the themes important to them.[11] The relatively free flow of discussion and debate between the members of a focus group offers an excellent opportunity to listen to local voices[12] and to gain insight into participants' conceptual worlds on their own terms.[13]

In this research I was concerned to learn about normative constructions of mothers and workers and how these women negotiated these constructions in their daily lives as 'working mothers'. The focus group discussions were public fora, in which women shared their experiences with each other and with me, thus the discussions had the potential to have a normative effect, generating agreement on a normative construction of motherhood. One interesting, and unanticipated feature of the focus group discussions was the tension generated when some women recognised or accepted different discursive strains that were not identified by other women. In fact, it emerged that the women, to different extents, recognised the competing and conflicting discourses of neo-liberalism, individualism, feminism and motherhood and this generated considerable disagreement, tension and lively discussion in many focus groups. The fact that they did not recognise a single normative construction of mother or worker, but recognised several, demonstrated how they contested, refused, accepted or accommodated these discourses in the ways they combine mother-hood with paid work. These disagreements were the starting point for analysis, and formed the basis of interviews with the same women conducted a year later.

Organising focus groups was difficult, primarily because of par-ticipants' (un)availability. Finding times that would suit women who were attempting to accommodate the focus group discussion in between their obligations to employers and to their families was not easy. For each group, I approached women from different industry sectors and whose children were in different schools, so that participants would be unlikely to be acquainted with each other. Where possible I then selected women who worked in full- and part-time employment. After that, decisions were based on women's availability to attend the group discussions and the avail-ability of the venue. Five focus group discussions were held with thirty women, between February and April 2005.

Interviews

In order to locate women's intersecting inequalities at the level of Irish society and to explore how the relationship between the social relations of mother and worker intersect with the institutions of workplace, family and society, and were experienced by individual women, I explored these issues with the same women in semi-structured, one-to-one interviews. The interviews were very important in allowing for a 'contextualisation of experience'[14] and a closer look at the multiple dimensions of inequality within women's lives.[15] I conducted twenty-four semi-structured inter-views with individual women, sometimes in their homes, and sometimes in mine. These were conducted between January and April 2006. In the period between the focus group discussions and interviews, there had been many changes in women's circum-stances. One woman became pregnant, one had a baby, two women changed jobs, one moved house, and two had separated from their husbands. Six women were not contactable, which suggests their circumstances had changed, or they were no longer interested in participating in the study following their contribution to the focus group discussions. All the women who participated in interviews had reflected on their participation in the focus group and some wished to clarify or change some part of their earlier contribution. Some women wished to question further some aspect of 'working motherhood' they had not considered prior to participating in the focus group discussion. All participants claimed to have found focus group discussions informative, and to have found it thought provoking to have met other women who are 'working mothers', as all participants expressed their ignorance of the ways other women combine motherhood with paid work.

The group discussions and interviews represent new empirical data and are important cultural constructions in themselves. They are necessarily mediated by my selection from the transcripts, my interpretations of the transcripts and my theoretical concerns. I am distanced from the accounts by my position as researcher and interpreter. My interest stems from my experience as a mother in employment. Letherby[16] argues this is not unusual, as many academic research projects bear an intimate relationship to researchers' lives. However, I acknowledge that not all employed mothers share the same experiences. Hartsock[17] argues that one's position in the social hierarchy in relation to other groups potentially limits or broadens one's understanding of others. It is also important to note, as Letherby[18] claims, the interests and priorities of the researcher and the researched are likely to be different. Respondents have different motivations for being involved in social research: sometimes they wish to help the researcher; sometimes they wish to 'set the record straight'; sometimes they wish to 'get something off their chest', or even to 'educate the world'.[19] I asked all the women why they participated in the study and the most common response was that they wanted to know how other women combined motherhood with paid work and if there was a 'right way' to be a 'working mother' in Ireland.

Data analysis

There are different voices in the women's narratives in the focus groups and in the interviews. In the public focus group discussion, the women clearly drew on dominant discourses and were aware of the public nature of the discussion, and stressed their efforts in relation to caring for their children and appearing to valorise motherhood. However, in the private interview situation, women revealed more about the difficulties they experience combining motherhood with paid work, as well as intimate details of their relationships with family, employment and wider social networks. In this study, there are differences in the statuses of the data from the focus group discussion and the interview, which reveals the women's awareness of authoritative discourses in the public forum of the focus group, and their privately held views in the interview situation.

In order to apply a feminist methodology that acknowledges the intersectional position of 'working mothers' in Ireland, I decided to start at the level of discourse in order to reveal the ways the participants understood dominant motherhood discourses. As noted in Chapter 2, following Foucault,[20] women, mothers and workers are subject positions constituted through discourse, rather than preexisting discourse. The concept of discourse shows how the fixing of meaning is never a neutral act, but always privileges certain interests. Thus, the question of what discourses prevail and whose interests they serve are most important.[21] This is not to discount the importance of material or economic issues, but to emphasise the importance of culture and discursive power.

Social structures and phenomena are experienced and understood at the level of individual subjectivity, and expressed in stories about lives. Narratives can show how people actively, and sometimes knowingly, take up positions in certain discourses, and how they are positioned by other people, and by social structures and discursive practices. I recognise that there are many competing discourses which gave rise to contradictions. In this analysis, I embraced these contradictions and the tensions they produced. I examined them rather than tried to control or resolve them in order to 'produce an awareness of the complexity, historical contingency and fragility of the practices that we invent to discover the truth about ourselves'.[22]

What is at stake then, in the analysis of the women's own accounts, is the ways in which the classed and gendered formations of 'mother', 'worker' and 'working mother', 'operate between [the] abstract structures and concrete specifics of everyday life'.[23] The focus is on the dynamics of the criteria used for what is seen as the 'truth' of the matter in the accounts.[24] How come certain things can and cannot be articulated? How are particular 'truths' authorised and accorded legitimacy by participants? What is produced or made possible in and through these accounts? How is experience, as Rose asks, 'cut . . . in certain ways, to distribute attractions and repulsions, passions and fears across it?'[25]

Following Gray, I considered how certain languages of description, explanation and judgement came to acquire the value of

'truth' and the kinds of actions and techniques that are made possible by these truths.[26] This approach challenges any essential
unified interiority of the subject prior to its expression in thought,
conduct, emotion and action, which in turn cannot be understood
outside of their relation to certain knowledges and expertise.[27] The
accounts are analysed to identify the 'truths' that are discursively
invoked to explain why things are seen and constructed by women
in particular ways.[28]

Excerpts from the group discussions and interviews are given
an independent existence as texts that are brought together to
produce readings of how the categories 'mother', 'worker' and
'working mother' are constituted in a local study.[29] This is not to
present evidence of the women's experience; when experience is
constructed as incontestable evidence, the discursive construction
of experience and its contextualised conditions of production are
ignored.[30] Individuals do not have experience; instead it is subjects
who are constituted through experience.[31]

Group discussions allowed participants to share their understandings, opinions and views in their own language and allowed
me to be a participating observer to the interaction of the women in
the group. This provided insights into the ways women talk about
and experience 'working motherhood' and the shared way they
made sense of these experiences. Focus group interactions revealed
not only shared ways of talking, but also shared experiences and
shared ways of making sense of these experiences, which offered an
insight into the commonly held assumptions, concepts and meanings of 'working mother', as well as participants' awareness and
engagement with or rejection of dominant discourses and norms.

The focus groups were designed to reveal dominant discourses,
participants' experiences of inequalities at the level of the individual as well as revealing the range of diversity and difference
within the group. Therefore, I found applying a discourse analysis
to the focus group transcripts was useful because 'it is in discourse
that power and knowledge are joined together'.[32] To begin this
analysis, I concentrated on agreements and disagreements between
participants in focus group discussions. Areas that were contested
indicated strong views, and women felt variously threatened or
supported by particular discourses. There were some areas of
unanimous agreement, suggesting that the women had taken up a
particular discursive position and identified with it in a variety of

ways. The women demonstrated the effects of norms of 'ideal mother' and 'ideal worker' on their lives by sharing many examples of the ways they balance responsibilities to work and home. Areas of agreement were illuminating in outlining the contests between participants to demonstrate their self-regulating and self-normalising behaviours in terms of their desire to conform to normative constructions of motherhood.

Areas of disagreement outlined the extent to which the women subscribed to or opposed dominant discourses and discursive strains. It was expected that the discourses the women would draw on when sharing experiences of being 'working mothers' would include motherhood, caring and working; however, analysis of focus group transcripts revealed that discourses of neo-liberalism, feminism, motherhood and individualism differentially influence women's concepts of 'worker' and 'mother' and these are internalised by women in various ways. It was in the disagreements that women's attachment to, or refusal of, these discourses were revealed. One of the striking aspects of the disagreements and contested issues in the focus group discussions was the challenging and defensive behaviour of some women. During focus group discussions the women were forced to confront different ways of being mothers and workers. This led to a search for validation of participants' own circumstances, values and choices. In some discussions, some women were unable to validate their own or other women's choices when confronted with alternative ways of being 'mothers' and 'workers' and this created considerable tension.

To analyse the transcripts, I modified the 'voice-centred relational method',[33] which views subjects as relational beings, situated in a web of complex social relationships. The method is designed to 'translate this relational ontology into methodology and into concrete methods of data analysis by exploring individual's narrative accounts, in terms of their relationships to the people around them and their relationships to the broader, social, structural and cultural contexts within which they live'.[34] The first reading sought to identify the discourses women draw on. Following analysis of the focus group discussions, which revealed the influence of discourses of motherhood, feminism, individualism and neo-liberalism on the women's lives, the interview transcripts revealed the extent of each individual woman's attachment to or refusal of these discourses. In a similar way to the voice centred relational method, the second reading explores the women's relational and individual concerns. I specifically sought to identify whose concerns mattered most to women, and if these concerns changed in different times and situations. The third reading located these relational and individual concerns within a wider social nexus and sought to identify the operation of power at the intersection of relational and individual concerns with family, workplace and society. Finally, I read the transcripts for evidence of women's agency in the ways they combine motherhood with paid work. While this approach is similar to the voice centred relational approach, the significant difference is the emphasis on dominant discourses, because of the relevance of discourse as a political process in this intersectional research.

In order to reveal the patterns and the configurations of inequality, following Ferree and McCall,[35] a comparative analysis of both focus group and interview analyses facilitated identifying the patterns of inequalities women experience by combining motherhood with paid work. Some patterns are experienced by all women because of the intersection of motherhood with paid work, while other patterns are experienced by women in similar occupations and family situations.

Limitations of the research

One of the inherent characteristics of case studies is that they facilitate the construction of detailed, in-depth understanding of the complexity of the interrelationship between phenomena, events and meanings in specific contexts. A limitation of case studies is that the findings are not generalisable to wider contexts. However, treating these thirty women's everyday lives as a sociological problematic facilitated exploring the interactions between women and wider social structures and relations. This 'working mothers' standpoint reveals the operation of power at individual and societal levels and the operation of patriarchal power through discourses, which uncovers the symbiotic relationship between categories and intersections, and which creates and maintains inequalities and privileges for 'working mothers' in one middle-class Irish suburb. This research does not claim to represent the complex inequality experienced by all 'working mothers', but it does reach out from the experience of women to explore gendered power relations in Irish society.

CHAPTER 4

Making the 'right' choice

This chapter explores the choices women make and the constraints women experience by combining motherhood with employment. Power operates through dominant discourses and shapes women's 'choices' regarding the ways they combine motherhood with paid work. The choice to engage in paid work outside the home or to have a career conflicts with motherhood for many women, given the way paid work is organised. Electing to engage in paid work requires that women be free to perform as 'ideal workers' unencumbered by care responsibilities. Careers and working outside the home are entwined with the individualism, rights and freedoms of liberalism. This can be seen in the language of choice that has come to prominence in recent years in political discourses and policies. 'The idea that we are autonomous human beings who can choose the kind of personal life we wish to live has become a deeply entrenched one'.[1]

In contemporary societies people are charged and burdened with choices about how to live their own lives and create their own biographies. Lash claims the contemporary individual 'is characterized by choice, where previous generations had no such choices . . . he or she must choose fast, as in a reflex'.[2] It can be argued that Lash overestimates the lack of choice in previous generations and the amount of choice available to contemporary individuals. However, there is a perceived decline in the significance of categories of identity such as nation, religion and class, reflecting changes in the order of discourse.[3] These forms of authority are being replaced by the authority of the individual who is involved in a process of self-invention.[4] At an individual level, men and women 'can and should, may and must, decide for themselves how to shape their own lives'.[5] At the institutional level, people are linked into the institutions of the labour market and welfare state, legal system, educational system and state bureaucracy which have emerged with modern society. These institutions produce various regulations that are addressed to the individual and they demand and promote people's active steering of their own lives. 'We are, not what we are, but what we make of ourselves . . . what the individual becomes is dependent on the reconstructive endeavours in which he or she engages'.[6]

Within assumptions of rational choice one has a list of options and carefully selects the most appropriate within the ordinary constraints that exist, of time, money or information. Within rational choice theory, therefore, the individual is conceptualised as primarily motivated by the rewards and costs of their actions and the likely profit they can make. Rational choice 'assumes that individuals maximise their utility from basic preferences that do not change rapidly over time'.[7] Within individualist conceptualisations of choice, the amount of choice available to individuals in most areas of their lives contributes to high expectations in all areas. Schwartz argues, because we have more options, we have an obligation to make the 'right' choice:

> When you have no options, what can you do? You will feel disappointment, maybe; regret, no. With no options, you just do the best you can. But with many options, the chances increase that a really good one is out there, and you may well feel that you ought to have been able to find it.[8]

The 'right' choice

Women experience pressure to engage in paid work, and also pressure to fulfil the demands of intensive nurturing. The burden of choosing the 'right' way to combine motherhood with paid work was a significant pressure on participants in the current study. Many women mentioned seeking the elusive 'right' way of combining motherhood with paid work as their reason for participating in this research; other women said they wanted to find out if other women had discovered other, better and easier ways of being a 'working mother' in Ireland. Making the 'right' choice is important to women. However, the choices the individual makes may be based on rational analysis, but desire may subvert rationality.[9] 'Working mothers' are constituted through discourses of neoliberalism, which produce the desire to participate in paid work and the development of children's knowledge and skills; feminist discourses, which produce the desire to participate in paid work and public life; discourses of individualism, which produce the desire to exercise autonomy and motherhood discourses, which produce the desire to be available to their children and fulfil the demands of intensive nurturing.

Anna demonstrates her anxiety about making the 'right' choice, following her decision to reduce her working hours in order to be available to her children:

> One time I did feel torn, I suppose, is when I actually made the choice to go part-time and about a week later, they [children] all wanted to know when they were going back to Mary's [childminder]. You know, why did I bother? Because they loved going down there, you know. So, I felt, God, had I made the right choice? (Anna, interview).

Anna desires to be available to care competently and professionally for her children because of her positioning within motherhood discourse, and she chose to work part-time. She was disappointed with her children's reaction to her reduced working hours, which suggested they were happy with the childminding arrangement. 'In some ways it kind of has backfired on me because they keep wanting to go back to the childminder' (Anna, interview). As Anna describes it, her decision 'has backfired', suggesting that her engagement with motherhood discourse has been challenged. This is disappointing for Anna as she enjoyed working full-time: 'I enjoy work, but it's trying to get your teeth into something in three-and-a half-hours. You know, you're no sooner cranked up than it's time to go home again. So, from that point of view, I miss the days' (Anna, interview). Her positioning within motherhood discourses suggests she should be available to her children, but her children did not respond as expected to her availability. Anna also identifies with individualism and neo-liberalism discourses and enjoys work. She exercised the option to work part-time, because she may have perceived part-time working to be more compatible with the demands of motherhood as motherhood discourses suggest. However, as Anna regretted being unable to immerse herself in work in her reduced hours, she may also have recognised the discursive strain of achievement in discourses of individualism. Anna says her decision 'has backfired' because her children did not appreciate her reduced hours in terms of her availability to them. She was understandably torn between competing discursive strains, and is not altogether satisfied with her decision to reduce her working hours.

Similarly, Jean described being torn between work and home. '[I] feel torn. You're a bad mother because you're not at home all the time and you're a bad colleague because you're not at work all the time' (Jean, focus group). In many respects modern society is characterised by greater choice and opportunities for agency on the part of women than were earlier times[10] and much of the focus of debate around care and women's employment has drawn on ideas of individualism, autonomy and 'choice'. 'Affluent and liberal modern societies provide opportunities for diverse lifestyle preferences to be fully realised [so that] women [have] genuine choices as to what to do with their lives.'[11] Anna demonstrates the dominance of motherhood discourse in influencing her choice to work part-time, thus marking part-time working as more accept-able, and compatible with spending more time with her children.

Hakim considers that women have genuine opportunities to realise their lifestyle preferences and calls this 'preference theory'. She explains that women have three dominant preferences: to be 'home centred', with very little attachment to the labour market; 'adaptive' whereby women's participation in the labour market is 'irregular' based on their home commitments; or 'work centred' whereby women have high levels of career commitment. Hakim argues women's recently found capacity to exercise 'choice' is a reflection of their preferences.[12] She has argued that research on the decision to return to work or not, and attitudes towards child-care show that women's choices are determined first by a woman's values, and only second by practical issues such as the availability and cost of childcare. Duncan also found that women, when forced to prioritise, positioned themselves on a continuum with home at one extreme and work at the other.[13] Hakim argues that policy research and predictions of women's choices will be more suc-cessful in future if they adopt the preference theory perspective and first establish the woman's distribution of preferences between family, work and employment. Although Hakim admits that the social and economic context can have some influence, lifestyle preferences are, in her view, the principle determinant of women's employment choices.[14] In this way preference theory neatly operationalises the individualisation view of late modern society in women's choice of employment behaviour. Giddens supports Hakim's claim that 'modern women [have] real choices between a life centred on family work and/or on paid work' as a demonstration that 'we can no longer learn from history', because 'individualization has been the main driving force for change in late modern society'.[15]

However, as McRae points out, any contextual constraints are in practice ignored by preference theory.[16] Women's lives are bound by cultural and social expectations of gender roles, particularly when women are mothers, as well as practical considerations concerning economics and childcare. While individualism suggests a high degree of personal choice, people still live out their lives dependent on institutions. An over-emphasis on choice underestimates the extent to which most women, and especially mothers, live out their lives within very real constraints. As Yolanda describes her situation: 'I have no choice really. I have to [work], I would nearly be the main earner in the house' (Yolanda, focus group). This lopsided emphasis on choice is evident in Hakim's so-called 'preference theory'.[17]

Angela demonstrates that practical considerations as well as her positioning within dominant discourses are experienced as constraints: 'I had terrible, terrible guilt when they were younger and terrible feelings of I wanted to be at home and I wanted to be at work. When I was at work I wanted to be at home and when I was at home I wanted to be at work; there was a fierce confusion' (Angela, focus group). This 'confusion' reveals the tension between discourses which conflict and the way they are experienced by women who have taken up subject positions as 'mothers' and 'workers'.

It is not disputed that attitudes will shape individual behaviour, or that particular sets of attitudes to work and family may be found across a range of social positions and education levels, but it would seem unwise to assume that women's employment behaviours may be primarily accounted for by the hypothesised existence of different 'types' of women, as 'preference theory' suggests.[18] It is not possible to examine women's preferences without exploring the availability of subject positions deriving from dominant discourses. Women are obliged to choose between motherhood and paid work or make decisions about ways to combine the two. One may feel autonomous and free to choose, but the power of regulatory discourses means that such choice is both forced and of false appearance. This is because 'the subject's positioning within particular discourses makes the "chosen" line of action the only possible action, not because there are no other lines of action, but because one has been subjectively constituted through one's placement within that discourse to *want* that line of action' (original emphasis).[19] The subject positions which women may take up are made available through these discourses, but not all subject positions are equally available. Individuals have differential access to particular discursive positions and discourses have different gendered and classed implications; we can only 'pick up the tools that are lying there'.[20] In this way, choices are understood as contextualised within the specific regulatory discourses to which we have access. Thus, preferences and choices cannot be decontextualised. We need to 'conduct a critical scrutiny of preference and desire that would reveal the many ways in which habit, fear, low expectations and unjust background conditions inform people's choices and even their wishes for their own lives'.[21]

The rhetoric of choice

Kate has a very busy life, with four children and a demanding career. She claims to be exercising her autonomy by maintaining her commitment to her career:

> It's a choice. I choose to do these things. I'm not good at saying no, that's my problem . . . I don't know how I would even define my hours of work. I don't know how I would calculate my hours of work really . . . It's not really a decision for me . . . It's not a choice for me to be part time. No, my workload is much greater now than it ever was at any other time in my career, but it was never a choice to be part-time or full-time (Kate, interview).

Kate suggests if she wants to pursue her particular career, she has no choice but to make a full-time commitment to it. However, Kate has been subjectively constituted through her placement within discourses of individualism to *want* that line of action.[22] Kate has invested heavily in her career and describes her working hours as 'forty plus' per week. She volunteers for extra work, gives media interviews at all hours and on two occasions she has been abroad for work, and brought her four children with her for five and six months respectively. It is the nature of her work and the culture of the organisation that progression in her career is dependent on demonstrating a high level of commitment, which Kate does. However, Kate claims that she chooses to work as hard as she does. She could take life at an easier pace, but she does not. 'It is self-inflicted. I know there are people in my position, in the kind of job that I do, who take life at an easier pace than I do. And I could do it that way, but it's just not for me' (Kate, interview). Kate perceives she has a choice and like the people she mentions above, she could choose to 'take life at an easier pace'. However, she does not select this option, because of her positioning within individualism discourses: 'It's just, I guess, an ambition in me. And it's not material success and it's not to be self-important and it's not that I'm egotistical, or anything like that, it's just that I am actually so interested in anything anybody asks me to do, that I say "God yeah, that's really interesting, yeah, I'd like to be involved in that"' (Kate, interview).

Choosing to work and having the opportunity to work does not mean combining motherhood with paid work is necessarily easy. There is a gender order in society that pervades organisational culture and privileges male ways of working and organising. The social relations of gender are embedded in complex ways in both the formal and informal workings of organisations and are concealed beneath apparently gender-neutral policies relating to targets and performance. These ways of working disadvantage women occupationally and socially in ways that are made invisible by being presented as both normal and inevitable.[23] Kate has an almost impossibly busy life, yet she describes it as her 'self-inflicted' choice. Clearly her positioning within individualism discourses influences her choice to attempt to behave as an 'ideal worker', even though she has four children, and experiences practical difficulties by combining her career with motherhood. Within Foucauldian discussions of governance at a distance, agency is perceived to be the simultaneous act of free will and regulation. In the act of 'choosing', and experiencing this choice as an individual act of will, we are submitting to the requirements of particular regulatory discourses. 'At any given time, the future will seem open which accounts for our sense of freedom, but it is being made in the present by the projects that we discursively endorse and the activities which we engage in'.[24] When mothers use choice rhetoric, they are being realistic in a society where the best jobs require ideal workers to have the ability to command a flow of family work few mothers enjoy.[25] The subject position of the agentic person who can make rational choices, act upon them and experience themselves as 'continuous, unified, rational and coherent'[26] is mainly available to middle-class males; thus men have greater access to discourses of autonomy.[27] Autonomy and choice are traps that will only further ensnare women, because the gender order in society and family prevents many women from exercising 'free' choice, yet the individualist burden of exercising choice applies to women as well as to men.[28]

Joy has decided to prioritise her children over her career while they are young and describes very busy days working from home at market research and being available to her children. 'There's this absolute about you're a "working mother" or you're not a "working mother" . . . every mother works, not every mother earns . . . And I think the pressure is there to work, to be honest . . . Just to be a mother is not enough to be a successful woman' (Joy, focus group). Joy acknowledges neo-liberalism and individualism discourses and her choice to recognise and conform to motherhood discourses. Consequently she observes pressure on women to participate in paid work and perceives that motherhood is less valued than, in her view, it ought to be, in contemporary Irish society. The influence of discourses of individualism is evident in Joy's account, and she claims society does not regard women who work full-time in the home as 'successful'. The conflict between discourses of individualism and motherhood are evident in Kate's and Joy's accounts. Joy perceives that her choice to prioritise spending time with her children over pursuing a career requires promoting and defending. While women's right to participate in the workforce is key to feminism, there have also been vibrant debates concerning the protection of women who choose to stay at home and in particular greater economic recognition of the work women carry out in the home has been the subject of several Irish feminist campaigns, such as Wages for Housework in the 1970s and the National Women's Council's childcare campaign, which incorporated childcare services for stay-at-home mothers.[29] However, despite these vibrant debates and energetic campaigns, none of the suggestions were adopted by the state. In Ireland, as elsewhere, in the popular imagination, feminism is linked with the glorification of paid work and the devaluation of family work. The progress liberal feminism made was more obvious in the public / employment arena, which alienated many women who chose to stay at home and rear their children. 'This leaves many women confused once they have children. When they feel the lure and importance of family work, they are left with the sense that feminism has abandoned them.[30]

However, feminists have also pointed to women's unequal position in the family. Oakley exposed the reality of the 'homemaker' role and the nature of housework,[31] while Bernard spoke of the 'wife's marriage' and the 'husband's marriage',[32] identifying the very different experience that people in a family may have of their relationship. Hartmann[33] and Hilliard[34] identified the potential for conflict that arises from the fact that the family is not so much a unit as a group, within which individuals have differential access to resources. Joy also maintains a part-time commitment to paid work and does market research in the mornings and at night in order to be available to her children during the day. 'It's working at sprint all the time . . . so it's constant; it's just like(.) It's a hamster wheel' (Joy, interview). She too describes her busy days as her choice, 'and I know, I bring it on myself' (Joy, interview). Even though Joy prioritises motherhood and being available to her children, she also recognises individualism discourses, and engages in paid work outside the home. This way of combining motherhood with paid work has been described as 'Chameleon Motherhood',[35] because such women work hard to minimise the visibility and impact of paid work on family activities and vice versa, working part-time or by night. Thus Joy is able to perform both at home and at work without social sanction.[36]

For Anna and Joy, reducing their hours in paid work limits their earning power, career prospects and independence; thus they experience inequality with women who pursue careers full-time. However, these women spend more time with their families and children and presumably experience less pressure and guilt. This choice is available to them because both are partnered and economically comfortable so they have the option to recognise and engage with motherhood discourses by working part-time.

Kate describes combining motherhood with paid work as 'hugely difficult' on a practical and emotional level, because there are conflicting obligations on women who combine motherhood with paid work:

> Being a mother is fine and being a professional is fine, but it's trying to marry the two. It's the tension between the two is the difficult bit. It's not either of them on their own that's difficult,

it's trying to combine the two that's hugely difficult and not
only on a practical level I suppose, but also on an emotional or
a psychological level (Kate, interview).

In Kate's account the construction of motherhood and career as
polarised contributes to the constraints she experiences by making
efforts to combine the two. These constraints manifest themselves
in practical and emotional difficulties for Kate. Florence also
noted, as currently constructed, the roles of mother and professional worker are incompatible: 'I can't be a career woman and
have children . . . you can't go up the promotional ladder, not in
nursing, and stay part-time . . . basically you have to stay full-time
if you want to go places, so therefore, I sacrificed that side of
things' (Florence, interview).

Women's lives are more nuanced and textured than the simple
polarisation of paid work and unpaid care would suggest and
women themselves stress the value they place on both activities.
Women articulate their desires for autonomy, for social and
economic independence, and their desire to work towards self-
actualisation. Women also articulate their love for their children
and their desire to care and spend time with them. Women who
are 'working mothers' have difficulty experiencing autonomous
action in the face of motherhood discourses. Women with dependent children are neither autonomous nor free to make choices
that advance only their own interests.

The rhetoric of choice is central to the neo-liberal agenda: we
are all the agents of our own choices. Not only the 'at risk' girls
and young women, lone parents and those with little cultural
capital – the 'reflexivity losers' – but also those claiming to be more
successful. The women who complete their schooling, obtain university degrees and professional training – the 'reflexivity
winners' – are faced with conflicts in their personal lives that
increasingly appear as individual decisions, as investments even.[37]
Kate's conflict appears as an individual decision, but is the
outcome of Kate being socially produced as both mother and
worker, and her multiple positioning within both discourses.

Crompton[38] has also criticised theories that have emphasised
the contemporary and overwhelming significance of choice, particularly for women. Beck[39] described people as being freed from
historically inscribed roles; however, Hughes[40] argues that the
extent to which historically inscribed roles have in fact been

transcended has been exaggerated, particularly in respect of mothers. The reality of intimate relationships is that entering into them successfully entails time, negotiation, trust, vulnerability, altruism and the relinquishing of a degree of individual freedom. This clearly suggests a certain tension between an individual's autonomy, their commitment to others in a family grouping, and the demands of work.[41]

For many women, the achievement of autonomy is both tenuous and ambivalent because desire is constituted through the discourses which one is the subject of and subject to. Women are subject to, and the subject of, discourses of motherhood, which position women as responsible for their children. Women are also subject to discourses of individualism which position women as autonomous, agentic people. 'Working mothers' desire autonomy and motherhood, therefore they both exercise agency and are also constrained in their decisions to combine motherhood with paid work. In the choices of 'working mothers' we see

> the doubled sense of 'subject' (subject/ed *to* and subject *of* action) . . . [which] allows for an individual who is socially produced, *and* 'multiply positioned' – neither determined nor free, but both simultaneously (original emphasis).[42]

In examining women's choices to combine motherhood with paid work, it is possible to see the exercise of agency, as well as the cultural sanctions and structural inequalities that women encounter as constraints on their freedom to make these choices.

Choice and Constraint

Women who are mothers experience constraints on their autonomy and freedom to choose the kind of personal lives they wish to live because motherhood limits women's freedom. Mothers experience gendered expectations not only to be selfless, nurturing and caring, but to find caring for others fulfilling and rewarding. However, individualism discourses produce the desire to develop successful and rewarding careers as well as economic self-sufficiency and mothers are also expected to contribute financially to their families.

Some women attempt to achieve autonomy, self-sufficiency and self-fulfilment through productive paid work, but motherhood is a significant limiting factor. Jean made a reluctant choice to reduce her hours of work to meet gendered norms in relation to the mother role:

> From a career point of view, I've made all the sacrifices. He [my husband] hasn't you know. Because I suppose I would have been better qualified than he would, in my area, than he would in his. But yet, I made the choices to go part-time, because I was the mother (Jean, interview).

Jean is a chartered accountant, and better qualified than her husband. Applying instrumental rationality would mean that her husband should take reduced hours, because she has higher earning capacity and can contribute more materially to the family: 'My job is a better paid job than his job, do you know what I mean, my job even though I work less hours, but that's just the way it is' (Jean, focus group). Furthermore, Jean suggests that she would have liked to continue working full-time, rather than reducing her hours: 'I would have stayed full-time' (Jean, interview), which suggests that she really did not want to reduce her hours. This is not what happened and she reduced her hours of work. However, while Jean acknowledges gendered pressure on her to reduce her hours, she also claims this decision is her choice.

Many women spoke about the difficulty of fulfilling their obligations to work because of their commitment to their families. One way to cope with the practical and emotional difficulties of combining motherhood with paid work is for women to limit their career options, or reduce their working hours, or both. Some women compromised their careers because of family commitments. Eithne believes she would be unable to meet the demands of a more challenging role and she has limited her career options: 'I think if I hadn't children, I wouldn't be in that job, I'd have moved to a more demanding job a long time ago. So I do make compromises based on my family situation' (Eithne, focus group). Kate maintains a full-time commitment to her career and navigates conflicting priorities which result in practical and emotional difficulties for her. These women are privileged in that they are very aware that they are free to make choices, even if these are within constraints. Women's awareness of constraints gives them moments of freedom or the possibility to consider alternative options. Their awareness of being constrained reveals to women their scope for making choices, and this possibility creates freedom.

However, some women, especially those parenting alone, perceive no choice in their decision to participate in paid work, and see it as an economic necessity to provide for themselves and their children:

> I work purely for money . . . when Jack was about three I went job sharing, and it was absolutely fantastic, it was brilliant I loved it . . . I did part-time, and I did that for about three years and then my marriage broke up. So, I had to go back [to full-time work](.) And I wouldn't be there. No way. Absolutely no way. I'd prefer not to be in full-time work (Jane, interview).

For Jane working full-time is not a choice but a necessity to provide materially for herself and Jack. However, being solely responsible for rearing her son and working full-time, according to Jane 'is impossible and it's wrong you know, and then when you are on your own, bringing to school, collecting, everything, everything you are responsible for' (Jane, focus group). Her use of the word 'wrong' to describe being responsible for 'everything', demonstrates that she perceives her situation, parenting alone, as unfair:

> Yeah. And feeling really, kind of, pissed off about it I suppose, in that, because we have to do it. Whereas before, when I was [part-time], I enjoyed it more when I had the choice. But once the choice was taken away from me, suddenly everything that I wanted, I didn't want it then anymore. It was 'this is drudgery, it's you know, I have to pay all the bills, I have to do [everything] (Jane, interview).

Jane has less freedom than Eithne or Kate, because women who parent alone experience a greater economic obligation to participate in paid work, but there is no lessening of their responsibility for children. Interestingly, the new-familialism strain of motherhood discourses do not promote full-time intensive care of children by mothers who are not married. Women who perceived an obligation to generate family income regarded it as a constraint on their choices regarding the way they would combine motherhood with paid work. For these women, working is a chore which is resented as it is an economic necessity in order to fulfil obligations to provide economically for their children. 'The "right to choose" means very little when women are powerless'.[43] Therefore, in Jane's account of combining motherhood with paid work, there is a sense of fatalism, far from the notion of individualistic self-invention.

Despite the moral opprobrium increasingly accorded to the employee rational economic actor/citizen as one who is not only autonomous and rational, but also market-oriented, consuming and calculatingly self-interested, the fact remains that a large part of humanity at any given time are not self-financing consumers (notably children, people who are very frail, unpaid carers, people with work-constraining disabilities and those who are ill).[44] Lone parents who are supporting dependant children are also not self-financing consumers.[45] Therefore, 'claims about the market as a suitable or even crucial vehicle for the exercise of autonomy proceed without inquiry into what actually makes human autonomy possible'.[46] The market does not acknowledge or accommodate dependency and Jane experiences inequality relative to other women because she parents alone, which is reported to cause practical as well as emotional difficulties for Jane.

Feminists have also taken up the liberalist discourse of choice. 'Although differences [between feminisms] still exist . . . the more interesting point is that significant similarities exist as well. And at the core of *all* the differences remains "the" liberal feminist recognition of woman as an individual with "rights" to freedom of choice' (original emphasis).[47] While it is not disputed that women should have rights and entitlements to freedom of choice, feminists struggle with the dilemma of choice, in part, because of an overarching concern about the paradigm of the rational economic man and the atomistic concept of liberal individualism. 'Rights' can only be realised within favourable social and economic conditions and at any given time, some women will have little, or no, choice.[48] If a woman is free to choose to engage in mothering or paid work, this suggests she has autonomy and control over the direction of her life as individualism discourse suggests. Feminist's challenge to sexism and male dominance both in public and private domains explicitly relies on individualism to claim women's human subjectivity and equal entitlement, but feminism finds it almost impossible to challenge motherhood on individualist terms.[49]

While women navigate their own ways in choosing how to combine motherhood with paid work, mothers' choices are subject to public scrutiny and sanction and the interest taken in women's choices regarding combining motherhood with paid work is an intrusion to which no other worker or male parent is subject.

Motherhood is a high-profile, public role and women experience public scrutiny, from non-mothers, mothers, men and women, families and friends. 'All your peers have an opinion on it [motherhood]. All age groups, it's both your parent's generation and your siblings and your friends and everybody seems to have an opinion on what choice you made or didn't make' (Eithne, interview). 'Mothers have no shortage of critics, but precious few friends'.[50] 'Not even world leaders and presidents are subject to the same amount of judgment and derision as mothers are, and everyone has an opinion . . . And they are not scared to share it'.[51] Women who chose different ways of mothering are also reported to be critical of working mothers: 'Other mothers judging, you know. We are all enemies in a way. Well, this pressure does come from other women and I think we fool ourselves to think it doesn't' (Avril, focus group). Hakim argues that 'there are no major constraints limiting choice or forcing choice in particular directions'.[52] There are major constraints limiting and forcing women's choices, because some choices are marked as more acceptable than others, particularly when women are mothers. This scrutiny constrains women's freedom to make choices. However, the 'pressure' Avril experiences from other women suggests their different subject positioning within different discourses, revealing the conflict and contradictions inherent in the discourses women choose to recognise.

Participants found that intensive motherhood discourses are promoted in the media and widely taken up in society. Jean describes her friends' attitudes to her working: 'Other friends of mine who don't work . . . say "why bother having children if you're going to work?" "Do you not feel bad when you're not there when they come out of school?" (Jean, focus group). Yolanda also identified this pressure from the media: 'You know the way you'd hear or read things about "working mothers", and "why did they bother having kids if they're going to go out and work?"'(Yolanda, focus group). The expression 'why bother having kids if you're going to work?' was mentioned again and again by women, suggesting that a dominant social message women had internalised is that women either mother full-time or work full-time, but not both.

Kate reported experiencing criticism from her colleagues at work: 'Yeah. People often make negative comments, about the fact that my life is so busy, that it's really my own fault, that I should have stopped after two [children] (Kate, focus group).

> I think every decision you make as a parent, whether you work or don't work, whether you(.) Whatever you do with your children, people either agree or disagree . . . people do sort of point it out to you as well . . . You know, I think mothers feel very guilty about it because there are so many choices they have to make and they feel that whatever choice they make somebody will say 'Oh!' [critically] when you tell them what you did (Eithne, interview).

Women must make choices, and the visibility of motherhood puts pressure on women to make the 'right' choices between discursive strains which conflict. This is an inequality with non-mothers, who are not subject to the same pressure, scrutiny or sanction. Society suffers from 'motherism' as opposed to 'sexism'.[53] This public scrutiny and the promotion of intensive motherhood in the media[54] puts pressure on women, not only to choose, but also to choose a socially acceptable way of combining motherhood with paid work.

Grace described the difficulties of working at management level and the gendered expectations of male colleagues that professional women with children should not work:

> I was the first woman in that company to go out on maternity leave, who was [at managerial level] . . . And then, what I found is that when you came back to work [after maternity leave] was that they were all watching you, to see 'is she going to fall apart?' You know, 'is she going to be able to manage this now?' You'd come in – in the mornings and they'd say 'oh she's on time this week' . . . And the comments people would make, the personal comments that people felt they had the right to make, never ceases to amaze me (Grace, focus group).

Grace provides an account of the gendered expectations of her colleagues and their interference in her personal life, which she felt transgressed professional and common courtesy, demonstrating that motherhood is the property of everyone. This might suggest that perhaps it is only women who experience a conflict when combining paid work and parenting, given the relatively recent opportunities and choices available. However, in some workplaces it is only acceptable for women without children to work. In Grace's account, her male colleagues waiting for her to demonstrate her inability to fulfil working and mothering roles, contributed to the difficulties of combining motherhood with paid work. Grace subsequently left that employment in the private sector and moved to a public sector role that better facilitated balance between her work and home life. Interestingly, almost half the women in this research work in the public sector. The state, is of course, obliged to observe equality legislation, however, flexible working arrangements are not equally available to participants even within the public sector. Those in senior positions were less likely to work reduced hours or avail of flexible working arrangements in either public- or private-sector organisations. In 2013, the Irish government prohibited flexible working for Assistant Principal or higher roles in the public service.[55] The take up of flexible working arrangements is gendered and, as Grace noted, fatherhood did not impact her colleagues' commitment to employment in the way motherhood was expected to impact hers:

> They all had the security blanket themselves, that's what I felt about it at the time . . . If one of their children was sick you never knew about it, because it all happened outside of work for them. Very much so. Whereas you were bringing this into work and they didn't necessarily want to know about it (Grace, focus group).

It is evident that Grace's male colleagues are privileged by having stay-at-home wives, which enables these men to behave like 'ideal workers', unencumbered by care responsibilities. In many organisations 'ideal worker', cultures persist, despite the numbers of women and mothers in paid work. As Cockburn argues, mothers' employment creates 'practical difficulties for managers, increases the proportion of women in the labour force and brings an unwelcome domestic odour, a whiff of the kitchen and nursery into the workplace'.[56] Thus, in some organisations, women experienced resentment and interference from colleagues who suggested women were not fulfilling their obligations to work by becoming mothers.

'Working Mothers' and Choice

Women draw on intensive nurturing strains in motherhood discourses in relation to reducing their hours in paid work to spend time with their children. Women draw on the discursive strains of autonomy and choice in neo-liberalism and individualism discourses in relation to developing careers. Combining motherhood with paid work causes women practical and emotional difficulties.

Women describe themselves as 'torn', because working and caring are governed by different values and women also are aware of practical constraints on their freedom to make choices in relation to combining motherhood with paid work.

For every inequality, there is a privilege. Women with partners, with higher education levels and with greater earning power are privileged in that they have the choice to reduce their hours in paid work in order to prioritise motherhood. Women who reduce their hours of work in order to better balance employment and motherhood limit their careers, earning power and independence. There are inequalities and privileges in the amount of choice available to women and the extent of the obligations they choose to recognise. Women who maintained high levels of commitment to work reported experiencing emotional and psychological difficulties because of the difficulties combining a full-time career with motherhood creates. Women may choose not to perform as ideal workers, but they do not choose the marginalisation that accompanies that decision.

Women are hurt by the hard choices they face. However, once the focus shifts away from women's choices to the gender system within which these choices are made, the realistic limits to women's choices are revealed. Gendered expectations in family, workplace and society shape both the patterning of mothers' wishes in respect of employment as well as their capacities to realise their preferences because of their maternity. Allowing women the 'choice' to perform as ideal workers without the privileges that support male workers is not equality.[57] Families, workplaces and society continue to promote older hierarchies and traditional gendered inequalities through motherhood discourses, which expose the real limits to women's 'choice' to combine motherhood with paid work. Women internalise the pressure to find a socially acceptable way of combining motherhood with paid work – the elusive 'right' way – which demonstrates public scrutiny of mothers.

Women have little option but to make sacrifices, because 'ideal mothers' and 'ideal workers' are constructed as polarised in Irish society. Women's choices are determined at an individual level by the social relations of gender, class and marital status because political, material and social inequality leads to class and gender differences in outcomes. Women who have professions and are partnered are privileged on the basis of class and therefore have more options, and therefore may be able to make better choices. This leads to inequalities between women, which results in resentment between women, 'the mother war', and conceals the deeply patriarchal social structures which put clear and effective limits on the choices women are free to make.

Even though legislation to facilitate women's employment has been in place since 1973, with increasing rights and entitlements to equal pay, maternity and parental leave (Appendix 2), the structural and social changes necessary to support women's employment have not materialised. In fact, labour market activation policies have developed significantly, while policies for supporting unpaid care have seen modest development. In Ireland, women have been waiting a long time for men to participate equally in caring in the private sphere, and the expectation of women's primary role as carers continues to persist. Given that dual-earner arrangements are now the norm, this delay is considerable and reflects the strength of Ireland's attachment to deeply patriarchal, traditional gendered roles for women and mothers.

All women spoke of 'my choice'. As Warner argues, 'if you have been brought up all your life, being told you have wonderful choices, you tend, when things go wrong, to assume you made the wrong choices – not to see that the 'choices' given to you were wrong in the first place'.[58]

This is one pattern between intersectionality and discourse, configuring women's choice to combine motherhood with paid work as each woman's personal responsibility or problem, thus maintaining the inequalities women experience as private affairs. However, these private troubles are in fact public issues, but are maintained as private troubles through each woman's illusion of choice. Mills argued that a trouble is a private matter; it occurs when values cherished by an individual are felt by her to be threatened. A trouble can be resolved by the individual's wilful activity. An issue, however, Mills argued, is a public matter, when some value cherished by publics is felt to be threatened. An issue transcends the local environment of the individual and concerns society as a whole, the historical and social institutions and their interrelation in that society.[59]

However, by making choices which women regard as private matters, women's choices conceal the essentialism that underscores many of the norms deriving from dominant discourses, in particular 'ideal mother' and 'ideal worker' norms. Discourses operate to constrain the choices available to women, so no woman can make a 'free' choice, free of constraint under these conditions. Women's decisions regarding the ways they will combine motherhood with paid work frequently amount to no more than a series of unsatisfactory trade-offs masquerading as choice.

CHAPTER 5

Reflexive moral reasoning

Choice always means the assumption of responsibility and making choices involves making claims about the individual's construction of the self as a moral actor. Because individuals must construct their own lives, they are constantly faced with moral choices, such as whether or not to use contraceptives, and whether or not to have an abortion.[1] Bauman argues the most fundamental condition of modern society that tends to suppress the influence of morality is the dominance of a certain mode of reasoning, namely the logic of means towards ends or instrumental rationality.[2] In rational decision making, the criteria of effectiveness and efficiency have replaced the moral criteria of good and evil, deriving from neo-liberal and individualist discourses.[3] However, Bauman also claims there is a heightened interest in ethical debates in postmodernity for two reasons, the first being the effects of the pluralism of authority. Since there is no single authority which can be called on to provide unequivocal answers to questions, individuals must negotiate with one another and they must reach an understanding on the rules they agree to recognise. Secondly, there is the centrality of choice in the self-constitution of post-modern individuals who are self-governing, and have the freedom and discretion to make decisions about the way they live their lives, following their own individual guiding principles. This individualism requires reflexivity, and is also a fundamentally moral concept insofar as individuals must choose a way of being in the world.

Morality in decisions to work

Choice, desire and morality are linked. Desires are integral to the various discourses through which each person is constituted and are not necessarily amenable to change through rational analysis.

78

Some women felt a moral obligation to make an economic contribution to society and Eithne and Grace spoke about the investment in their education and their perceived moral obligation to seek a return on that investment. The notion of investing in careers and the obligation to seek a return on that investment speaks to concepts of individualism and the 'responsible citizen', inherent in discourses of neo-liberalism. Eithne has two children and works full-time; she said she felt a moral obligation to use her education and had always expected to continue in employment after the birth of her children: 'Because you decide to go into higher education and because you decide to do a doctorate, yes, I think there is that implicit understanding that you'll use it and you'll work with it' (Eithne, interview). There is morality in Eithne's choice to use her education: 'Because you've been supported through your college education by both the state and by your parents' (Eithne, interview), and she feels obliged to provide a return on others' investment as well as her own. Likewise, Grace also believes she should seek a return on her investment in her education: 'And yes, when you are younger you feel the need to get something back for having put all that in' (Grace, interview). Grace reported that many of her peers perceive a moral obligation to work for equality, for feminism and for other women. Grace claimed her generation would have been the first with the opportunity to work in male-dominated areas, and many of her peers felt compelled to succeed in that environment: 'That you must do it for women, to be an example . . . You have been given these gifts, and you should do it, because it's the right thing to do for other women, to change the world' (Grace, interview). Thus Grace mentions the liberal strains in feminist discourse, that women are as entitled as men to participate in the public sphere. However she does not claim this for herself, but for her cohort at university, having modified her views following motherhood. Warner also noted that the 'Girls Who Could Have Done Anything' are now dealing with the 'harsh realities of family life in a culture that has no structures in place to allow women, and men, to balance work and childrearing'.[4]

Similarly, Jasmine has a career and believes she has a moral imperative to challenge gendered assumptions and provide a feminist example for her children: 'I'm rearing two girls, I do think it's positive role modelling for them to see me going out to work, and being seen having my own [independence]' (Jasmine, focus group). Eithne, Grace and Jasmine all perceive moral obligations to participate in paid work. The discursive strains of developing careers and investing in one's future deriving from discourses of neo-liberalism and individualism are evident in Eithne and Grace's moral reasoning. These women have made economic and emotional investments in their education and training and are making rational choices to maintain their contribution to paid work in order to obtain a return on that investment. Jasmine also sees an obligation to continue in paid work to provide a role model for her daughters, thus the discursive strains of independence and autonomy are evident in Jasmine's moral reasoning. While these women perceive moral obligations to participate in paid work, it should be noted that these women are privileged; they are all partnered, professional women with careers.

Gina reported being conflicted, because she too had invested in her career and felt obliged to seek a return on that investment. However, Gina currently job-shares, working one week on, one week off, and while she feels this meets one set of moral obligations it is at the expense of the other: 'Part of me then does feel that you totally give up, you have totally given up your career and "what did you go to school and college and do all that for and you're going to turn around and give it up?"' (Gina, interview). Clearly working half-time is not totally giving up, yet Gina perceives she has abandoned her career because she too recognises competing discursive strains and achieves a compromise by job-sharing. However, anecdotal evidence suggests that it is not possible to advance a career while working less than full-time.

Nevertheless, many women who reduced their hours of work also feel moral obligations to their colleagues and employers. Grace reduced her working hours because she felt her children were disadvantaged by her working full-time and she wanted to spend more time with them; however, she also has a moral obligation to fulfil the requirements of her role and a commitment to her colleagues:

> What we were trying to achieve really, is more contact time with the kids and to be able to do the after-school thing. So the afternoons, really, was the option. And the reason then that I went for the two days full time was that I really couldn't do my job properly with just working mornings. There's certain elements of my job that I need a full day to do it. So I knew that it

would be a disservice for me to pretend that I could do my job by just working mornings. I really couldn't (Grace, interview).

Grace demonstrates that rather than working mornings only, which would have been her ideal choice, she elected to reduce her hours in a different pattern so as not to compromise her role. Jean has also reduced her hours of work to satisfy gendered moral norms, but she continues to feel a moral obligation to her colleagues when she is not at work:

I feel guilty for walking out the door when I'm at work, because, like, my job is not the kind of job that you can share. It's not the sort of thing you can chop up and give to somebody else, and really, I suppose, squashing a full-time week into a part-time week. And then, if I have to, I'll bring work home on the laptop and log on or whatever. I mean sometimes, the odd time, in the evenings or weekends. But I sort of feel, because I have a group of people working for me, sometimes I feel guilty when I have to say 'well I'm off now it's quarter past three and I must get my children sorted out' (Jean, focus group).

Jean has a position of responsibility with colleagues reporting to her and she perceives she is letting her colleagues down by leaving them to work in her absence. Gina, Jean and Grace have made working arrangements which attempt to recognise the competing discursive strains of pursuing careers and providing maternal care for children in a way which satisfies their obligations both to home and to work. While many women feel moral obligations towards their colleagues, many women also experienced the disapproval of their colleagues for continuing to work full-time when they became mothers: 'One . . . gentleman told me I was irresponsible to have four children in the first place, so(.) All my own fault' (Kate, focus group). Kate experienced moral opprobrium from her colleague who considered Kate 'irresponsible' as both a mother and a colleague, because her decision to maintain her career and have four children did not meet with his approval. However, Kate has also acknowledged that she could work at an easier pace, but chooses to be highly committed to her career – demonstrating the impossibility of being committed in both spheres.

Interestingly, some women saw their participation in paid work as fulfilling the moral obligation to provide materially for their children, as part of meeting children's needs: 'If they [children] want some things, you have to work to pay for them' (Aisling, focus group). Similarly, Brona claims to be very stressed working full-time as a factory operator, working three twelve hour shifts a week, with a husband she describes as 'useless' and an unreliable child-minder. She claimed, 'I'm a bit resentful of work at the moment, because I feel I'm killing myself working' (Brona, interview). Brona resents work, not the unfair burden of managing home and three children, with little support. This resentment of work speaks to the dominant maternal discourse that mothers' place is in the home, but Brona also reckoned her income is necessary to properly meet her children's needs:

> I have to pay money for insurance for his rugby this week and the tennis classes, that's ninety-five this week for just one child. When you see the cost of three lads, doctors, anything that's out of the ordinary(.) All those classes and sports, they all cost money (Brona, interview).

Reflexively Brona decided she has no option but to continue 'killing' herself working for the economic contribution her employment makes to the family, because 'If I give up, we would have to give up an awful lot of that' (Brona, interview). Brona frames her choice in terms of meeting children's needs. Gatrell argues that mothers who feel guilty about a wish to leave their children with others in order to be able to work, may find that this burden is eased if their earnings are construed as essential to family maintenance.[5] These women perceive an inequality with women who can financially afford to reduce their hours in paid work. Some women perceive they are not meeting obligations to motherhood because of their participation in paid work and many women appreciate it would be easier to give up or reduce their commitment to paid work, particularly in the middle-class area of the study. Jean has reduced her hours, and acknowledges it would be easier in the middle-class area to conform to the dominant practice of giving up work altogether:

> It's when I see people in the morning, people I went to school with, and you might be under pressure. You might be facing into a difficult morning, let's say, you know. And you see these women and they are out power-walking, having dropped the kids to school. And I'm saying 'I would have been one of the intelligent, inverted commas, ones in the class, who got lots of honours in the Leaving Cert, and there, these women are out power-walking in their designer tracksuits, and I'm the fool rushing to work to get abuse for the morning, with sort of pressure and stress and everything like'. And I'm saying 'where did I go wrong?' (Jean, interview).

Jean comments that women who mother full-time in the local area enjoy personal time when their children are in school, and she acknowledges that her life is more difficult in many ways than the lives of those women who do not engage in paid work – 'where did I go wrong?' (Jean, interview) – implying that these other women's choices are right. The notion of man breadwinner and woman homemaker implicit in much of the motherhood discourse is evident in Jean's account of the local area. As Dillaway and Paré argue, these ideological prescriptions reinforce an equation of 'good' mothers with economically privileged, married ones, in that women with children should not have to work for pay because they should be married to husbands who earn family wages.[6] However, reflexively, Jean has decided, the difficulties of combining motherhood with paid work notwithstanding, she intends to continue in paid work:

> Quite possibly, if I was out power walking, I might get fed up of it after a week or two and I'd probably be, well maybe I'm just saying this to console myself. But I think it's, are you motivated to have a career? Are you happy to stay at home? I don't know if it would be enough for me to stay at home (Jean, interview).

Jean's reflexive deliberations demonstrate the difficulties of combining motherhood with paid work, both of which are morally inscribed. The relationships between career ambition and personal happiness are presented as opposing choices, which reveals the competing discursive strains in dominant discourses and which contribute to the 'mother war' for women who make different choices. While Jean does not condemn other women's choices, there is a discursive strain in individualism discourse that suggests that the career of full-time wife, mother and homemaker has ceased to be an adequate life project.[7] Jean has invested significantly in her career and has reduced her working hours to fulfil the desire to be available to her children, as motherhood discourses suggest. However, individualism discourses produce the desire to have a career, and Jean has reduced her working hours, performing her role in less time in order to maintain her career. Some women who reduced their working hours regard professional 'working mothers' as a legitimate dumping ground for their anxieties about individualisation; however, Jean, as a professional 'working mother', regards the affluent women who are full-time in the home as having a far easier, more comfortable lifestyle. However, 'a major cost of not working when one's children are young is that one may thereby miss out on what could be an adequate life project – i.e. a full and satisfying career outside the home'.[8] Lifestyles and material possessions set up differences amongst women who come to be defined by what are constructed as their mutual differences.

Morality in decisions to care

The moral imperative to undertake care work in all forms is much stronger for women than for men.[9] Women are moral actors, and recognise 'obligations that present themselves as necessary to be fulfilled but are neither forced on one or are enforceable'.[10] It could be argued, however, that in traditional and new-capitalist discourses of motherhood, and with the emergence of child's needs discourses, these obligations are actually enforced given the conditions shaping women's lives:

> Yeah, whenever it's discussed in the media, it's all about 'getting women back into the workplace'. It has never crossed any of the writers' minds that any woman would choose to put the focus on the home for the child's first three years, for the critical developmental period of that child's personality. That's never crossed anyone's mind that, well, you know(.) And it comes across as a very strong message that I've picked up on (Joy, focus group).

Joy identifies with the strain of intensive mothering in motherhood discourses and consequently provides intensive care for her children, not just for the child's first three years. Joy, however perceives that 'getting women back into the workplace' is a particularly strong media message, suggesting that there is only one dominant message regarding women and employment. In this case study, the majority of women in the area mother full-time, and it is interesting that Joy regards the media as predominantly endorsing neo-liberalism and individualism discourses, when in fact much coverage is given to both arguments advancing motherhood and child's needs discourses in the media.[11] However, only one other woman in this study suggested that she (and other women) would rather not work: 'I really do think cost is the major thing. Most of us would rather not have to work I'm sure' (Anastasia, focus group). Every other woman in that focus group disagreed, and all suggested their employment and their mother-hood are important components in their reflexive biographies.

Jean and Eithne compromised their careers to fulfil obligations to the mother role and some women who reduced their hours of work perceived a reduction in their personal autonomy. Exactly half the women researched had reduced their hours of work, fol-lowing motherhood. A key trigger in women's compromises is the morality they attach to making decisions regarding the ways they will combine paid work with motherhood and the guilt women feel if they perceive they are not satisfying gendered moral norms:

> That's one of the reasons I felt [I had to give up work] that, for me, the guilt, that and the fact that and nearly crashing the car because I was crying so hard driving away from it, five morn-ings, you know, every day. I simply couldn't, couldn't do it. I felt I was putting my need for(.) I don't know, fulfilment beyond her [baby's] need for development. So I had to, as you said, prioritise (Joy, focus group).

For Joy there was a simple choice to make between mothers' fulfil-ment in paid work, or baby's need for development. By working full-time Joy perceived she was putting her needs ahead of the child's, and she subsequently gave up her job. Now she works part-time in a flexible way at evenings and weekends to be avail-able to her children during the day. One way of reconciling the dilemma between meeting obligations to care and engaging in paid work is for women to recognise only one dominant discourse and have one clear unambiguous subject position. However, it was evident in the focus group setting that women had chosen different ways of combining motherhood with paid work, with Joy being the only woman in six who had reduced her hours of work in that par-ticular group. Therefore it was provocative to state to five women with full-time jobs and careers that mothers who work full-time prioritise their own needs over those of their children. Many women are not fulfilled in paid work, and many babies develop perfectly well with other caregivers, yet the juxtaposition of mothers satisfaction and baby's development was highly emotive and created considerable tension in that focus group discussion.

In Ireland as elsewhere, women's choices are framed in transi-tion from status to effect. In popular culture and the media it is commonly claimed that women 'choose' to give up work and stay home to rear their children because this is most effective for family functioning; not that women stay at home because motherhood discourses dominate in a patriarchal society. This is a shift in justi-fication of gender discrimination: from a system where gender arrangements are described in the language of hierarchy to one in which they are described in the language of emotion; from an open acknowledgement of male entitlements to one that justifies them as the optimal path to self-fulfilment for women as well as for men.[12] Joy has decided to prioritise her family now and con-centrate on her career when her children are older: 'I'm feeling very happy at where we are from a family and children and that's working, it's working well. It's taken a lot of effort to get it to this point and I'm very happy with it and I wouldn't change the way we have it at the moment' (Joy, interview). Joy describes the con-sequences of her choice in emotional terms, she is happy now that she has prioritised her children over her career. Joy anticipates spending more time on her career when her children are older, suggesting that at some level she also recognises autonomy as a discursive strain in individualism discourses.

Women who are mothers rarely act in their own best interests, because morally inscribed motherhood charges women with priori-tising the interests of their children, particularly when they are babies:

> I used to find when the kids were younger, you were giving them a lot of time, and you had very little time for yourself. I found anyway, you know, that I was less likely to give them to somebody else, even if they offered to child-mind. I'd prefer do it myself, sort of thing. Because I'd feel guilty if I was away from them (Amy, focus group).

Women enjoy spending time with their children and many women, like Amy, would elect to spend time out of work with their children rather than engage in other pursuits. The decisions women make regarding work and care suggest little evidence of their being atomised individuals exercising unencumbered lifestyle choices; women take decisions about how parenting might be combined with paid work with reference to moral and socially negotiated views about what behaviour is 'right and proper'.[13] These decisions are gendered because they deal with notions of mothering; they are moral in providing answers about the right thing to do in relation to motherhood, and in relation to employment; and they are ration-alities in providing a framework for making decisions.[14]

The choice of the necessary

Bourdieu describes the ways in which expectations and aspirations of subordinate groups are scaled down to what is possible, or as he puts it 'the choice of the necessary'.[15] People form dispositions, he claims, which engender aspirations and practices compatible with their available options: 'The most improbable practices are excluded, either totally without examination as *unthinkable*, or at the cost of the *double negation* which inclines agents to make a virtue of necessity, that is *to refuse what is anyway refused* and to love the inevitable' (original emphasis).[16]

While Jean claimed to exercise autonomy over her decision to reduce her hours of work, her account suggests she was refusing what was anyway refused because she acknowledged gendered societal pressure on the mother to reduce her hours. All women claim to have made 'choices' in determining the ways they will combine motherhood with paid work, but the reality is that many women's decisions amount to a series of compromises because the choices are not entirely free and many women make decisions to combine motherhood with paid work under duress. Duress is not just limited to paradigmatic threats of the 'your money or your life' variety. The robbery victim's freedom to choose does not increase her welfare because she was forced to choose between her money and her life.[17] Discourses of individualism offer no self-referencing definition of duress; it is not identified by the presence or absence of 'true' consent. Rather, duress is judged on the basis of a normative assessment of the quality of the choices available. What distinguishes the conventional doctrine of duress from the feminist argument regarding a woman's consent to engage in employment or motherhood or combine the two, is where the moral baseline is drawn. It is not enough that a person has consented; she must also have had normatively acceptable options from which to choose. Is it normatively acceptable for 'working mothers' to have to choose between career and motherhood because these are constructed as polarised in Irish society? Although much of the pressure to choose between motherhood and paid work is framed by a discourse of equivalent choice between career and work in the home, for many women who reduce their hours of work, their time at home with children is circumscribed by drudgery, while the promise of autonomy and fulfilment in careers is also not met for many women. Women with partners are privileged in that they can reduce their hours of work, reduce their income and limit their career plans in order to provide more direct care for their children. There is a part-time premium in that part-time workers have more control over their working time and suffer less from stress and health worries than women who work full-time.[18] However, there is also a part-time penalty, with lower earnings and pension entitlements and this 'choice' maintains these women's unequal position at home and at work. Women experience gender inequality because only women are mothers, and fatherhood is not reported to carry the same public scrutiny and sanction as motherhood does.

Many women are navigating their way between competing dis-cursive strains and making 'decisions, possibly undecidable decisions, certainly not free, but forced by others and wrested out of oneself, under conditions that lead to dilemmas'.[19] For many women, their choices result in compromises, trade-offs and sacri-fices. Faye has a very involved, committed career as company director and said it was never even a possibility that she would consider reducing her hours of work because of her children:

> I just knew that was it with the company, you just(.) It was the sort of position that you had to be there. And if you wanted to go in and lead something, you just had to be there in terms of full-time. So, that had a big influence on my choices going forward. And I suppose my wanting to have children, that was always there (Faye, interview).

In Faye's organisation, full-time commitment is required to reach a level of responsibility. However, Faye also wanted to have chil-dren, and her 'choices' to combine motherhood with paid work were influenced by practical considerations: 'I wanted two chil-dren . . . I felt that's what I could, not so much cope with, but that's what I wanted in life. And I wanted to work full-time, and I didn't want to kind of be compromising' (Faye, interview). Faye demon-strates her reflexivity, choosing to have two children enables her to maintain her commitment to family and career. Workplaces and careers which demand employee's full-time commitment create practical difficulties for 'working mothers' and Faye and Kate describe very busy lives maintaining 'ideal worker' commitment to their employing organisations, while combining their careers with motherhood. This does not suggest that motherhood is less important to women with high levels of career commitment. It does mean they experience more practical difficulties, and that they experience emotional difficulties in the form of guilt. Rubery, Smith and Fagan found there is a polarisation in the workplace between women with, and without children, with only the latter being able to pursue a career.[20] However, in this research, women demonstrate they are able to combine motherhood with careers, but with different degrees of compromise and difficulty.

Yolanda, on the other hand, would like another child, but reflexively is considering her situation:

> At the moment my worst thing is . . . It's a big decision – I wouldn't mind having a third child, but I'm just wondering, how in God's name would I cope? And I'm saying now, am I letting this, am I going to in ten years' time, going to be saying why didn't I? . . . But I'm saying right, how am I going to manage [financially]? I can't give up work, it's not [possible]. I could job-share. I cannot give up in the situation . . . it's not an option. No, it's not (Yolanda, focus group).

Yolanda's reflexive decision-making demonstrates the conflict she is experiencing. She would like a third child, and is considering the economic and practical difficulties that a third child would mean for her family. As she is the main earner, these considerations are not insignificant. Women's lives are interdependent with their children, their partners, their colleagues and wider social networks. Women describe that they make compromises based on their family situations. It is possible to see the power operating through discourses of motherhood and is evident in families and workplaces which reinforce the gendered order of caring, and which create moral dilemmas and inequalities for women who attempt to combine motherhood with paid work. This dilemma arises and is maintained from the relationship between discourses of motherhood and discourses of individualism, because individualism assumes women have a full appreciation of the implications of their choices and are able to recognise and act in their own best interests, while discourses of motherhood demand the sublimation of women's interests to those of their children. The decisions of 'working mothers' are still made rationally, but with a different sort of rationality to that assumed by individualism discourses.

Reflexive moral reasoning

Women see morality in relation to their commitment to paid work and morality in relation to motherhood. 'Working mothers' demonstrate they make choices to combine motherhood with paid work by engaging in gendered reflexive moral reasoning.[21] Participants in this study reflected on moral concerns in relation to their children, families, employers and their colleagues. They reflected on moral concerns in making an economic contribution to society, in relation to seeking a return on the investment in their education, providing role models for their daughters, and they reflexively made decisions about the ways they would combine motherhood with paid work, and engaged in moral reasoning during these reflexive deliberations. This is one way women can reconcile the consequences of their decisions and the dilemmas these decisions create.

By recognising morality in their decisions to combine motherhood with paid work, women exercise agency, but also contribute to the dominant discourses which reinforce the polarisation of working and caring and which create intersecting inequalities for women who try to do both. However, women's moral reasoning reveals that their 'choices' are frequently made under duress, because the conditions under which the choice is made are not of women's own choosing. It is duress for a woman to be forced into limiting her career options, limiting the number of children she has, reducing hours of work, reducing her income or working under 'ideal worker' conditions because of gendered expectations in the workplace and society, a lack of fatherly support, and public scrutiny and sanction. As reflexive social actors, women employ techniques of resistance and self-governance by making gendered, reflexive, moral choices which conceal the public and private gender regimes operating in families, workplaces and society.

Women make choices in conditions not of their own choosing between morally inscribed motherhood and morally inscribed participation in paid work, with little social support. These choices are neither free, nor morally sound. Women are obliged to make the best choices that lead to the greatest satisfaction for all, therefore women engage in reflexive gendered moral reasoning in making decisions to combine motherhood with paid work. However, while women's moral reasoning is an attempt to exercise agency, it conceals the stark reality that women make choices under duress, and the inequalities or privileges a woman experiences as a consequence of her choice are constructed as her own fault, or her own achievement. One consequence of experiencing inequalities and privileges and blaming herself for them is that women experience emotional distress caused by the doubts and insecurities of making impossible choices under structural conditions beyond their control.

Women present their decisions as freely chosen, but in reality, women's decisions frequently amount to little more than a series of compromises masquerading as 'free' choice. Women are not empowered by moral reasoning, but in fact are constrained by it, as it provides women with the illusion of choice, masking the clear and defined limits to women's participation in the public sphere and the persistence of the gendered order of caring. Women's moral reasoning perpetuates gendered assumptions regarding women's role in families and in the workplace. Because, as Warner argues,

> All this moralizing we routinely do is a ridiculous waste of time and energy. And it also rests upon assumptions that have no basis in reality. Chief among them is that mothers do what they do most of the time out of choice.[22]

CHAPTER 6

The myth of motherhood

In Irish society there is much rhetorical valorising of the mother role, yet when women take up the subject position 'mother', there is little support and considerable sanction for women. For middle-class women in particular, there is a strong command to be 'moral mothers', to care competently and professionally for their children.[1]

Oakley termed the motherhood ideology, 'the myth of mother-hood', which, she argued, contains three popular assertions:

> The first is the most influential: that children need mothers. The second is the obverse of this: that mothers need their children. The third assertion is a generalisation which holds that mother-hood represents the greatest achievement of a woman's life: the sole true means of self-realisation. Women, in other words, need to be mothers.[2]

This myth provides a useful explanatory framework for the ways in which the women in this study regard motherhood, for them-selves and in wider society. Women demonstrate they internalise the myth in their decisions to combine motherhood with paid work and despite the influence of discourses of individualism, feminism and neo-liberalism, in early twenty-first-century Ireland, the myth of motherhood is still very relevant. Each of the assertions is exam-ined in their accounts of combining motherhood with paid work given by these 'working mothers'.

Children need mothers

One strain in motherhood discourses is that of intensive mothering. There are three main tenets of intensive mothering, to which all women must adhere if they are to be viewed as good mothers: (a) childcare is primarily the responsibility of the mother; (b) childcare should be child-centered; and (c) children exist outside of market valuation, and are sacred, innocent and pure, their price immeasurable.[3] As the primary caregiver, the mother is ideally best suited to comprehend her child's needs and can interpret and respond to those needs intuitively.[4]

The norm that children need their mothers was internalised by participants and Eithne claimed 'they [children] do need their mother . . . there's nothing you can do about it' (Eithne, focus group). Eithne suggests that children only need their mothers, but that it is a biological given that cannot be changed. Amanda demonstrates that she too has internalised the powerful normative assumption that mothers provide the best care for children: 'It's about the mothering of our children that we do as well. I know Dads are very, very good, but they don't do that same softness and that same gentleness' (Amanda, focus group). Similarly, all women described themselves as being the one to care for children when they are sick, even when husbands volunteered: '[P]art of you, inside you says "oh well, this is the mother's job, this is something I must do" . . . it's not that he wouldn't want to do it, it's because it's "the right thing to do"' (Grace, focus group). Grace uses moral language – caring for sick children is 'the right thing' for mothers to do, because it is 'the mothers' job', – demonstrating the way the gendered order of caring is presented as natural and inevitable. Brona described the emotional distress she experiences going to work when her children are sick: 'But if they are sick, and the babysitter's minding them, you know, there's nothing like yourself, like. You have to get on with it, but you feel terrible, going to work when they're at home sick, you know' (Brona, focus group).

Even though Audrey has the career in her family, she too believes the mothers' primary role is as carer: 'I don't have a childminder this week, and my husband is taking half days to collect the kids from school, and I mean, 'tis he would be doing the things, he's doing the things you know, that I should be doing' (Audrey, focus group). When I asked Audrey why she felt she should be looking after the children rather than her husband, she replied, 'things I'm supposed to be doing' (Audrey, focus group), demonstrating the way the differences between the genders have been naturalised. All women in this study perceive the obligation to care for their children themselves, because of the persistent norm that children need their mothers Apart from the societal pressure on women to provide intensive care for their children, women love their babies and some found it difficult to leave small children in order to go to work:

> They used to cry in the morning and stuff like that, and that stays with you for hours, having them dragged off your legs and stuff like that you know. And I have vivid memories of that when they were smaller now I have to say. But(.) And you're not the better of that for the day really (Grace, focus group).

There is no doubt that women love their children and can experience distress leaving them when they are small. However, it was reported that older children also expect their mothers to be at home and available 'Because even though my children have always known me to work, and they've always, certainly in the last five or six years known me to be away, regularly away from home, they don't like it, they still don't like it, even though they're used to it, they're still not comfortable with it' (Kate, interview). Families and society vigorously promote the norm that children need their mothers. This contributes to the guilt 'working mothers' experience, regardless of whether or not they adjust their paid work to suit their motherhood by reducing their hours of work.

Women may compete in the labour market if they are contributing to their families, but must not relinquish their primary responsibility for caring. Richardson found that attitudes vary according to whether a woman is seen as having to work to help support a family, or alternatively, is going out to work to satisfy her own needs and interests.[5] The public condemnation of women who appear to prioritise careers over families, or to work for material gain, is indicative of the opprobrium poured on rational economic actors, and mothers who attempt to perform as rational economic actors are perceived to be failing as women and mothers and are roundly condemned: 'That's the stigma of being a working mum' (Agatha, focus group). The normative assumption that children need mothers is evident in the criticism of women who do not work outside the home. Women were aware of this criticism: 'I would think then that there would be another category of mothers who would say you are neglecting your children by working' (Aisling, focus group).

Many women who work full-time are aware of the criticism of other women, and recognise pressure to prioritise their children's needs over their own, which causes women to justify their decision to combine motherhood with paid work:

I never feel cheated in not being with my children all the time. I feel I have been there every step of the way for them and I feel that I know more about them than anybody else. That I would be the expert on them, no matter what and that, just because I'm not with them a few hours every day, doesn't mean I don't know exactly what they get up to and what they're like (Eithne, interview).

Because Eithne maintains her commitment to paid work, she is obliged to affirm that her children's needs are being met by her. Fathers are not reported to share this obligation. Women experience guilt because they perceive they are not properly satisfying moral obligations to their children, which is not shared with their partners. This is a gendered inequality because combining paid work with fatherhood was not reported to carry the same moral obligations that combining motherhood with paid work does for women. In fact, not having to do caring is part of the patriarchal dividend, something that accrues to men by virtue of being a man, even if men do not set out to avoid it.[6] This masculine privilege is created and maintained by the power of motherhood discourses, which promote the myth that children only need mothers.

Mothers need children

Letherby argues that motherhood is regarded as a privilege and a duty, a natural consequence of marriage and proof of adulthood.[7] Rich claims motherhood ideologies and discourses frequently identify women as mothers first and women second, and she argues that motherhood is only one part of female process; it is not an identity for all time.[8] Nevertheless the idea that mothers need children in order to be truly feminine is a powerful normative assumption. Letherby and Williams claim that having a child is central to femininity, that without this desire or ability, women are unfeminine and abnormal because society still takes for granted that '"woman" equals "mother" equals "wife" equals "adult"; and this presumption remains part of medical, political and public discourse'.[9] Conner also claims that mothering is 'the activity that above all, completes and confirms feminine identity'.[10] Thus, women's identity is linked to their ability to mother and women who cannot or do not wish to reproduce are placed in a relationship to motherhood, even if a negative one.

Joy identified with this and enjoyed the feeling of importance and being needed that motherhood provided when she had her first child: 'when I just had one, I perhaps did feel that I was the be all and end all' (Joy, interview). Eithne claimed she had always wanted to become a mother: 'It [motherhood] was an experience I wanted to experience in my lifetime, to . . . be pregnant and have a baby' (Eithne, interview) and finds motherhood enriching and rewarding: 'I absolutely adore being a mother and it has enriched my life way more than I expected it to . . . I didn't expect it to be as fulfilling as it actually is' (Eithne, interview). This suggests that some women themselves do not recognise a need to be mothers, until they become mothers themselves. There is no doubt that motherhood can be enjoyable, but the public scrutiny of motherhood and the pressure to conform to norms of mothering frequently ensures that 'mothers' needs are occluded in favour of the child's'.[11]

Parental leave is unpaid leave, to facilitate parents caring for young children. Introduced in 1998, it was initially fourteen weeks per child under age eight; it increased to eighteen weeks in 2013. Leave is available to either parent, but at the employer's discretion. Audrey took all her parental leave when her children were young in order to spend as much time as possible with her children at that stage: 'You enjoy seeing them grow and get big and having the time with them and not missing it . . . Taking them to school and taking them to playschool and going to birthday parties, that's all a great time really, and a great time for the mother as well' (Audrey, interview). Audrey derived pleasure from attending to her children when they were small. The power operating through motherhood discourses is evident in Audrey's account. Perhaps being with young children is only 'a great time for the mother' because it conforms to gendered expectations, and there is a certain comfort in that. Norms of good mothering suggest women have little choice but to conform to prevailing norms or risk social sanction, but as Lawler states 'neither pleasure nor choice indicate an absence of authority or of the operation of power'.[12] The normative assumption that women need to mother and will find it fulfilling is clear in Audrey's description of spending time with her children when they were young. However, Audrey was only able to do this by working in a job she 'didn't want to do' while her children were young:

> I worked then, I worked in a Monday to Friday job, in a job really that I didn't want to do, but I did it because my husband was doing shift work, and I worked so that I would be off every weekend with the kids . . . So at least I was going to be

there every weekend and I had no night duty or anything. So I did a Monday to Friday job, and I was there in the morning at eight o'clock and I was home in the evening by five (Audrey, interview).

Audrey worked in a job which ensured her availability to her children every weekend and every evening after five, as well as taking all her parental leave in order to be available to her children. Even though Audrey had compromised her career by taking that particular job, she still reported feeling conflicted when going to work when her children were small, as this did not meet her needs as a mother: 'I didn't really like it, no. I mean the first six months I suppose I cried going to work thinking about him [her child]. But I had to do it and I knew that I had to do it. We couldn't manage otherwise and I was able to continue working' (Audrey, interview).

All women in this study claimed to enjoy motherhood and to find it fulfilling and rewarding. Motherhood provides women with cultural capital, particularly in the middle-class area of the study and there is a particular pressure generated by middle-class, full-time-in-the-home mothers in the local area, which creates difficulties for women who also engage in paid work:

I really love being a mother and I think, I think I'm good at it. We try hard to parent our children very well and I really(.) I'm surprised at how much I enjoy being a parent to my children, and I really love that part as well. And I suppose that's the worst thing, missing out on you know, meeting other parents at the school . . . I'm dropping them at half past eight, because the school opens at half past eight, and I'm gone, you know, and she's the first in the classroom, and I'm gone, the times I'm dropping her, So you do feel that maybe they are losing out on something by you being a 'working mother', but I think in the long run it will balance out. I do, you do feel that it's a downside for me at the moment that I do feel I am missing out on things by working full-time, but still not enough for me to actually give up (Eithne, focus group).

Eithne demonstrates her enjoyment of motherhood and her concern that her daughter is 'missing out on things' because Eithne has no opportunity to develop relationships with other mothers and children at the school. The conflict in discourses is evident in Eithne's account of how she loves being a mother, but the downside of being a 'working mother' is insufficient for her to actually give up work. While all the women claimed to enjoy their children, many women sought visibility as mothers. Grace had just reduced her hours of work in order to be able to collect her children from school three days a week and to spend the afternoons facilitating their activities: 'Oh God, and you arrive to the school and suddenly everyone's saying "her mom's there, her mom's there" and you're just thinking "oh my God, what kind of mother am I?" you just have to pick them up from school and you're after making their whole week' (Grace, focus group). Grace was conscious of the public scrutiny of mothers, and how their presence or absence was visible and drew comment. The expression 'what kind of mother am I?' was very telling in terms of the way Grace believed good motherhood is synonymous with being visible at the school gates and in the community as well as her perception that she was not meeting the requirements of the 'good mother' role, by not being available to facilitate her children's after-school activities. Both Eithne and Joy are involved in mothering organisations – the Irish Childbirth Trust and La Lèche League – which also promotes and affirms their motherhood.

The greatest achievement of a woman's life

During focus group discussions, women expressed different opinions regarding women who mother full- and part-time and while all the women claimed to find motherhood enjoyable, fulfilling and rewarding, their participation in paid work set up differences between them. Some women regarded their paid work as important components in their reflexive biographies: 'You are more than, you are not defined solely as a mother, or a partner, or wife, you have your own job' (Eithne, focus group). 'Isn't that sad? The way you say it "not just a mother"' (Florence, focus group).

Amy claimed she had always wanted to mother, but initially expected motherhood to fit around her career. However, she now finds motherhood more rewarding than her career: 'it's what you get back, maybe I'm getting more back from my children now than I am actually from my career' (Amy, interview). Likewise Aisling claimed that having four children, while being very busy, was rewarding and fulfilling: 'I don't think you can say that we're constantly giving, giving, giving to the kids and not receiving anything back' (Aisling, interview).

Colleen assured herself, and me, that our participation in paid work would not be detrimental to our children, or society, and we are fulfilling our maternal obligations:

> It's not a bad thing that we are 'working mothers'. We are not reneging on our duty as a mum . . . What you put into your kid now, you're going to reap at the end of the day, somewhere down the road, just by seeing that they are a great, moral upstanding person (Colleen, interview).

Colleen clearly sees motherhood as a duty to her child and also to society. This reflects the view that women are responsible for raising the next generation as well as preserving the family as the central social unit. Colleen was anxious to confirm that she is fulfilling these duties, even though she is engaged in paid work. Colleen spoke about prioritising her son's needs over her own while he is young:

> It doesn't matter what marital circumstance you're in, you will make that decision [to prioritise her child's needs]. His [needs] rather than mine anyway . . . That's the whole thing. It's not forever, they're only little for a very, very short period of time. They only really need us for a very short period of time, thirteen, fifteen, seventeen years. Like if you think about it, it's not very long (Colleen, interview).

Colleen believes her son needs her to prioritise his needs over her own, and she is prepared to suspend her need for individual time for seventeen years and, as she is parenting alone and working thirty-two hours a week, this is particularly acute. However, in contemporary Ireland, with the dominance of intensive nurturing discourse, 'this loss of self, this self-sacrifice wouldn't even be mourned as a loss. It would be embraced, with open arms, and celebrated – as though it were the highest evolution of all the forms of motherhood that had come before'.[13]

Beck argues it is a defining characteristic of contemporary western societies that individuals experience pressure to become what one is, and especially to demonstrate to family, friends and colleagues, that one has truly 'made it' and achieved success in personal and professional lives.[14] Joy believes she has 'made it' personally and she will make it professionally by having the status a career will bring her in the future:

> It's not that I don't see myself as having a career. I see it as being modular. That's just the way I feel. I have to compartmentalise that part of my life as being on the back burner for now, and that I will have it all, but not necessarily all at the same time (Joy, interview).

Joy believes her decision to prioritise caring for her children over her career is the optimal path to fulfilment for Joy. However she also acknowledges that this requires compromise, and 'having it all' is possible, but not all at once:

> This [motherhood] is my priority. This is the way I prioritise my life. And other people prioritise their lives in different ways, and everybody makes the best choice they can . . . Well, this has worked for me, and if I don't voice it, somebody else might not be aware of this being an option for them'. Somebody else might not say 'hang on a second, you know, you can have it'. The phrase I would use is that I think it is possible to have it all, I do, just not necessarily all at the same time. That's what I'm aiming towards. I think I've got it all. But I don't have the status. If I carried on working, I would have the status symbols and the status of being in a professional role (Joy, interview).

Joy describes how she had returned to work after the birth of her first child, but found the experience too stressful, because she perceived she was not adequately fulfilling the mother role: 'I wasn't happy because I felt I wasn't giving, I wasn't delivering the goods the way I was used to delivering the goods, and I felt "God, I'm letting the side down here", I felt I was letting the side down' (Joy, interview). There is a religious tone to the way Joy speaks of her children: 'I can devote the time to them' (Joy, interview). Many participants framed motherhood discourses in religious or moral terms (e.g. duty, giving and devotion), particularly in relation to their obligations towards their children. Joy chose to work more flexibly at market research, which she juggles around her children's needs, because she chose to prioritise the mother role and she reconciles this with her expectation that she will return to her career when her children are older.

All women in this research identified with the myth of motherhood and many mothers assured themselves, and me, that they were satisfying their children's needs, their own needs as mothers and that they found motherhood fulfilling and rewarding, the greatest achievement of a woman's life: 'Mothers are so, so important, and we are so important as mothers' (Florence, focus group).

The Mother War

Women's different ways of combining motherhood with paid work results in 'the mother war'.[15] Women who work outside the home, women who reduce their working hours, and women who mother full-time blame and criticise each other for different ways of parenting:

> Nothing rankles the mother in the home, who has made a huge financial [sacrifice], who has sacrificed a career path and sacrificed some personal aspirations to hear 'oh but I have to work' from somebody who's wearing Prada sunglasses and Jimmy Choo shoes. And I have met them, 'Oh but I have to work, we have a huge mortgage' and I'm thinking 'Hello? The glasses? The shoes?' (Joy, interview).

Joy is conscious that she has made sacrifices to be available to her children, and the outward trappings of wealth from a woman who claims to 'have to work' for economic reasons irritates her: 'If status is something that I miss, and I do on some level . . . Who doesn't? I mean who wouldn't like to be perceived well, as having done well for herself and having fulfilled potential?' (Joy, interview). Johnston and Swanton found that despite fulfilling their ideologically defined gender roles, many stay-at-home mothers feel pressured to return to work 'they feel they are constantly suspect because they do not work'.[16] Joy's paid work is invisible, which might contribute to her perceived lack of status. This suggests that Joy recognises the discursive strains of self-actualisation in discourses of individualism and personal economic success in discourses of neo-liberalism. The contradiction between discourses of traditional self-sacrificial motherhood and discourses of individualism and neo-liberalism are evident in the difficulty Joy has in accepting another woman's choices. Women who prioritised their children claimed superior moral authority and many of these women were also highly critical of women who continued to work full-time, suggesting these women were not fulfilling their obligations to motherhood by meeting their children's needs. Because she is available to her children by working evenings and weekends, Joy uncritically assumes women who work full-time are working purely for material gain and does not acknowledge that some women might work for economic necessity or to make an economic contribution to society, and might also experience emotional as well as practical difficulties in combining motherhood with paid work. Agatha perceived this criticism from members of her family who do not engage in paid work outside the home: 'The mothers who don't work(.) well, to me anyway, because I'm one of a big family and I have a lot of in-laws and sisters and . . . they suggest, I'm not saying that they are [perfect], [but] they suggest that they are more or less meeting the standards of a perfect mother' (Agatha).

Many women did not consider that other women might be happy in paid work, achieve job satisfaction and fulfil their ambitions, as well as being mothers. It is at least conceivable that it is beneficial for children to have a mother who is fulfilled in work who might otherwise be anxious and frustrated if she were not participating in paid work. Amy works part-time, two days a week and feels she has achieved balance:

> I'd be a terrible full-time mother because I'd need to get away totally from that and talk about something else and meet different people and if that wasn't happening during my week, I'd be, I'd just be a really frustrated mother really, you know. At least this way, I can get away, I can do my [work] I can have nice chats with other people and I can communicate in a totally different way. It gives you another identity within yourself and then when I come back to the kids, I can actually take on a different role . . . I think one enhances the other really, you know. I don't think I could do it without one or the other, you know. I think they work well together (Amy, focus group).

Amy, like many women in this study, has reduced her hours, and enjoys her time spent in paid work, acknowledging that not participating in paid work would be frustrating for her. However, it was possible for Amy to reduce her hours as she works in the public sector. Similarly Grace moved from private to public sector employment after the birth of her second child, and has subsequently reduced her working hours to better balance work and home. In comparing her situation to other mothers working full-time, Grace observed women who work very long hours at their chosen careers may benefit materially, but at the expense of not satisfying their obligations to their children:

> I'd say that most of these people then are very well paid and they have a lot of material things and they can probably do a lot of very nice things. But I think eventually it will catch up with you, that you will realise what you've missed, and all the years that have gone by, that you haven't seen them [children] and you haven't been there for [your children] and you don't get them back (Grace, interview).

There is a warning tone to Grace's observation 'It will catch up with you'; Folbre comments that in economics the term selfishness is often used in such a way as to imply that it is more rational than altruism.[17] Utility-maximisation is linked to the individualism and competitiveness of markets. Women who are perceived to assert their self-interest risk transgressing norms of femininity. Women who pursue careers may therefore find themselves in a contradictory position when attempting to combine careers with motherhood. In respect of the division of resources within the family, discourses of motherhood require women to put their children first. Not to do so can reap severe sanction[18] as evident in the disapproval of Grace and Joy of women who pursue careers.

Women are compelled to make choices in relation to combining motherhood with paid work and to take responsibility for the outcome of their choices. Women's participation in paid work has not guaranteed men's participation in the home and has caused a backlash which is evident in intensive mothering discourses and the persistence of the myth of motherhood. Many participants framed children's needs in terms of children needing their mothers' care and time, and many women who had prioritised caring for their children by reducing their time in paid work condemned other women's choices and joined the public scrutiny and criticism of full-time 'working mothers'.

The Myth of Motherhood

Women experience inequalities because of gendered obligations promoted in the myth of motherhood and in this research, many women claimed to experience guilt because they were not always available to their children, as the myth dictates. Women internalised the myth that children need mothers, and the pressure to meet this need resulted in many women reducing their hours in paid work. Women also experienced inequality because they were expected to undertake greater responsibility for caring than their partners. The women believed that mothers need children and experience inequalities by reducing their working hours or working in jobs they do not enjoy, in order to meet their need as mothers to be available to their children. They had also internalised that motherhood is the greatest achievement of a woman's life and spoke about motherhood in religious terms (sacrifice, vocation and duty). In order to conform to the myth, one woman worked evenings and weekends in order to be available to her children during the day; another was prepared to suspend her need for personal time for up to seventeen years; another worked in a job she did not like for up to a decade, in order to find a balance between paid work and motherhood which prioritised the maternal role.

The power operating through dominant mothering discourses produces the desire to spend time caring for children and conceals the backlash against women's progress and the patriarchal power operating through these discourses which sets clear and defined limits on women's ability to combine motherhood with paid work. These discourses are also evident in the state's neo-liberal agenda. Changes in tax and welfare legislation which facilitate gender equality have only been introduced following pressure from the EU and effective lobby groups, such as the trades unions and non-governmental organisations mostly concerned with women's and children's rights.[19] Nevertheless, there is resistance to measures which encourage women's participation in paid work and a backlash encourages women to provide direct care for their children in the early years.[20] The 2013 state's report on early childhood care and education, *Right from the Start*, suggests that mothers returning to work within six months of childbirth may be negatively related to children's cognitive outcomes, especially if this is on a full-time basis. The negative associations of early maternal employment with children's outcomes are largely observed among children in intact families or in families with parents with high levels of education.[21] The association between maternal employment and chidren's cognitive outcomes is in fact small and not universally observed, yet it is worrisome that the expert group on early years care and education would highlight a position which discourages women's employment, reflecting the dominance of intensive nurturing as a discursive strain.

The condemnation of 'working mothers' by women who choose alternative ways of working and mothering sets women in opposition to each other and reflects the conflict between discursive strains of achievement and autonomy on one hand and intensive nurturing on the other. This conflict is reflected in the fact that the women in this research are aware of their privileges and therefore do not complain about the inequalities they experience because the myth makes women feel guilty for working outside the home in the first place. Women who are 'working mothers' do not campaign for change in family, workplace or society, and suffer the inequalities they experience in silence. They are compelled to make choices in relation to combining motherhood with paid work and to take responsibility for the outcome of their choices. Many women who had prioritised caring for their children by reducing their time in paid work condemned other women's choices, experienced moral authority and joined the public scrutiny and criticism of full-time 'working mothers'. A pernicious aspect of the myth of motherhood is that 'the mother war' is not just confined to mothers; women's forms of mothering are subject to public scrutiny and sanction. Many women in the study reported experiencing criticism from colleagues and other family members, while criticism of 'working mothers' is a regular media item. Constantly experiencing criticism regarding their lifestyle choices is an inequality that full-time-in-the-home mothers, non-mothers and fathers do not experience. Families, workplaces and wider society therefore continue to promote ideas of intensive mothering and traditional gendered values regarding mother's place in the home, which makes combining paid work with motherhood stressful and difficult. It would be possible for women to provide direct care for their children during the early years if maternity, paternity and parental leave provisions were improved. This would facilitate early years care of infants by those mothers who wish to provide direct care for their infants as well as encouraging fathers' involvement in their children's care. This might reduce one ground of conflict between women who engage in paid work outside the home and those who do not.

The persistence of the myth of motherhood demonstrates conflicts and contradictions between individualist and neo-liberal discursive strains, combined with a neo-liberal state which promotes women's employment. The neo-liberal changes which have taken place in the economy and society, with changes in tax and welfare systems to facilitate women's and mothers' employment, have had little corresponding change in the family and society. There is a weak path dependency between social policy and social attitudes, demonstrating that Ireland maintains a deeply conservative, patriarchal culture, which is promoted in intensive motherhood and child's needs discourses and evident in women's identification with the myth of motherhood.

CHAPTER 7

Childcare

Childcare is central to women's ability to participate in paid work. Sourcing, arranging and paying for suitable, safe childcare is essential if women are to engage in paid work outside the home. Exploring the childcare landscape and women's childcare arrangements reveals the persistence of the gendered order of caring in Irish society, in families and in households. The state does little to meet families' childcare needs, which creates difficulties for women who combine motherhood with paid work, because caring is seen in families and society as predominantly a female concern and a private responsibility.

Childcare provision

Childcare and the provision of childcare have received considerable attention from a range of interests including government in recent years. Landmark developments included the introduction of regulation of pre-schools in 1996, the appointment of the first ever Minister for Children in 1994, the first National Childcare Strategy in 1999 and the establishment of the National Children's Office in 2000. The Centre for Early Childhood Development and Education (CECDE) was founded in 2002, a Children's Ombudsman was appointed in 2003, a new Office of the Minister for Children was established in 2005, and in 2006 a new National Childcare Strategy (2006–2010) was launched, with a budget of €575 million.[1] The Irish National Action Plan for Social Inclusion (2007–2016) includes the long-term goal that 'Every family should be able to access childcare services which are appropriate to the circumstances and the needs of their children'.[2]

In 2006, Síolta, the National Quality Framework for Early Childhood Education, was published to provide quality standards in pre-school childcare and applies to private, self-employed and

106

community facilities as well as registered private childminders. Discourses of children's rights and early childhood education have also informed policy and since 2010, the Early Childhood Care and Education Scheme (ECCE)[3] has provided limited free pre-school places in pre-school services that provide an appropriate educational programme which adheres to the principles of Síolta. Children aged between the ages of three years and two months and four years and seven months enrolled in pre-schools receive free pre-school education of three hours per day, five days each week for thirty-eight weeks. The pre-school receives €64.50 for each of the thirty-eight weeks, which equates to €4.30 per child per hour. In 2013, the Department of Children and Youth Affairs published *Right from the Start*, a report of the Expert Advisory Group on the Early Years Strategy.[4] The report makes fifty-four recommendations across ten themes, which include increased investment, supporting families, access to services, and training, professional support and regulation of providers. Thus far, these recommendations have not been adopted.

In 2000, as part of the National Development Plan 2000–2006, the government introduced the Equal Opportunities Childcare Programme (EOCP) to increase the supply and quality of childcare throughout Ireland.[5] In 2000, the Equal Opportunities Childcare Programme (EOCP) was initiated to continue until 2006. The EOCP provides funding for private, community and voluntary childcare sectors. Private childcare and self-employed providers receive funding to establish and staff childcare centres, grant assistance is given to community-based childcare facilities through thirty-three County and City Childcare Committees and the EOCP also recognises the role of the National Voluntary Childcare Organisations (NVCOs)[6] and allocates funding to this sector to develop and support their childcare programmes. The EOCP has been succeeded by the National Childcare Investment Programme 2006–2010, which aims to provide a further 50,000 childcare places over the duration of the programme. In addition, the EOCP makes funding available to the County Childcare Committees to enable them to organise training, networking and information activities to create an awareness of quality among small-scale childminders.

However, small-scale childminders are specifically excluded from the notification process required under the Child Care Act (1991),[7] while the Childcare Regulations[8] make provision for the voluntary

notification by childminders of their childcare service to the Health
Services Executive (HSE). Under the Child Care Act (1991), a person
minding more than three pre-school children from different families
is obliged to notify the Health Services Executive (HSE);[9] however,
childminders who are relatives, or caring for children from only one
family, or caring for three or fewer children from different families,
are exempt from the notification process. Childminding Ireland provides training and support to small-scale childminders who register
their services. In Budget 2006, a new Child-minding Relief was introduced whereby a child-minder who looks after up to three children
in her own home can earn €10,000 tax free, provided their total
income from childminding does not exceed €15,000 in a year.[10] The
total income limit remains at €15,000 in 2014. Private childminders
are still the most popular form of childcare, yet the state does little to
regulate or support this informal sector.

There is little data on the extent of private childminding in
Ireland. One recent estimate based on 2007 data, suggests nearly
50,000 children in Ireland are cared for by private childminders,[11]
while the OECD estimated that 75,000 children were placed with
37,900 childminders every working day in 2002,[12] the majority of
whom are not regulated. At the end of 2011, the number of paid,
non-relative childminders registered with the HSE was 257, while
1,250 childminders were 'voluntarily notified' to the City/County
Childcare committees.[13] The government is not directly involved in
childcare provision but is a facilitator of community childcare and
private childcare through provision of capital grants to crèche
providers. Overall, in 2012, between day care, sessional and part-
time services, there are just over 4,300 childcare facilities regulated
by the HSE.[14] According to Fine Davis, the government is delegating
provision to a plethora of private sector, public sector and community groups, through the provision of capital grants: 'It is basically
saying to the marketplace and community: "You do it." It is saying
to parents: "You find your own childcare, you pay for it".'[15]

The government's position encourages the increasing marketi-
sation of childcare on the American model, whereby parents with
good financial resources will buy childcare on the formal market
and selected 'excluded' communities will be the recipients of government largesse for subsidised childcare. Perhaps this is what the
more farsighted members of government actually want, influenced
by industry interests, because this maintains childcare as a private

issue and facilitates capital accumulation for private sector providers.[16] This market-based model is predicated on individual choice and the notion that choice will create a demand to which the market will respond with supply. The notion of childcare services as a public good with individual and societal benefits has been advocated by the OECD, who advised the Irish government that public spending on early childhood services would be 'adequately compensated by enhanced social cohesion, improved educational levels and productivity in the next generation, greater gender equality, increased tax returns from women's work and by savings in health and social security expenditure'.[17] The National Economic and Social Council (NESC) also advised the government on the importance of childcare as a public good with individual and societal benefits,[18] yet the state has consistently focused on issues of supply, coordination and quality, and avoided the issue of affordability, despite expert recommendations from the OECD, NESC, the National Economic and Social Forum (NESF), and the National Women's Council of Ireland (NWCI).[19] The most recent set of recommendations from the Expert Advisory Group on the Early Years strategy also regards children as a public good and recommends increasing investment from 0.44 per cent of GDP to the international benchmark of one per cent of GDP over five years. Other recommendations include extending paid parental leave; strengthening child and family support through a dedicated 'child and family service'; demanding governance, accountability and quality in all childcare services and enhancing and extending quality early childhood care and education services as a comprehensive strategy for all children aged 0–6 years in Ireland.[20]

However, in an EU study of childcare, Ireland ranked lowest in terms of childcare supports and maternity leave[21] and was ranked the worst of the original fifteen member states in terms of public childcare provision. Compared to most European countries, childcare provision for pre-school children in Ireland is and has been uncoordinated, variable in quality and in short supply.[22] There have been some recent improvements in provision,[23] though Ireland still has the highest net childcare costs as a proportion of average earnings in the OECD.[24]

In contrast, in Denmark, where childcare is seen as a public good, social cohesion and gender equality are evident. Funding of pre-school services is greater than two per cent (2.1) of GDP while in

Ireland it is less than half of one per cent (0.44). This expenditure is evident in the rates of children in regulated childcare. In Demark, twelve per cent of children less than one year old and eighty-three per cent of one- to two-year-olds access regulated childcare, while in Ireland, between ten and fifteen per cent of children under three have access to regulated childcare.[25] In Denmark ninety-four per cent of children aged between three and five accessed regulated childcare compared with fifty-six per cent of children aged between three and six in Ireland. This is also reflected in labour-force participation rates of mothers: in Denmark seventy per cent of mothers with children aged under three and eighty per cent of women whose children are aged between three and seven years are in the workforce; in Ireland fifty-seven per cent of women whose youngest child is aged under three years, fifty-two per cent of women whose youngest child is aged four to five years and fifty-eight per cent of women whose youngest child is aged six or over are in the workplace.[26]

The lack of state support and childcare provision in Ireland has created a situation whereby childcare has been positioned as a private issue for families to resolve themselves.[27] This is what the OECD has termed a 'maximum private responsibility'[28] model of childcare, 'in which the joint problems of childcare, family life and labour force participation are entirely private concerns which are left to the individual to solve'.[29] In practice, 'the individual referred to here is usually the mother'.[30] As Lynch and Lyons argue, the reason at least one member of a household with children is forced to leave employment is because childcare is privatised and costly.[31] Furthermore it tends to be women who leave employment given the strong moral imperative on women to be primary carers.[32] Despite extensive debate and an array of promises from within the political system, public provision and support for childcare services is abysmal.[33] The childcare debate reflects a lack of political and societal consensus about where mothers should be on the employability continuum.[34] Whether or not they engage in paid work, women are still regarded as responsible for the practical and emotional labour required to care for family members.[35]

At the level of the individual, the government provides child benefit which can be used towards childcare costs, even though it is available regardless of the economic or employment status of the mother. In every budget from 2010 to 2014 the rates of child benefit have been cut. In Budget 2015, it was increased by €5 per child to

€135 per month, which represents an overall reduction of nineteen per cent on the 2009 child benefit rate of €166. In Budget 2006,[36] an Early Childcare Supplement was introduced, which was a grant of €1,000 per year for each child up to and including age five. This grant was available to all children in the state regardless of the employment status of the mother, but it was designed to assist with childcare costs for employed mothers. However, the Early Childcare Supplement was removed in 2009[37] which suggests that in times of rising unemployment, there is no further need to facilitate women's or mothers' employment and women's work is less important than that of the male breadwinner. In theory it was replaced in 2010 with the Early Childhood Care and Education Scheme (ECCE).[38] Less advantaged parents have access to limited childcare places in community providers, while high costs, inaccessibility and lack of provision mean middle-class families struggle to source and retain suitable childcare. Barry argues: 'there is a continuing assumption of the provision of care, primarily by women, in households or through the private market place'.[39] The low level of public provision and the lack of statutory support for women in the home and childminders reinforces these assumptions.

The government's position reflects conflicting policy coalitions, deriving from neo-liberal discourses on the one hand and traditional motherhood discourses on the other. There continues to exist in Ireland a highly ambivalent attitude to women's place in society, which serves to lessen and divide childcare financing. Although referred to as the Equal Opportunities Childcare Programme (EOCP), the major childcare programme in Ireland has never acquired, in the eyes of mainstream society, a frank 'equality of opportunity for women' label. EOCP and other gender measures continue to co-exist in Irish society with more conservative views about 'the family' and the role of women, views that are reinforced in the 1937 Constitution:[40]

> Because of government attention to two voting constituencies, EOCP has been tracked over the first six years of its existence by parallel expenditure on mothers-at-home – a nice example of policy incoherence: on the one hand, government provides financing for childcare services to allow women access to the labour market and to take in charge the early education of young children from disadvantaged backgrounds; on the other, it funds a parallel policy designed to keep women in the home to care for children.[41]

The government's ambiguous position in relation to the EOCP provides an example of the way neo-liberalism is deployed in a contradictory and ambiguous way,[42] encouraging women's employment and at the same time maintaining women's place in the home.

Childcare arrangements

Women spend considerable effort on making childcare choices, because certain forms of caring, namely 'love labour',[43] cannot be provided on a hire and fire basis.[44] Because private childminders are not regulated, choosing childcare is one of the most difficult and important decisions a 'working mother' has to make in relation to combining motherhood with paid work. The choice women make in relation to childcare is gendered, because overwhelmingly women are responsible for making this decision, and childminders are invariably women.

Amanda spoke about the stress involved in finding a childminder who would work in Amanda's home from seven in the morning and she noted the responsibility for arranging childcare in her family is gendered:

> That was a huge stress for me, trying to hold onto a babysitter who would come in – in the morning, at seven. It was impossible to get and the fear of losing them, because, I felt it was my responsibility. My husband would not be involved in getting the new childminder. I don't know what other people's experience of that would be, but it was always me. Me who would put the ad in the paper, [me] who would ask around (Amanda, focus group).

Care work is gendered. In families it is the woman who finds and engages childminders, and in all cases, childminders are women. All the women in the study were responsible for managing and organising caring, even if they did not do all the day-to-day hands-on caring work.[45] Eithne describes her husband's gendered expectation that she would be responsible for childcare. Before their first child was born they discussed childcare arrangements:

> And Tom said 'OK, so we'll send the child to the crèche, Monday to Friday and you can mind the child Saturday and Sunday' and I'm there, 'No'. He said: 'What do you mean. No?' And I said 'You are off during the week, you know, you might be working Saturday and Sunday night, but you are off

Monday and Tuesday, so you can be minding the child Monday and Tuesday'. 'But I've stuff to do!' I said, 'What do you think I have at the weekends? I have stuff to do too!' And he, you know, it took him a few months to come around to the concept that he'd have to parent when he was off, because he loves his time off in the middle of the week, because he was 'doing stuff'. There was lots of 'stuff' he could do (Eithne, focus group).

Tom does now care for both children when he is off during the week and enjoys it; however, it was not his expectation that he would be involved in childcare because of gendered expectations of the mother's role. All women in this research acknowledge gendered obligations to care, and this affects their decisions about how they will combine working and mothering, and the childcare arrangements they make. They spoke of the stress involved in finding childminders, particularly women who were not from the local area and did not have family support nearby:

I had to find a childminder. I remember I came back here and there was no sort of [available register]. And I wasn't from [the local area] and my husband wasn't from [the local area] and it was the most stressful two years of my life, almost to the stage where I would, very, I almost gave up work, and it was a real struggle I must say (Amy, focus group).

In Amy's account, the lack of state provision of childcare had a direct negative impact on her participation in paid work. Amy described being very committed to her career in England and holds the lack of quality childcare directly responsible for her decision to reduce her hours in paid work following her return to the area of the study. However, the issue of childcare has not actually prevented women from entering the workforce: 'Irish women, and in particular Irish mothers, are entering the workforce in increasing numbers without the help of formal childcare'.[46] In families, childcare is the responsibility of individual women, who source, arrange and pay for childcare and have full responsibility for its success or failure. Collette described the most common situation, whereby men are interested, but women have the responsibility for arranging care:

I'd say my husband would be very interested in making sure we have the right person . . . Yeah, he would get involved, but yeah, at the end of the day, I think it is utterly I think the mother's responsibility (Colette, focus group).

The Women's Health Council[47] argues this inequitable burden has been found to cause women significant physical and emotional distress and Amy, Amanda and Collette demonstrate the gendered inequalities they experience because they have responsibility for sourcing and arranging childcare. Many women claim the lack of regulated care has led to trial and error in their childminding histories:

> When I had my first baby I was looking for a childminder, going back to work after maternity leave. And I had bad experiences. And from then on I said, 'never again just the one person', because you don't know what they get up to when you're not there. So I always looked for a situation like a Montessori school where there was a teacher and an assistant teacher, so that they were, I suppose, checked by somebody else, at all times (Sabine, interview).

Women are concerned with the quality of the care children receive, both the 'love labour'[48] carers perform as well as the material tasks and work involved in caring so that children's physical, social and emotional wellbeing is not compromised when women leave their children in the care of others. In a study of middle-class families' childcare arrangements, Vincent and Ball found that the discourse of familialism strongly influenced childcare choices. This discursive strain 'asserts that one to one care by the mother in the home is the best form of care, and if this is not available, it should be mimicked in other forms of care'.[49] This generates pressure on women to choose the 'best' care for their children. Sabine demonstrates that a more public, pre-school environment is preferable to her than a private childminder because she has concerns about its invisibility. However, women are also concerned about availability when selecting childcare. Crèche and pre-schools are open every week of the year but will not accept children when they are sick, as opposed to childminders who may not be available every week of the year but generally will care for children if they are sick.

There is an unfounded assumption that crèche care is impersonal and formal with children not receiving the individual attention they would in a home environment, because it is regarded as commoditised caring on an industrial scale. There was widespread condemnation of crèche care by women who engaged childminders or family members:

And this business of children being in crèches from eight o'clock in the morning, till eight o'clock at night, five days a week, and(.) I don't think that's right. You know. I mean a child didn't ask to be brought into the world, and it most certainly didn't ask to be dumped into a crèche for forty-something hours a week you know (Grace, interview).

Grace engaged a childminder, and even though she was not entirely satisfied with her own childminding arrangements, she nevertheless felt they were superior to those women who engaged crèche care. There is a gendered inequality in the way women experience public criticism for using crèche care, even though crèche care is regulated and arguably safer. Women who used crèche care generally explained their choice with reference to its availability every week of the year, which is the only form of child-care to guarantee this.

There is an interesting paradox surrounding crèche care. Popular views regularly link 'dumped' with crèche, and crèche care is commonly seen as inferior to childminder care. 'It goes against the whole thing about having a child if they're going to be sitting in a crèche from nine to six all day long' (Gina, interview). Yet, the government regards provision of childcare places through capital grants for crèche providers and crèche places for disadvantaged children as all that is necessary to facilitate women's employment and frames success in childcare policy in financial or market terms. However, it became apparent in 2013, in a television documentary by the national broadcaster, RTÉ, that the government regulation of crèche facilities is 'light touch' and falls short of guaranteeing quality care for children.[50] The programme showed children in crèches being manhandled and neglected by staff who appeared to be poorly trained. Therefore, women's concerns regarding crèche care are not without foundation. This media report into several facilities revealed that the childcare system is 'poorly regulated, deeply flawed and occasionally dangerous'.[51]

In a newspaper article the same week, journalist Victoria White added to women's concerns by citing research to support her argument that children should not be cared for in crèches, strongly advocating a familialism position and telling parents (women), that the lack of a strong emotional bond between individual carers and individual children in corporate crèches creates an environment favourable to child welfare abuses.[52] The government response was to establish a Child and Family Agency in 2014, which brings a range of child and family support and welfare services together in one statutory body, and which includes pre-school inspections.[53]

Women retain responsibility for the choice of childcare and for making the best choice within extremely limited options. Both Freya and Eithne combine crèche care with other forms of care. These are the only two women in the study who use crèche facilities despite crèches being the focus of state intervention. Freya has her older two children minded by an au pair, while the baby attends a crèche. Eithne combines family care with crèche care, whenever her husband is available, and Eithne's girls attend a crèche, one for the full day and one for after-school care. Eithne found public scrutiny of motherhood extends to childcare and she found crèche care is roundly condemned:

> And you know, we get a lot 'Oh, you have them in a crèche?'
> ... A lot of people don't think crèches are very good for the child, in terms of the child's development. In that they don't get the one to one care that they would get in a home environment. And that your child is deprived somewhat by being in a crèche, or that you dumped them in the crèche from eight in the morning to six in the evening, day after day (Eithne, interview).

As caring is gendered, these difficult choices are women's responsibility and choosing crèche care is a socially unpopular decision that women are obliged to defend. Women's desire to have their children cared for and loved by their carers led to many women claiming to have preferred family care to engaging a paid childminder or crèche to care for their children. However, only eight women managed to achieve this at any stage.

Kate described herself as 'fortunate' in being able to access family care, which is provided by her sister. However, the care of female relatives reinforces the gendered order of caring:

> She [my sister] collects them from school, she keeps them, she'll do their homework with them every day. She brings them to, or collects them from, activities after school. So she's like their surrogate mum, I suppose really. And it's great that she's my sister, it's wonderful (Kate, interview).

Kate reported that when her children were younger, she engaged au pairs, but when the children started going to school, changed to her current arrangement. Employing an au pair is a particularly middle-class childminding arrangement and three women in this study engaged au pairs at some stage during their childminding histories. Six women combined family care with paid care; Jean has her older child minded by her own mother, while her younger two go to a childminder's home. Similarly Yolanda's parents come to her home two days, and her children go to a childminder for the other days. Six women described their husbands as being actively involved in the care of their own children, which may suggest men are challenging traditional gender norms and valuing care. This is consistent with the national data. In 2008, men spent on average four hours and forty minutes per day on paid work and just under two hours per day on caring and housework.[54] Joy only works when her husband is home in the evenings and weekends to care for their children. Faye's husband is taking parental leave one day every week, while other husbands are available to older children after school.

In a minority of cases, women's care patterns changed with the birth of their second child. Four women had their own parents minding the first child, but moved to childminding or a combination of crèche and childminding when the second child was born. Jasmine had her sister-in-law caring for her children when they were pre-school age but now combines after-school care with her husband, who has recently changed to working nights:

> I suppose I'm very lucky now at the moment, because Patrick is working in a different job now and he's working mostly at night, and he collects them mostly in the afternoon and that gives me the freedom not to be rushing home from work either, you know, that I can take an hour. Whether it's to do a bit of extra work after school, or, you know, just to meet a colleague for a cup of coffee or something. So I'm kind of lucky enough at the moment, you know (Jasmine, interview).

While Jasmine is privileged in relation to childcare because her husband is available to care for their children during the day, there is an inequality which arises from this position; Jasmine and her husband rarely spend time together. Both Eithne and Joy, whose husbands are involved in caring for their children, also reported spending very little time together as a family, as one parent was working while the other was caring for the children.

Having family available for childcare, while regarded as a privilege by Jasmine and Kate, is completely arbitrary and maintains caring as a private issue. Family caring also means that the caring is not commoditised, and fits with traditional expectations of caring as outside the remit of the market. With the exception of six women who described their husband's involvement in childcare, all other care was provided by grandmothers, sisters, paid child-minders and crèche workers, who are all women. Joy believed only family care was good enough for her children, and claimed women who went outside family for childcare were neglecting their children, by 'dumping' them: 'So and so's dumping their children to be reared by other women . . . and I felt so strongly about it . . . it just felt so deeply uncomfortable for me' (Joy, focus group). This was quite a strong statement to make in a focus group discussion where women had discussed their distress regarding sourcing childminders, children's unhappiness with childminders, women's stress in managing work while worrying about childcare and women reluctantly reducing their hours of work because of unsatisfactory childcare arrangements. In this research, family care is the most preferred form of childcare, followed by private child-minders, and then crèche care, reflecting similar findings to Vincent and Ball's research with middle-class families in the UK.[55]

Unregulated childminders

The women in the study were concerned that the people they engaged as childminders would care for their children to the same extent as they themselves, did. However, sourcing and retaining suitable childminders was a great concern for the women, because they were unable to participate in paid work unless their respon-sibilities towards care of their children were satisfied. Sourcing carers who will care for children, physically and emotionally to the level women desire is difficult, because registered childcare is pri-marily available in the form of crèche care. However, most participants expressed a preference for more personal forms of care and sought individual childminders who would develop long-term relationships with their children. A private childminder is the most common form of care the women in this study utilised. Fifteen women engaged childminders either in the minders' homes or in the women's homes, while four other women engaged childminders in shared arrangements.

Childminding Ireland reports that 'Childminding has been a hidden part of the economy for a very long time, so we're not surprised at the numbers . . . it also suits society to have it this way, to have cheap, accessible childcare available'.[56] There is an implication by Childminding Ireland that because childminders are not registered, they are providing an inexpensive service. There is also an implication that childcare is accessible. It is not. The lack of statutory support and intervention has created a largely inaccessible and inequitable childcare market in Ireland. Because so many childminders are not registered with the HSE, the invisibility of childminders, both in the formal economy and in society, makes it difficult for 'working mothers' to make and retain satisfactory childcare arrangements, which suit themselves, their children and their childminders.

Sabine had a distressing experience with a private childminder:

> Because, now we had a childminder here and the whiskey was going down and one day I came home and the child had a stain on the bib, that was cough bottle, adult cough bottle . . . with alcohol in it, given to the baby (Sabine, interview).

Brona also had a difficult experience:

> When she was minding my children, that she brought them to her house and she used to be having sex with her boyfriend upstairs, and they caught her . . . 'they were naked in the bed'(.) That was only last year. [The children's ages were] three and four (Brona, interview).

Amy had a situation that was dangerous, and which had a long-term effect on herself and her family:

> I suppose just the care here isn't good, you know . . . Safe childcare. Safe. I think, like you know, we don't know what our children are going into, and we don't know where it's going to take us if anything within that is going to change our lives forever, I think. And for me, that's what happened. My first childcare placement here was with somebody who changed, utterly changed my whole life. It was a bad, bad experience. It was just one experience, but it was one sort of thing, that certainly before that I would have thought, 'it's ok to be a "working mother"' or whatever you know. And then I suppose I started to look at the other kids that were being in care, I started to look at the crèche . . . where babies are being left off at eight o'clock in the morning. And with my second child, who was ten months at the time, I chose not. I didn't want that kind of care for him, where he'd be put into a room, even though again, you know, I wanted him to have one to one care,

but that proved to be a mistake you know. So it was a price I paid, that I didn't expect that I had to pay, and I suppose I resent the fact that there was no(.) There was nothing in place to prevent that from happening (Amy, interview).

Choosing childcare is gendered, and as women demonstrate, the responsibility for this choice rests with women and if the choice, as in Amy's case, does not work, then Amy blames herself for making a bad decision. However, Amy also acknowledges the failure of the state to regulate private childminders and put structures 'in place to prevent that from happening' (Amy, interview).

There are different discursive strains evident in Amy's account. Small-scale private childminding is the most popular form of childcare deriving from discourses of motherhood, and Amy is critical of crèche care. However, neo-liberal discourse suggests crèche care is a market led response to childcare demand. The state supports provision of crèche places, yet women's preferences for more private, home-based arrangements are not acknowledged in the state's childcare policy. Paradoxically, crèche care is the only type of care that is regulated in Ireland, and the absence of regulation of private childminders raises questions about the reluctance of the state to address this issue. O'Connor and Murphy argue this delay in developing a childcare policy, combined with the lack of state intervention to support parenting and care work has reinforced women's disadvantaged position in society.[57] Care work continues to be seen, and addressed within a policy context, as predominantly a private concern and a female responsibility.[58] In all paid care arrangements, childminders are women, and all 'working mothers' have responsibility for sourcing, arranging and paying for childcare, demonstrating the way caring work is gendered, even if it is commoditised somewhat by being undertaken by paid care workers.

Class contributes to inequality between women and the cost of privatised reproductive services such as childcare can create and maintain class and gender inequalities for poorly paid 'working mothers'. Brona works a shift schedule of three twelve hour days each week: 'There's a month of Monday, Tuesday and Wednesday and then a month of Thursday, Friday, Saturday' (Brona, interview). Brona's husband works a regular Monday to Friday week and I enquired why Bona's husband would not care for the children on the Saturdays Brona works: 'She [childminder] usually works on a Saturday. Well, even if he didn't want to work on a Saturday she wants her money. You know, she wants that set money. He, actually, some Saturdays he'd have nothing to do and he'd go off killing time' (Brona, interview). Brona demonstrates that she pays her childminder on a daily basis, rather than calculating an average rate based on three days one month and two days the next month. This reflects the instrumental nature of the relationship between Brona and her childminder. However, the fact that Brona's husband would 'go off killing time' if he was not working in order to maintain this arrangement demonstrates that childcare arrangements are Brona's responsibility and he has little involvement in care in their home. Connell found men's 'collective choice not to do childcare reflects the dominant definition of men's interests and in fact helps them keep predominant power'.[59] As Lynch and Lyons argue, the challenge in realising social change is that patriarchal practices of caring do not have to be re-configured in every individual case or in every household; they are already encoded in the norms of femininity, masculinity and domesticity.[60]

Clearly, paying for childcare is also Brona's responsibility: 'So I'd be wasting fifty-five euros, but I have to pay it out, but I understand that . . . But it's a bit of a waste though . . . the third day is a bit of a balls in one way' (Brona, interview). Mahon found women incurred replacement costs for childcare which increased with the number of children. When taxation and childcare costs were subtracted from their wages, many found it was not economically viable for them to remain at work.[61] The gendered order of caring has not changed because of women's participation in paid work, and women are obliged to arrange and pay for care of their children, with most not questioning these gendered obligations.

Brona was unable to pay her childminder more than fifty-five euros a day, and acknowledged this restricted her choice in terms of available childcare: 'If I'd a better job I'd consider giving way more money, I'd love to be able to, but my job doesn't [pay me]' (Brona, interview). Average hourly childcare costs at the time of the research were €4.90 for pre-school children and €6.00 for primary school-going children. Brona has two school-going children and one pre-school child; if she was to pay the average hourly rate she would be paying €202.80[62] per day, which is almost four times what Brona currently pays. Brona also found it difficult to continue justifying her participation in paid work in economic terms: 'other people with bigger wages are fine, I do think it's very hard for the likes of us to stay working, to have the incentive to stay working' (Brona, interview). She also observed that many women change their way of working to avoid childcare costs: 'there's a lot of women that give up, and go working at night, but they're at home all day then and working at night so they don't have to pay a babysitter' (Brona, interview), which Brona would do, except her job does not lend itself to this.

As is evident from Brona's account, the division of care labour is gendered and classed. Lynch and Lyons found those who are poorer cannot afford prohibitive childcare costs,[63] thus, women with little disposable income are limited in the childcare available to them, and class and gender interact to ensure both these 'working mothers' and childminders earned less, so reproducing class and gender inequalities. The impact of inequality in the caring sphere has negatively impacted on women's position in other spheres of life and has served as a basis for their subordinate position in economic, cultural and political systems:[64]

> Families with young children need affordable childcare if parents are to work. If childcare eats up one wage so that there is little or no financial gain in going out to work, parents (most often mothers) are less likely to seek a job. But how people manage life at home also plays a big part in the equation. Many systems still implicitly regard childrearing as a mother's responsibility: everywhere women are doing more unpaid work than men, regardless of whether they have full-time jobs or not.[65]

The feminisation of care has not been contained within the family, but has also been reflected in paid care work. Much of the paid employment which women have taken up in recent years has been in caring jobs of all kinds. One-third of participants in this research are employed in caring professions.[66] In all cases, childminders are women, therefore gender and class inequalities are reproduced in the childcare arrangments of 'working mothers'.

Sabine is from another European country and she became a mother in Ireland and was appalled at the low level of state support for working parents:

> It's really hard to be a 'working mother' in Ireland. Very hard in Ireland in particular . . . Because I see my friends [in home country], my family and my brother's wife, and they have a lot

> more options you know, and cheaper options. A lot more
> cheaper options, a lot more [is] state funded (Sabine, inter-
> view).

'To have good public services, including caring services, a state must invest in them'.[67] Women who attempt to combine mother-hood with paid employment experience difficulties sourcing, accessing and affording safe childcare because of the lack of state provision, support or regulation of private childminders. These women's different views on childcare and the dilemmas they experience are not idiosyncratic. Discussions on mothers' websites Rollercoaster[68] and Magic Mum[69] reveal that women's dilemmas in relation to finding and choosing the best care for their children are widespread:

By arguing that the market will self-regulate, the state legit-imises the gendered order of caring. The state's lack of childcare provision and its lack of regulation creates inequalities for 'working mothers', because they are charged with full responsi-bility for choosing childcare and being responsible for their choices in a situation where the state is less than helpful.

'Working Mothers' and Childcare

The availability of safe, affordable childcare is essential if women are to combine motherhood with paid work. These women's per-ceptions of appropriate childcare are partly influenced by spatial and financial constraints, as well as their understanding of what 'people like us do',[70] the local moral geographies of childcare.[71] Women's preferred form of childcare was family care, the next most popular form of childcare was private childminders and crèche care was the least preferred form of care. However, family care is arbitrary, private childminders are unregulated, and crèche care is a socially unpopular choice.

Depending on the different positions women find themselves in, some are better able to deal with the lack of regulated childcare than others. Women who availed of family care consider them-selves most fortunate; however, in the majority of cases, family care was gendered. In this research, the women were responsible for choosing, arranging and paying for childcare and experienced inequalities in families where care of children – by the women themselves, or by paid carers – is the responsibility of women. When childcare arrangements are unsatisfactory, women take the blame for poor decisions. Similarly, crèche care is unpopular, and those women who avail of crèche care are obliged to defend their decisions, which is paradoxical in a situation where crèche places are the focus of state intervention in childcare.

Women's childcare decisions are made in constricted circumstances. The most appaling inequality women experienced is that their children were unsafe in the care of private childminders. This inequity is the responsibility of the state. However, individual women and children bear this inequality because of the lack of support and regulation of private childminders.

Society continues to promote the gendered order of caring and women bear the responsibility of caring for children and arranging childcare if they engage in paid work. All childminders are women, therefore the gender system has not changed because of women's participation in paid work. Women make care arrangements with little social support and class and gender intersect to limit the childcare options of women with fewer resources. However, there is some cause for optimism in that some fathers are involved in the care of their own children, yet this maintains caring as a private issue and fits with societal views about caring being outside the remit of the market.

The childcare landscape has not co-evolved to facilitate women's employment and, as is evident from women's accounts, there are persistent gendered assumptions about women's place in the home. The lack of state intervention to support parenting and care work has reinforced women's disadvantaged position in society because the state persistently regards care work as predominantly a private concern and a female responsibility. The state has resisted measures which will facilitate provision of adequate, affordable, accessible childcare, demonstrating that women's participation in paid work has generated no corresponding change in the childcare landscape, and, regardless of the desirability of women's participation in the formal economy, the state nevertheless maintains caring work as women's private responsibility.

CHAPTER 8

Who cares? – childminders

The relationships between mothers and childminders are complex, hierarchically ordered, occasionally exploitative and sometimes emotionally competitive. Women's narratives reveal their relationships with the women they engage to care for their children and their different valuations of care when undertaken by themselves as mothers and by paid care workers.

As the care sector has grown, women have formed an ever larger majority of paid care workers.[1] In keeping with the low value assigned to caregiving in the private sphere, this sector is characterised by low pay and poor working conditions, devaluing the care in economic and employment terms.[2] The net effect of not recognising the work dimensions of caring is that it is 'not seen as producing anything of great value, although it does'.[3] However, as Oakley argues, '[W]hen almost everything else has a cost and a price, the concept of 'value' becomes wholly economic; terms such as 'value', 'labour', 'production', 'reproduction', and 'work' have all been hijacked into the service of economics.[4] In neo-liberal society, there is a focus on outcomes in terms of children's development. This means that almost professionalised tasks may be easier to commodify, such as supervising homework or taking children to activities, and there is a case for substantially improving the conditions of this commodification to preclude exploitation.[5]

Women bear disproportionate responsibility for care work, in the informal world of the family and in the formal world of the care economy.[6] Some private childminders do not enjoy the benefit of contractual employment because their care work is invisible, unrecognised and undervalued. The childminders' tax free allowance of €15,000 for minding up to three children in the woman's own home[7] reflects a wage of €7.21 per hour for all three children, based on a forty-hour week. This is eighty-three per cent of the national minimum wage and equates to earning €2.40 per hour per child. This reflects the low value the state places on care and care workers.

The National Childcare Strategy Report of the Partnership 2000 Expert Working Group on Childcare recommended that 'All those providing childcare services for one or more children, in addition to their own, including persons employed by the parent/s of the child, either in the child's home or in the childminder's home, should be required to register.'[8] To date, this has not been implemented. The report also recommended that childminding income should be disregarded when eligibility is being determined for social welfare and ancillary benefits such as medical cards. A further recommendation was the introduction of personal tax relief for parents, who would receive relief at the standard tax rate based on receipts. These recommendations have yet to be implemented.

Relationships with childminders

According to the National Association of Private Childcare Providers (NPCP), Dublin has just twenty notified childminders even though it has a population of one million. Limerick, with a population of 184,055, has fifty-three notified childminders, while Cork has just three notified childminders for a population of 481,295.[9] Women's preferences for personal forms of care are not acknowledged in the state's neo-liberal market-based approach to childcare, which provides grants to crèche providers only, while thousands of children are placed with childminders every working day, making it the most popular form of childcare in the state.[10] However, there is little regulation of this service. Only 257 childminders are registered with the HSE, as childminders who care for fewer than three pre-school children, from different families in their own home, are not subject to any regulation, mandatory training or Garda clearance. Barry claims there is a growing crisis in care provision, linked to both lack of availability and high cost in the context of low-level public provision of childcare services.[11] 'Looking for a childminder is difficult, and obviously finding the right childminder is difficult and keeping the same childminder is also difficult. Obviously there is a cost issue as well – it's much higher with two children' (Collette, focus group).

The quality of childcare is a major concern for parents and satisfaction with the arrangement in respect of the emotional wellbeing of the child has been found to be at least as important as economic considerations.[12] Faye appreciates the difference her childminder makes to the quality of her life:

> This woman, is just like, probably one of the most important parts of our lives, bar the immediate family . . . Once again I realise how absolutely lucky I am with her, and I think these are the last kids she's going to mind. She's kind of in her mid-fifties now, but like that, she does all the dropping off to school, and the collecting, all the dancing and the tennis and she does all of that. So, the guilt comes in sometimes that I'm not there to do that and(.) I hear where Sheila took the kids today, she did this, and she took them to McDonalds and she took them to the party and all of that, but you kind of have to move along with it as well. That's a lucky kind of side. Every day I wake up and think how lucky, how great this scene is you know, at the same time (Faye, interview).

Guilt and luck are linked together in Faye's account. She experiences guilt because she is unable to take her children to activities, but luck because Sheila is able to do it. Avril feels even the terms 'childcare' and 'childminding' do not do justice to the relationship involved:

> Thinking of it as childminding, I think, is [wrong]. I never think of it like that, I think of it as what's benefiting for the child . . . I think that even no matter if it's five hours or ten hours, it has to be a very secure environment. And that has to be right for the child . . . Maybe that's the first relationship that has to actually happen. You know, I would think you have to like the person, you have to respect them and you know, work with them, that it is something you are both taking on together. That's certainly, you know, what I would think is paramount to the whole thing because I don't think, if there isn't a relationship there it will fail, and that's definite (Avril, focus group).

Clearly Avril sees the arrangement with her childminder as a cooperative one, based on mutual respect. The job of caring for children is 'something you are both taking on together' (Avril) and the relationship between mother and childminder is more than an employment one. To facilitate the 'relationship' they are 'taking on together', Avril finds spending time with her childminder very important for herself, the children and the childminder:

> I would be there for a lot of the time with her. For half a day a week I am there with her . . . I work within the house with her for that half day and I always did that. And I just felt that that was good for her and good for me (Avril, interview).

There is also, of course, an individual responsibility for employers of carers to act ethically[13] and many women do: 'I pay her well and I look after her well, so it definitely works both ways' (Amelia, interview). Women were also concerned that their children would value their childminders and Audrey was quite upset that her elder two children did not treat their childminder appropriately:

> I suppose the biggest thing I would find now, at this stage, where the kids are getting a bit bigger, is the disciplining of them really . . . You tell them they have to respect her and everything and we've probably got over that now, they are better now with her . . . I felt bad about the way they treated, they way they answered her back a couple of times. I felt, my goodness, is this their attitude? Is this the way they're turning out? . . . But I mean at least she brought it to my attention and we were able to deal with it (Audrey, interview).

Avril, Amelia and Audrey describe their satisfaction with their childminding arrangements which they reported had been in place for some time. While there is a hierarchical relationship between mothers and childminders as in all employment relationships, these women demonstrate they value their childminders and the work they do, and they employ their childminders on equitable terms and conditions:

> The lady who used to do all my cleaning and everything, eleven years ago, I used to pay eighty pounds a week. Well it was all my housework done and everything. She was fabulous and then I used to pay her for her holidays. But then she was kind of a poor lady anyway, so she came from a poor background and her husband wasn't working. She was a fantastic worker, she was fabulous, you know and I used to love to give her the money because I felt, it was kind of giving it to a good cause, that she would spend it well or whatever, you know (Anita, focus group).

Anita describes 'my housework . . . and everything', demonstrating that one gendered worker replaced another, and Anita was happy to pay the woman, because in addition to being a 'fantastic worker', she also deserved to be paid as a 'good cause'. Anita does not describe it as 'paying' the woman, but 'to give her the money', which suggests Anita felt she was being altruistic and generous, not that the woman was providing a service for which she was entitled to be paid. Some women's valuation of caring work reflects the wider societal view; caring is invisible and not regarded as 'work' because it is carried out by women, in the private sphere of the home.

In Ireland, workers who are employed in the care sector have the same status as semi-skilled workers such as bar staff, goods porters and mail sorters, which is the second lowest occupational ranking.[14] If care workers are employed in domestic situations in private households, they are classified as unskilled workers at the bottom of the occupational ranking index.[15] It is not surprising, therefore, that 'service workers, especially those who have worked as domestics, are convinced that "public jobs" are preferable to domestic service'.[16]

The National Association of Private Childcare Providers (NPCP) reports that the free preschool year (Early Childhood Care and Education Scheme) has increased administrative demands and academic requirements on childcare providers. The government currently pays providers €4.30 per child per hour, or €64.50 each week for the thirty-eight weeks of the programme per child. The state does not pay providers holiday pay for their staff, even though providers, as employers, are required by law to pay holiday pay to their employees; consequently, many staff are laid off during the summer months. That implies an annual salary in the region of €15,000–16,000 for somebody working in a sessional service that operates two sessions a day during term times.[17] A recent survey of centre-based services found average wages to range from €10.10 per hour for unqualified staff to €11.24 for graduates.[18]

The Office of the Minister for Children has requested that all pre-school leaders achieve a minimum of FETAC Level 5 in childcare and, in order to achieve the higher capitation grant of an extra €10 per child per week, HETAC Level 7 has been deemed necessary.[19] Currently, only twelve per cent of those working in early childhood care and education services in Ireland have degree-level qualifications.[20] The majority of qualifications are at Level 5 on the National Framework of Qualifications. Since 2012, it is also reported that many providers seek staff on the state's JobBridge programme, which pays the worker €50 on top of their jobseeker's allowance; consequently, one in four childcare workers does not hold a basic qualification.[21]

Eithne's experience of crèche care is positive and her children are cared for competently and professionally. But, Eithne observed the employees in the crèche where her children are minded cannot afford to take unpaid maternity or parental leave, because care workers generally earn less than other types of workers:

> Several of the girls who work in the crèche have had babies within the last twelve months, and they were all back to work after . . . [statutory] maternity leave. They didn't take any of the unpaid leave that they were offered, couldn't afford it obviously. And they don't talk about taking parental leave or anything (Eithne, interview).

The women working in Eithne's crèche may not be very well paid, but they do enjoy employment contracts, and are entitled to all the legal protections afforded to employees. However, like other care workers who earn little, they cannot afford to take the unpaid maternity and parental leave which many of the mothers of the children they care for enjoy. Eithne acknowledged she is privileged in comparison with the carers of her children. She could afford to avail of unpaid leave, while the women in the crèche who cared for her children could not, demonstrating that the employment conditions of reproductive workers may not be particularly favourable.[22] McKay notes that certain powerful groups and actors benefit from, while simultaneously devaluing care, because of the way it is not valued in social or political systems;[23] evidence of the neo-liberal state and the influence of neo-liberalism discourses on the commoditisation of care. There is a stark inequality between Eithne and the crèche workers who care for her children and Eithne acknowledges this inequality. However, both Eithne and the 'girls who work in the crèche' (Eithne, interview) are not members of the powerful groups and actors who benefit from devaluing care. The owners of the crèche, to whom Eithne pays a significant proportion of her salary, are the beneficiaries. The 'girls who work in the crèche' are paid a fraction of Eithne's crèche costs. There is a symbiotic relationship between professional 'working mothers' and care workers, and Eithne's acknowledgement of the inequality between herself and the 'girls who work in the crèche' demonstrates the intersecting inequality, whereby both professional women and careworkers are produced hierarchically in relation to each other. As Dhamoon argues, regardless of whether a specific relation of penalty or privilege is constituted by a subject marked as dominant or subordinate, we all occupy differing degrees and forms of privilege and penalty and are therefore always and already implicated in that structure.[24]

Commodification of caring

As women participate more in employment, care is transferred more to the market and caring occupations are organised according to the rational economic model: how much time it takes to deliver particular care-giving tasks, and how much the time and the task are worth in instrumental terms. As Lynch and Lyons argue, the emotional work involved in loving another person 'is not readily transferred to a paid other by arrangement'.[25] To attempt to pay someone to visit a friend in hospital or share a meal with a partner is to undermine the premise of care: 'It is not possible to produce "fast care" like fast food in standardised packages'.[26] Badgett, Lee and Folbre argue that commoditising all caring will result in 'pre-packaged units of supervision' and a society where there is a lack of focus on the welfare of others.[27] However, in contemporary Irish society, care is also about time, and paid care is increasingly measured in terms of time as a commodity. In a focus group, Grace discussed approaching her childminder regarding Grace's plan to reduce her working hours:

> GRACE   My intention was to try and get her to stay with us and to do the reduced hours, and . . . what she said to me was 'what are you going to do if I don't do it?' So I said, 'Well, you know, we really haven't thought that far ahead, but if you don't, well, I'll try and get somebody else'. And she said 'Oh I'd hate to think of Katie dumped in with someone else' . . . 'Dumped' Not a word about Susan, of course. I could have sold her to the gypsies. She wouldn't have cared.
>
> FAYE   Doesn't that make you think what she thinks you're doing with your children is dumping them?
>
> GRACE   But this is it. That's what I was saying. So, it's at the back of your mind you see.

The low valuation of caring was evident in the way Grace's childminder regarded her own work. It was interesting that the childminder used the term 'dumped' in relation to a child she is currently minding, and to whom she is clearly attached. Grace is aware of this and bringing her children every day to this woman causes Grace distress. However, power relations are also evident in the relationship. Grace can arbitrarily reduce her hours of work without negotiation or notice, while the childminder can withdraw the service altogether:

> So I think maybe she had it too easy, really to be honest, for years . . . Whereas I think she kind of got a bit of a wake up call, and she realised – free money here for doing very little. So that has improved quite a bit, and the fact that they see less of her is a good thing I think now as well . . . the balance has come back into it. And I suppose the other advantage for me is that I'm very definitely now their mother, do you know what I mean? And she is in her role (Grace, interview).

Grace demonstrates the delicate dynamic in the relationship between 'working mother' and childminder. By reducing the time her children spend with the childminder, Grace is happy that she has asserted her role as primary carer. 'Control over time – our own and other peoples – is a form of power'.[28] By exercising this power, Grace also establishes new boundaries in the childminding relationship. According to Grace the childminder is 'doing very little'; however, this reflects the difficulty for Grace of influencing the form the care takes in her absence, as much as Grace's valuation of the care work itself. The relationship between 'working mother' and childminder is clearly hierarchical and emotionally competitive in some cases. Mothers can unilaterally change or reduce their hours in paid work, which has consequences for childminders' earnings and hours of work.

The women in this research were concerned that childminders would perform the material tasks necessary to properly care for their children, particularly participating in extra-curricular activities. Yolanda was concerned that her children did not have an opportunity to do homework properly in the childminders' home:

> They don't do the homework in the childminders' house, because there's too many kids up there, there's too many televisions on(.) I just said it at the start. I said, 'look, don't do the homework, I'll do it when I come home' (Yolanda, focus group).

This was reported to cause tension in the relationship between Yolanda and the woman who minds Yolanda's children and Grace was concerned that her children could not engage in sporting and social activities unless it suited the childminder's own children:

> I find now that in the last couple of years it is becoming harder and that I almost have to beg her now to(.) 'Would you mind taking her here and would you mind taking her there?' And sometimes she does it and other times she makes it very difficult. And, certainly last year and the year before it was very,

very hard, very difficult and(.) I found that my kids could only do things if her kids were doing it as well, because I wouldn't have to go and ask her to go and do an extra pick up or an extra collection. And I found that that was very hard (Grace, interview).

The childminding woman is also a mother, and this woman is 'mothering for income'[29] by taking care of Grace's children while simultaneously taking care of her own children in their own home. The difficulty Grace experienced with asking her childminder to take her children to after-school events reflects the power dynamic in the relationship, as the childminding woman prioritised the after-school activities of her own children. Where women took their children to childminders' homes, the child is a visitor to the minder's home, and has 'paying guest' status, maintaining the childminder's control of the home space. From being a site of private, unpaid caring, the home has also become a site of commoditised transactions and a site of paid work. Thus, choosing and paying for childcare involves a renegotiation of home and mothering for these women. While the home is a site of commoditised transactions, it also reinforces the mother's role as natural in the sense that women attempt to replace themselves in the home.

Interestingly, in cases where women engaged childminders to come into their homes, they reported having more satisfactory childminding arrangements, and generally employing their childminders on equitable terms and conditions. Perhaps this is because both 'working mothers' and childminding women are happier with caring for children in the children's own home, maintaining home as the 'natural' site of social reproduction, which is a discursive strain in motherhood discourse. Welcoming women into their own homes also demonstrates the trust implicit in the mother-childminder relationship. In either case, paying for childcare represents a shift from traditional paid production and unpaid social reproduction and the home/work dichotomy is variously shaped by these women's childcare choices and arrangements.

Some women did not recognise or reward the labour involved in childcare when undertaken by paid care workers. This is a strain of neo-liberalism discourse which promotes value for money and reduces care to a commoditised transaction. However, all women were anxious that care workers would do the material tasks involved in caring for children's physical needs as well as ensuring their children's acquisition of skills and knowledge. Children's development represents a strain of individualism discourses which requires investment in children's capital so that they will become productive, independent citizens. With the intensification of mothering, there is a focus on outcomes in terms of children's development and many women attempted to commodify the caring that childminders do. Some 'working mothers' were concerned that their childminders would provide emotional labour[30] and develop attachments to their children in order to replicate mother's care, which is a strain in discourses of new-familialism, suggesting that one-to-one care by the mother in the home is the best form of care, and if this is not available, it should be mimicked in other forms of care. This reinforces the notion of motherhood as a 'natural' relationship between mother and child. Grace was concerned that this emotional labour was not available to both her children equally and reported that her childminder treated Grace's children differently from one another. The older child was reported to be unhappy, which caused Grace distress and prompted her to reduce her working hours. However, the widely held view that mothers' care is the best care for children was evident when women were concerned that there was slippage between the mother's primary role as carer and the childminders' role as carer:

> At the end of the day they are your kids. They're not her kids, you know what I mean? And like, this is a job and her kids come first. If it was any other way, it would be wrong from her point of view. But of course, you see, you want it all, you know what I mean? You want her to cosset your kids the way you [do] and of course, she's not going to flipping do that, and if she did, you wouldn't like it either (Grace, interview).

Women want their children cared for, loved and minded by the women they engage as childminders, yet feel usurped when their children become too attached to childminders; they do not want their positions as mothers undermined. It is difficult to commodify caring. On one hand Grace describes the childminder's role in instrumental terms as 'a job', but on the other hand, she wants the woman 'to cosset your kids' and provide 'love labour'[31] for the children. Grace acknowledges the delicate dynamic in the mother-childminder relationship, suggesting that it is impossible to replicate mothers' care in a way that does not undermine mothers, while providing the desired level of care and affection for children.

Valuation of childminders

The most obvious evidence of women valuing their childminders is in the way they regard the issue of payment for the caring service provided. Women who commanded high salaries themselves could afford to pay their childminders higher wages, though not all did. Some women received loyalty and quality service in return for decent terms and conditions: 'I would say that most of my salary would go out on childcare. Definitely. You end up with very little at the end, very little at the end of the month' (Avril, focus group). Avril pays for childcare from her salary and in this research all women spoke of the cost of childcare as their financial responsibility. This is consistent with the findings of other writers who also found that childcare is a woman's expense, not a family's expense.[32] In fact, Mahon found the gendered responsibility of paying for childcare is a disincentive to women's participation in paid work.[33]

Colleen also believes childminding is a reciprocal relationship involving trust and responsibility on the part of both mother and childminder:

> I also don't stop wages for my childminder when I take holidays . . . If I take holidays I am taking him away from her, she didn't ask me for that time. I feel that she is entitled to get paid. I get paid sick pay, I get paid bank holidays so I don't deduct her any of those things. So it comes back to that trust thing. I want her to look after my son. I am very happy with the way she is doing it. I will pay her for those days. I think she is fully entitled to them (Colleen, focus group).

Colleen extends the benefits she receives in employment to the woman she employs to care for her son. While there is a hierarchical relationship between mothers and childminders as in all employment relationships, many women demonstrate they value their childminders and the work they do, and they employ their childminders on equitable terms and conditions, extending to their childminders the employment rights they receive from their employers. Aisling mentioned the risk of losing her childminder was a factor in her decision not to take unpaid parental leave:

> I have a fabulous childminder. And I wouldn't be willing to risk losing her, so I would have to pay her. I feel I would have

to pay her, while I would be off, not being paid, and it would be a very big financial burden to be paying out for full-time childminding that I wasn't using, when I wasn't being paid (Aisling, interview).

Aisling also demonstrates the difficulty of sourcing and retaining good childminding arrangements. Other women regard the work of childminding in more instrumental terms and only pay childminders for the hours actually worked, not paying holiday pay or sick pay:

Well what made me . . . very cross, when I actually got her she wanted to be paid for holidays, but I said 'no'. She was quite demanding about being paid for holidays . . . There was a week at Christmas when I only worked one day and at New Year's week when I only worked one day, and I only paid her for the one day. But she cribbed, big time, do you know. But, I don't know. I feel it's dreadful to be paying out a hundred and forty quid when you don't have to (Florence, focus group).

Florence works two twelve hour days each week, and pays her childminder €140 per week, or €70 euros per day, which equates to €5.83 per hour for minding three children, or sixty-seven per cent of the national minimum wage. Florence claimed 'it's dreadful to be paying out a hundred and forty quid when you don't have to' (Florence, focus group) because there is no obligation on her to observe employment rights in relation to her childminder. However, because Florence works two days a week, she has retained this woman to work two days every week, which prevents the woman from engaging in alternative paid work on those days. When Florence takes holidays, she is paid by her employer. However, Florence does not see the work as employment, but regards it in a more casual, invisible way. Likewise, Yolanda agreed to pay holiday pay when engaging her childminder, but now regrets it:

I have a week off at Easter and a week off at Christmas and four other weeks that I can take off during the year, and the arrangement that I made was that if I was off I'd pay her, but if she was off I wouldn't. But I'm sorry for that now, because I pay her six weeks a year for doing absolutely nothing (Yolanda, focus group).

In contrast to Aisling, who would pay her childminder full pay in order to retain her if Aisling took parental leave, Yolanda resents paying holiday pay to her childminder, even though holiday pay is a legal entitlement. Both Yolanda and Florence receive holiday pay from their employers but the nature of caring work, being in the home and invisible, does not carry the same entitlements as the formal employment relationships Florence and Yolanda enjoy. These women's views demonstrate the persistence of the gendered order of caring. Florence and Yolanda are kind and caring women, but uncritically accept the wider societal view that caring work carried out in the home is not valuable because of its invisibility. This invisibility leads to further inequalities for women who are caring for the children of 'working mothers' and reinforces the low value placed on care and care work.

It can be argued that the casual nature of private childminding is advantageous to employers and to childminders, because neither party has to commit to a contract of employment, or deal with the cost and administration of social insurance and income tax. However, materially more advantages accrue to employing households who do not have to comply with employment legislation or pay employers' social insurance, while childminders have no employment protection and, when the employment ends, have no entitlement to social security.

Earning and caring give access to different social rights and this leads to a dualism in social citizenship.[34] The treatment of unregulated small-scale private childminders is entirely at the discretion of employing women and households. There is a common tendency in policy and research to blame better-off women for exploiting poorer and low income women who care for children. However, as Lynch and Lyons argue, such an allegation is both profoundly gendered and sociologically misleading.[35] Caring is not simply a woman's responsibility, so men in households who hire women to care on exploitative terms are as culpable as their female partners. Weak labour laws and lack of enforcement of these laws also facilitate households employing childminders in domestic situations without regulation and proper wages. The problem is a neo-liberal policy one, not a personal one for individual women, but individual women are made to carry the moral responsibility because of the persistence of the gendered order of caring.

Vulnerable childminders

Women are aware of a black market in childminding and Brona claims her childminders have also been in receipt of welfare payments which supplement their childcare earnings. This excerpt from a focus group reveals women's awareness of the relationship between welfare and childcare:

> BRONA   There was six of them on-the-sick [receiving illness benefit[36]]. Once you get away with it after twelve months(.) they only call you every twelve months after that . . . They go out with . . . depression.
>
> AMY   You can start again and you can keep it going. I know somebody who has kept it going until her child was two or three, you know.
>
> BRONA   I think you get paid like a hundred and sixty, a hundred and sixty euros a week.
>
> JUNE   For staying at home.
>
> BRONA   It's still a hundred and sixty euros a week, every week for the rest of your life.
>
> FREYA   That's it.
>
> ANNA   And you're not paying childminders.

Many women do not want to leave their children when they are very small even if they could source and afford adequate childcare. One way of navigating the lack of childcare options is to claim illness benefit in order to generate an income while staying off work. This facilitates women being home with their children when they are small and retains a job to return to when children are older. Brona reported that two of her childminders who were claiming long-term illness benefit, had taken up childminding work:

> And both of them are on-the-sick, claiming all their benefits . . . And they've medical cards and everything . . . But you see, there's very little incentive for childminders as well. They don't get paid an awful lot. But someone that's on the sick, that wants cash into their hand, there's a whole underground industry there . . . Neither of the two of them have ever worked legitimately in their life. It's always been under the counter, you know. I can understand why they do that too though (Brona, interview).

It is easier for the state to pay illness benefit to many women than to address the issue of childcare with conflicting policy coalitions regarding women's place either in the home or in paid work. The Irish government refuses to support mothers in paid work with proper childcare provision or by regulating the quality of childcare, thereby ensuring that caring is neither seen as valued nor valuable and always a woman's issue. The women demonstrated their awareness of the government's ambiguous position in a focus group discussion:

BRONA   I think it's the Irish government putting their head in the sand. Do you know the way in some countries women who decide to stay at home get a nominal amount of money to stay at home? I think the government kind of know it's going on but aren't addressing it.

ANGELA   But I don't think you can just blame the government because at the end of the day we are all responsible for that. You have people there, needed for the services industry, very low paid jobs, who are they? The women. The women will go into the lower paid sector. And they're needed. So if there's a little small amount of those, and I'm not saying it's a small amount, but if there's a little fraction of those that are(.)

BRONA   Skimming.

ANGELA   Screwing the system, that's OK.

FREYA   I actually don't blame people in many ways, they're keeping the flow going.

BRONA   I don't know how to remedy it you know. Its sort of catch twenty-two. I can see why women do it, because it does, on the lower paid jobs, it doesn't really pay them to get a babysitter. It hardly pays me. But I'm just saying it's a huge part of society. The amount of money that goes on it, and the people that get away with it.

ANGELA   But it's still suiting the government, and it's still not costing them so much because the fact that the layer of people are being paid so little.

The women in this research were not critical of individual women who claim illness benefit and mind children, because they acknowledge these women are necessary to provide childcare which is in short supply. There is little official evidence of the black market in childminding; however media reports[37] and anecdotal evidence on popular websites (Boards.ie[38] and Ask About Money.ie[39]) reveals it is widespread. The National Association of Private Childcare Providers (NPCP) has claimed that 'crèche fees are constantly being compared to childminder rates – some of whom are charging as little as €3 per hour – while regulated childcare providers face ongoing pressure to upskill more staff, complete more paperwork and pay rates and insurance'.[40]

In focus group discussion these women suggested that the government turns a blind eye to the women who claim illness benefit to care for their own or other women's children, thereby legitimising this inequality. Some of these women supplement their childminding income with illness benefit, thereby reducing the cost of childminding for other 'working mothers'. However, as Angela noted 'we are all responsible for that' (Angela, focus group), demonstrating the symbiotic relationship between 'working mothers' in the formal economy and the women who care for their children in the black market.

The combination of welfare and black market is complex. All workers in the black market have no social security and no protection. These are 'the precariat',[41] those in precarious employment, working outside tax and social insurance networks with little or no job security, and little or no access to sick pay or pension entitlements or to other non-pay benefits. According to TASC, their rates of pay are generally lower than those of the regular workforce, and unsurprisingly, 'the precariat' is dominated by women.[42] Ireland ranks first in the EU-15 in terms of income inequality and twenty-three per cent of women have incomes that put them at risk of poverty.[43] Many of these women are employed as reproductive or caring workers. Childminders who supplement illness benefit with childminding wages have no employment protection at all. Private childminders enjoy no social protection as they are unregistered for taxation and social security and have no employment rights or protection under law.[44] Class and gender intersect to create and sustain inequalities for these women.

Not supporting and regulating childminders maintains childcare as a predominantly private affair and can result in childcare being precarious for both childminders, 'working mothers' and children. Many of these childminders are believed to be untrained and are isolated by their informal status from networks of registered childminders. Informal childminding arrangements are precarious for the minders who have no employment rights. Informal childminding arrangements with childminders who are not registered with the HSE, have had no training and no garda clearance are concerns for parents. Care arrangements may come to an abrupt and sudden end at the discretion of either the minder or the parents[45] and there are also concerns for the welfare of children in the care of untrained, unregulated childminders.

Working Mothers and childminders

Caring is maintained as women's private problem and this conceals the systemic gendered and classed constraints that make different childcare choices available to different women. In all cases, paid childminders are women, therefore gender and class inequalities are reproduced in the childcare arrangements of 'working mothers'.

Some women are privileged in that they have more resources to devote to childminding and receive quality service for employing childminders on equitable terms and conditions. However, the treatment of childminders is entirely at the discretion of individual women and employing households. Other women did not employ childminders on equitable terms and conditions, and thus created inequalities for childminding women. Women who had their children cared for in a crèche were aware that the women in the crèche could not afford to take unpaid maternity or parental leave, thus experiencing inequalities relative to the women whose children they mind.

Exploring women's relationship with their childminders reveals that allowing some women into the world of work, produces gendered, invisible care workers in the private sphere of the home. There is a symbiotic relationship between poor/welfare dependent women and caring work, which maintains poverty and gendered inequality. Women's responsibility for caring work in a society that legitimates exploitation of care workers (who invariably are women) produces domestic workers hierarchically in relation to 'working mothers'.

Liberal-individualist attitudes are evident in 'working mothers' employing invisible, inexpensive childminders without employment contracts. This arrangement maintains the black market in childminding, is bad for individual low paid childminders, for society and for women generally as it reinforces the low value placed on care and care work. The conflict between commoditising caring (arising from discourses of neo-liberalism which seeks value for money) and valuing care work (only when undertaken by mothers, arising from discourses of motherhood) results in 'working mothers' sometimes engaging in, and always being responsible for the poor conditions of childcare workers in Irish society.

Allowing women into the world of paid work, while maintaining women's responsibility for caring, has created a new, complex pattern of inequality between 'working mothers' and care workers. Women's choices in relation to childcare are gendered, in that women arrange and pay for childcare, and women are always engaged as childminders, whether they are crèche staff or private childminders. The failure of the state to regulate small-scale private childminders has consequences in terms of the inequalities experienced by 'working mothers', by childminders and by children. The state facilitates exploitation of childminders in tax and welfare systems. The treatment of care and care workers demonstrates the systemic mechanisms of domination that reinforce the gendered and classed regime of inequality for care workers in Irish society.

Women's participation in the public world of work has had little corresponding change in the gendered order of caring, and this reveals patriarchal power operating through dominant discourses, with caring being maintained as work of low value, undertaken by women in the private sphere. Consequently those who do caring work are generally not valued, with the exception of mothers who relinquish their positions in the public sphere to become 'new capitalist mothers'.[46] This is a pattern which divides and conquers all women because women collude in the propagation of the social and sexual divisions in which they are ultimately subordinate.

CHAPTER 9

Children's capitals

Childhood has become busy, scheduled, organised and productive and this is particularly evident in the middle-class area of
the study, where the dominant notion of mothering is associated
with full-time care. Participants' access to and aspirations with
regard to economic, social and cultural capital are markers of their
class position. Bourdieu's concept of capitals as a marker of class
stratification is helpful in exposing how 'working mothers' experience intersecting inequalities and privileges in Irish society on the
basis of class, and is more reflective of women's realities than
social class or socio-economic groups as defined in the census of
population. The influence of particular cultural norms specific to
location is also significant, as the acquisition of social and cultural
capital is significantly linked to social-class position. It was found
in national data, that three-quarters of nine-year-olds were
involved in some form of organised sports club or organisation,
while almost half of nine-year-olds were involved in structured
cultural activities such as dance, arts and drama; such participation increased substantially with the mother's level of education,
higher social class and greater family income.[1]

Motherhood has also become the focus of acute anxieties about
(re)productivity in the context of advanced global capitalism.
According to Pitt, the 'new capitalist mother' symbolises new discourses of maternal control and achievement, with such efforts
being geared, ultimately, towards the production of new generations of workers trained to master the complex informational
flows of global capitalist economies and cultures.[2]

> The tasks of birthing and raising future workers and con-
> sumers are increasingly presented to women as a curious and
> urgent mixture of career (with its own regimes of training,
> information and on-the-job surveillance) and sacrificial moral
> vocation.[3]

Ehrenreich also recognised the link between gender roles and class formation.[4] Much of what mothers do is designed to preserve and pass on what has been called the family's social capital,[5] their style of life and social position, and many mothers stay home to develop these skills in their children.[6] Feminist writers have highlighted that the contradictory economic pressures of the global economy, the creeping privatisation of political and social responsibilities for the rearing and, increasingly substantial portions of the education of children, all contribute to an increasingly pressurised and traumatised motherhood.[7]

This pressure and anxiety is evident in the development of a large consumer market for writers in the new literary genre of maternal confessional writers.[8] These writers highlight the paradoxical synthesis that fuses discourses of selfless motherhood with neo-liberal and individualist discourses of individual achievement and productivity. The inescapable conclusion urged on the contemporary mother is that she is the shaper of the psyche and personality of the baby and its future quality as a person/product will be her achievement, or conversely, her fault.[9] These writers expose the dissonant pressures heaped upon the 'new capitalist mother'[10] by the competing and conflicting discursive strains of selfless mothering, intensive nurturing, self-sufficiency and autonomy. These tensions are evident in maternal confessional writing which pursues the tensions, conflicts and contradictions of mothering and exposes the dilemmas of maternal ambivalence, and of cultural ambivalence about maternity. There is a backlash against even stating this ambivalence, and the significant opprobrium poured on mothers who have dared to write, let alone complain, about mothering is a firm reassertion of old 'truths' about motherhood: that maternal experiences are emphatically not subjects for theorising or debate, that their public airing is indecent and may even indicate pathology on the part of the woman concerned.[11] In Ireland, the strength of motherhood discourse is evident in a complete absence of criticism of the works of Enright[12] and Looney[13] in the popular press, reflecting the sacredness of motherhood in Ireland. Enright has written a dryly humorous memoir about pregnancy, childbirth and motherhood which is honest about the difficult, boring aspects of motherhood, but also celebrates becoming a mother. Enright precludes any negative reaction from her readers by commencing *Making Babies* with an apology for what is to follow 'Mothers should probably remain silent . . . sorry to everyone in advance. Sorry. Sorry. Sorry. Sorry.'[14]

There has also emerged a body of work concerning women who 'opt out',[15] which concentrates on professional, elite, middle-class women, and which reveals that women would really prefer to balance both professional and mothering lives, but workplaces are hostile to workers with caring responsibilities. In reality, most women are 'pushed out' rather than 'opting out'; nevertheless, the image of the high-profile woman who prefers family to career has gained ground in the popular imagination.

In Ireland, various strains of motherhood discourse abound, reflecting both traditional and neo-liberal values in what Keohane and Kuhling call a 'collision culture'.[16] Women are expected to pri-oritise motherhood, but not relinquish their obligations to engage in paid work and contribute economically to the family. Women experience pressure to invest in their children's acquisition of edu-cational, cultural and social capital[17] and this pressure is immense.[18] Berlant argues that to become a mother, for the suc-cessful late-capitalist woman, is to be suddenly charged with the production of the cultural and national future.[19] Ehrenreich observed middle-class mothers are required to produce children who will be disciplined enough to devote the first twenty or thirty years of their lives to scaling the educational and social obstacles to a middle-class career[20] and Quiney claims there is an expecta-tion that women will happily succumb to this pressure: 'one's own productive future, not only one's career, but also the right to signify as an individual or real person, politically and socially, will gracefully adapt or make way for it'.[21]

Mothers are as much concerned with the care of children as with passing on the family's social capital and in the middle-class area of the study, children's education and social activities are sites where women's social positions as mothers are publicly scruti-nised. Normative shifts in parenting standards have altered such that being a good parent today requires greater amounts of time and mothers are expected to cultivate children's intellectual and socio-emotional development with abundant time.[22] This is partic-ularly evident in this study and all mothers compared their mothering with full-time, stay-at-home mothers in the local area.

Giddens notes it is important to consider the power relations through which the time and space of particular social practices are mediated within a given locale.[23] Dyck[24] and Holloway[25] have shown how notions of mothering are learned and modified over time in particular local neighbourhoods, while Vincent and Ball found that middle-class mothers recognise particular class socialities and forms of social relations:[26]

> You can see generally, it is the wealthy women, or who are in wealthy situations who aren't working, at all, generally, like. I know that is a generalisation, but from what I can see, of the, kind of, full-time mums, they can afford not to work. And they have the mornings to themselves and you know, they have a nice lifestyle going on, once their kids are certain ages . . . It's almost like a snob thing now that I can afford to stay at home, and not work and have four kids (Freya, focus group).

There is a perceived status afforded to women in the local area who mother full-time and as Freya and Grace observed, it has now become fashionable for women in the area of the study to have large families:

> I think affluence is a big part of it, you know. But if you were just to take your own circumstances and look at the people around you, certainly I would think there's more of a status symbol in being a stay-at-home mother now. It's not seen as being, that 'oh, you've made the big sacrifice' or anything like that . . . it's the thing to aspire to be (Grace, focus group).

Sabine describes the traditional career trajectory for 'working mothers' in the area: 'most of our friends are not working, the mothers. They gave up or reduced to part-time and then gave up' (Sabine, interview). This pattern reflects the middle-class nature of the area, and the dominance of the notion that 'good' middle-class mothers are economically privileged, married, and do not work for pay because they are married to husbands who earn family wages.[27] It is difficult for these women to reconcile their positions as 'working mothers' with the norm that middle-class mothers are full-time in the home.

Educational capital

Most women attempt to be visible both at the schools and in the community, to facilitate their children's participation in school and sporting activities, and ensure their childrens' academic progress by their direct involvement in homework. All participants in this research described pressure to ensure children's homework is done properly in order to monitor their academic progress and to meet the school's expectation of parental involvement. In Ireland, eighty-two per cent of parents are concerned about their children's educational outcomes,[28] while the 'Growing up in Ireland' study of nine-year-olds found that seventy-two per cent of parents said that they or their spouse/partner helped the child with homework at least 'regularly'.[29] Jean and Colleen both claimed to reduce their hours in paid work in order to ensure their involvement in their children's homework and Jean and Anna admitted to finding home-work a particular pressure as both have three children. In 2012, sixty-nine per cent of primary school children and thirteen per cent of secondary school children were assisted with homework by their parents on a daily basis.[30] Avril has five children and reported that she is involved in her children's education, almost too much so:

> I would probably be too much focused on what they're doing and what they're not doing . . . Yeah. But I suppose that's just different strokes for different folks. I mean some people couldn't tell you their French teacher, and their English teacher, but sure I could tell you them all. And it's terrible, it's very bad, I said that to you. It's very bad, it's terrible, and it probably is an element of control really, do you know? In the fact that I make sure, I need to make sure that they're going to make it onto third level (Avril, interview).

As Williams[31] and Warner[32] argue, the increasingly visible imposi-tion of absolute responsibility for infantile sufferings and faults on the mother is symptomatic of the privatisation and individualisa-tion that accompanied the market-driven welfare reforms of neo-liberal economic policies. These have increased the burden on primarily female carers within families conceptualised as ideal private economic units in which to contain and conceal 'unprof-itable' relationships of nurture and dependency.[33] However, underlying this strain of 'new capitalist' motherhood discourse are class aspirations acknowledged today only in accepted codes; parents want their children to be successful and productive

> Professional middle-class parents . . . assume that their chil-dren are destined to do work like theirs – work that calls for innovation, initiative, flexibility, creativity, sensitivity to others, and a well-developed set of interpersonal skills.[34]

Middle-class values create a very particular pressure for women who attempt to promote middle-class values and aspirations in their children. Women's involvement in their children's education reflects national trends; sixty-nine per cent of children at primary school level get help with their homework from their parents daily.[35] However, Reay found that it is primarily mothers who 'help children with schoolwork, talk to teachers and network in order to uncover relevant information which will "give their child a head start"'.[36]

In the current study, the local area in which the schools are located has a particularly middle-class status and some women went to considerable effort to ensure their children's attendance at these schools. Gina spends her lunch time travelling from one suburb to another to ensure her daughter attends a particular school. It is also important for Gina to be visible at the school to facilitate her daughter's social activity with other children, so she collects her daughter from school during her lunch break: 'When I'm working then I never get to have a lunch break, literally, I spend the whole hour coming from work, dropping, collecting, and I might have a banana [for lunch] or something' (Gina, focus group). This puts significant time pressure on Gina to leave work every day, collect her daughter at school, deliver her daughter to her child-minder, and return to work through two busy suburbs, while having her lunch in the car.

Many women spoke of the difficulties they experience because of the school's expectation that there is a full-time mother in the home, with lack of notice for school closures, half-days, in-service days, and the expectation that mothers will be available to attend the school during the school day. For women who are unable to conform to these expectations, this can be distressing:

> I mean yesterday, I was to attend the parent-teacher meeting, but the teacher was sick, so she had to cancel it. So the secretary tried to contact me, and she said to my son, who's nine, 'It would be easier to contact Bertie Ahern [the then Taoiseach] than your mum'. He told me when he came home. He thought this was really funny. I found that . . . very disappointing. Yeah. But I was disappointed that she felt I couldn't be contacted. No, I didn't like that, because I felt I should have been able to, you know, it was my son. She wanted to contact me, if my son needed me, I should have been contactable . . . Well I felt it was quite a bit unfair. I felt, actually, I was a bit disappointed. Like, that was not a fair comment to make (Audrey, interview).

Audrey's distress that the school considered her uncontactable was considerable. She felt it was 'not a fair' comment to make about her mothering. Even though Audrey describes herself as having the 'career' in her family, she believes she should also be always available to her children. However, the school's attempt to contact Audrey demonstrates gendered expectations: 'Probably they did not have my mobile number, but I mean, certainly if they had rang my husband, he would have rang me and there would have been no problem' (Audrey, interview), but the school did not attempt to ring the child's father. Likewise, Tamsin experienced the gendered assumption that mothers are full-time at home: 'When David was sick, they keep phoning the home number. And I keep saying "But, I'm not at home" . . . he wasn't well at school and they phoned, and they said "We phoned the home number"' (Tamsin, focus group). Sabine also reported that 'when the kids get sick in school, the secretary in the school rings the mother. They ring the mother even though they have both our numbers, they never ring my husband' (Sabine, focus group). The schools expectation of mother being full-time in the home is evident in these three different schools ringing the home phone number, as well as in many other women's accounts in focus groups and interviews of unexpected school closures, demands for parents (women) to attend school and to participate in school-based activities during the school day. In one focus group, the schools' expectations were discussed:

FREYA   So often we see details on the newpapers or what-ever about childcare and they always show like somebody with this small baby, but it's school, is the thing.

ANGELA   The after school hours is the main thing.

FREYA   And the collections, and the unexpected days off.

ANGELA   That you are not told about.

ANNA   The in-service days.

FREYA   That's really the big thing, and you know our responsibilities around that are just huge.

ANGELA   They [schools] don't seem to have any awareness of the changes in families, even. They don't know and they don't want to know. They're very traditional.

In addition to expecting mothers to be full-time in the home, schools also have an expectation of parental involvement in children's education and women themselves are interested and active in ensuring their children's educational progress. It was found that parents with higher levels of educational attainment were more likely to help their children with their homework on a daily basis.[37] Grace reported that her children do homework twice: 'So they do it [homework] once in the childminders and then it all has to be gone over by the time you go home . . . But she doesn't do it properly in the childminder, I'd have to say she doesn't, so you have to double-do the homework' (Grace, focus group). Brona described ringing home to check on homework during the break in her shift at work:

> Actually Shane, at the moment, he was really struggling with his homework . . . but when I was at work I was worrying, I was saying he needs extra time. Do you know the guilt of that? And ringing home at six o'clock in the evening, 'Joe make sure you do the reading, make sure you do the reading.' 'Did your Dad do the reading?' He did it, only one page. And then the child is nearly asleep and I'm saying 'Come on, do this page' (Brona, interview).

Schools require parents to sign their children's homework and media reports also encourage active parental involvement in children's education and homework.[38] The schools' expectation of parental involvement is evident in the 'guilt' Brona experiences because of her inability to meet this expectation, due to her participation in paid work. In fact, over three-quarters of Irish parents feel that their working responsibilities impact substantially on bringing up their children.[39] All women in this research were frustrated at schools' expectations that mothers are full-time in the home and consequently provide very little notice for unexpected school closures, or requirements for parents (mothers) to attend the school during the school day. The persistence of this expectation and the schools' lack of accommodation for 'working mothers' creates physical and emotional difficulties and many women do reduce their working hours because of schools' expectations.

However, women who work outside the home, while retaining this responsibility, found it more difficult, as schools are a site where women's motherhood is visible. The schools' expectations of mothers' involvement also makes fathers' involvement problemmantic. Amelia reported that her husband felt excluded from the 'scene at the school', because it is predominantly women who are waiting at the school gates:

He collects them, say two or three days a week. And, the days that he collects them, he says to me, he always stands on his own. They [mothers] don't go near him and they all know who he is. They all know he's married to me and they all know he's Mike's dad, but none of those mothers go near him' (Amelia, focus group).

Amelia also reported that her husband was the only father who attended a recent parent/teacher meeting:

He went down to the parent teacher meeting. He brought the other two [children] with him and off they went. He came back to me and said 'I was the only father'. He was a bit embarrassed that he was the only father there . . . the people who were before him and the people who were after him were all the mothers, and he was the only Dad at the parent teacher meeting on his own (Amelia, focus group).

This expectation is gendered and reflects national trends; ninety-eight per cent of mothers attended formal parent-teacher meetings in the preceding academic year.[40] These gendered expectations and the practice of predominantly mothers' involvement in their children's schooling discourages fathers' involvement. It also makes visible the differences between women who work outside the home and those who do not. One difference is the perception that women who do not engage in paid work outside the home spend considerable time socialising at the school:

The non-working mothers who are down at the school, in their track suits, chitty chatting for an hour in the mornings and an hour prior to the bell going, they're always half an hour early. Always. They spend a fair chunk of the day there and I'm going, 'Oh no, I couldn't be here now, chatting away like this' . . . You know . . . there's a scene at the school, you know, I think if you're off, you're into that, if you're not working (Florence, focus group).

Changes in the order of discourse are evident in the expectation of mothers' involvement in their children's education and development of children's educational capital. This is a consequence of the state's neo-liberal policies, which have led to the privatisation and withdrawal of services, particularly in education. Women demonstrate they spend considerable time and resources ensuring their children's acquisition of educational capital, because of reductions in state spending on education and increases in the teacher/pupil ratio. Public spending on education in Ireland has fallen dramatically in recent years, from nineteen per cent of public expenditure in 1997 to nine per cent in 2011,[41] compared to an OECD average of thirteen per cent. Average class size in Ireland is twenty-four pupils per class, compared to an EU-21 average of twenty. Thus in Ireland twenty-two per cent of primary pupils are in classes of thirty or more and eighty-eight per cent of pupils are in classes of twenty or more. Only twelve per cent of pupils are in classes with fewer than twenty pupils.[42] The Irish National Teachers Organisation (INTO) said the fall in spending was hitting schools hard and argued spending cuts are directly responsible for cuts to school budgets, school staffing and special needs teaching hours. Furthermore, capitation grants, which are intended to be spent on the day-to-day running costs of the school (on items such as heating, cleaning, lighting, and the provision of teaching materials and resources), were cut from €190 per child in 2009 to €176 per child in 2012.[43] 'Ireland's education system is suffering the worst series of cut-backs and austerity measures',[44] consequently parents are facing higher rates of 'voluntary contributions' and are increasingly paying more money and spending more time on their children's acquisition of educational capital. In most instances, the parent who is most actively involved in their children's educational outcomes, is the mother.

A further complication for working mothers is the discretion each school has regarding its calendar. Ireland has a unique education system. The state does not run Irish schools directly. Instead it appoints patron bodies, almost all of them religious denominations, to run the schools on the basis of their own religious ethos. This 'patron's religious ethos' rule enables religiously-run national schools to influence the school calendar by observing religious holidays, which are not observed in the workplace. In addition, the dates for the start and the end of the school year have only been standardised since 2014.[45] Every school must be open for tuition for a minimum of 183 days at primary level and 167 days at post-primary level; however schools have discretion over mid-term and short breaks and discretionary days which can be used to close on religious or other holidays. Women with children attending different schools, because the majority of schools are same-sex in Ireland, or because their children are at both primary and second level, can find their sons and daughters and older and younger children having different school calendars, which creates additional scheduling difficulties for 'working mothers'.

In the 2002 Census (the most recent for which specific after-school care data is available), one in eight families stated they would prefer an alternative childcare arrangement, with after-school activity-based programmes being the most popular alternative suggested, with forty-six per cent giving non-availability as the reason for not availing of the preferred type of care.[46] In 2007, the Quarterly National Household Survey included after-school care in the same category with Crèche, Montessori and Playgroup, and in 2007, three per cent of all primary school children availed of this category.[47] As crèches, montessori schools and playgroups are designed for pre-school children, it can be assumed that only three per cent of primary school children in the state availed of after school activities. In this research, only one woman reported using after-school care at any stage. In 2013, a subsidised after-school childcare scheme was introduced to support low-income and unemployed persons to return to the workforce. The scheme provides for 6,000 subsidised after-school childcare places for certain social welfare income support recipients who enter employment, or who increase their days of existing employment, and have children of primary school age.[48] This initiative is a labour activation measure rather than an initiative to assist employed workers, but it does reflect the state's acknowledgement that after-school care is a necessary part of the care infrastructure and care provision.

The difficulty of facilitating the acquisition of children's educational capital and accommodating the school's expectation of a full-time mother-in-the-home results in many women reducing their hours of work. In this study, exactly half the participants in this study work reduced hours either by job-sharing, working part-time, or doing the same job in reduced hours, while half of all participants maintained their full-time commitment to paid work. Many women undertake considerable juggling to maintain their contribution to paid work as well as ensuring their children's acquisition of educational capital. The schools promote gendered values, and the expectation of a full-time-in-the-home mother creates pressure on women who combine motherhood with paid work. Because they are not always available when the schools require them, and do not devote the same amount of time to their children's education, many women report experiencing guilt.

Social and cultural capital

Gina was frustrated with the school's expectation that mothers are always available by being full-time in the home. In a focus group discussion she revealed: 'Something that really annoyed me this year was the Suzuki violin.[49] The mother has to come, once a week, twice a week for half an hour. So it's the elitist who don't have to work that do it' (Gina, focus group). Gina was particularly distressed about the violin lessons, and mentioned it again to me in interview a year later. Her concern was that full-time mothers in the area of the study can develop their children's cultural capital through violin lessons from which her daughter is excluded. Gina perceives she is treated unequally by being unable to facilitate her daughters' acquisition of cultural capital with violin lessons. Gina also perceives this inequity on behalf of her daughter who expressed a desire to play the violin.

Benn found the requirement to be visible in schools, sporting and social activities transcends material differences between women and regardless of their circumstances, all women are likely to be the parent responsible for dropping and collecting and the managing of children's activities.[50] The women in this study make considerable efforts to ensure their children participate in extra-curricular and cultural activities on a par with women who mother full-time in the area. Full-time homemaking mothers are visible at the schools and at children's extra-curricular and cultural activities, which is perceived to contribute to pressure on participants who do not have the same amount of available time for these pursuits; thus it is possible to see the power relations implicit in the way mothers ensure reproduction of class position. Society remains gendered and it is evident that childcare and children's development are considered the responsibility of women. The schools are particularly resistant to social change and while changes have occurred with women's participation in paid work, there is no corresponding effort to accommodate these mothers or these children by changing the organisation of the school system. These are gender inequalities because it is only women who experience this pressure.

Aisling and her husband are very busy every weekday and at weekends facilitating children's participation in activities: 'It is mad, it's hectic. But having said that, I still enjoy going to all these activities, it's not a chore it's not necessarily a chore' (Aisling, interview). Aisling derives some enjoyment from her children's participation in activities: 'The two older guys do a lot of activities they're very sporty and I suppose, part of it is my own thinking as opposed to the kids. I feel that I need to instil in them, it's just something in me, that you don't miss things' (Aisling, interview). Aisling hopes that their participation in activities will engender self-discipline in her children, so that they are involved in sport when they reach their teen years:

> And I mean, we're all encouraging them to be into activities, because when they're fifteen or sixteen, I don't want them hanging around street corners. And I want them involved, if at all possible, perhaps in team sports, that they'll feel a commitment, that they'll have to go training or whatever (Aisling, interview).

However, Brona experiences pressure because of her inability to facilitate her children to conform to the same cultural practices as their friends and neighbours: 'There's kids on our road now that have, every single evening they have an activity for an hour or whatever, be it scouts, this thing, that thing, drama' (Brona, interview). Brona's work schedule and available financial resources do not facilitate her children engaging in the same level of activity and this induces guilt: 'I actually feel like I'm a bad mother sometimes now when I hear these kids are doing this thing, that thing' (Brona, interview).

Women found birthday parties a particular pressure: 'I really have a problem with birthday parties during the week . . . I'm looking for someone to bring them, normally I can collect because it's over at five, but you don't want them to be missing birthday parties' (Yolanda, focus group). However, for some women there was no option, and their children did not attend some birthday parties, because it was not possible to make arrangements: 'but they actually do get over it . . . I have refused to let her go to birthday parties, I've actually just said "I'm sorry I'm not happy about you going to the birthday party . . . and you can't go, not this time." And they get over it, very fast, a couple of days, and the [birthday] kids don't mind, "sure they can bring me the present at school"' (Eithne, focus group).

Florence describes other mothers cultivating their children's friendships with her children, which she finds excessive. Florence observed that it is good for children to develop interests and friendships outside of school. However, as Florence observed, class is evident in the efforts of some mothers to ensure their children make particular friendships and acquire particular skills: 'You could run yourself ragged then five days a week, there's plenty of people out there who do it five days a week . . . Social climbing, you know, comes into it as well' (Florence, focus group).

Expectations have accelerated that parents should devote copious amounts of time to cultivating their children's development.[51] These expectations are gendered, however, and women devote more time than their partners to their children's acquisition of capitals. Class intersects with gender to ensure women's reduced ability to facilitate their children's participation in extra-curricular activities by virtue of unavailable time and unavailable material resources, thus class creates inequalities for children as well. Brona was also concerned that her children could not participate in activities to the same extent as neighbours' children. However, Brona's inequality came not just from unavailable time, but also economic constraints. This powerless responsibility is a source of extreme pressure.

Intensive nurturing and new familialism discourses suggest that mothers are solely responsible for their children's social, educational, physical and psychological development and to mother successfully women need to invest significant time and effort in caring for and developing their children. This is a major area where contemporary notions of gender are still rooted naturalistically,[52] because motherhood provides a degree of cultural capital to women for conforming to feminine and motherhood roles. In this research, women demonstrated that the local is a key element in the construction of meaning and identity and many went to considerable efforts to socialise their children into their local communities and in particular to reproduce their middle-class position through their children's participation in extra-curricular activities, in order to acquire social and cultural capital and to prepare their children to become 'exemplary capitalist winners'.[53] Women who engage in paid work outside the home find it more difficult to develop this cultural capital. The normative expectation of middle-class mothers' responsibility for the development of their children's capital is a discursive strain which is a key mechanism in the promotion of asymmetrical power relations between those women who engage in paid work and those who mother full-time in the home.

The local has significant meaning and importance to women and as Bennett suggests the 'local' is not a fixed spatial area, but 'a series of discourses which involve picturing the local and one's relation to it'.[54] Aisling demonstrates that 'the family' is both a relationship and a series of interlocking locations brought together through time and space, the management of which tends to be the responsibility of mothers, who undertake the regular and routine planning, anticipating, monitoring and rectifying that allow other family members to undertake a range of activities.[55]

> You know, today now we'll say, I came home, collected the two older guys. Came back here for half an hour. They did home-work and I brought the second guy to music, the first guy to tennis. Went down and collected the small guy and came back here. And then Tony came back here and then I had to go again to collect from . . . tennis. Tony collected from music, and then there was somebody else going out to football at six o'clock, so dinner had to be in-between (Aisling, interview).

Morgan has identified spatial time as 'the allocation of times in relation to specific spaces or locales'.[56] Aisling's scheduling of chil-dren's activities in spatially disparate locations means that children are subject to strict time discipline and an accelerated tempo which ensures that, even at a young age, children also have the experience of having 'no time'[57]. There is a widespread popular perception that children's lives today are much more institutionalised in the sense that organised activity for children with other children now exists in a wide variety of child oriented activities.[58] Since the economic sphere provides the dominant tem-poral mode, women in this study are subjecting children to strict timelines and routines, which creates more time pressure for 'working mothers'.[59] The pressure to develop children's social and cultural capitals is gendered and fathers were not reported to be as concerned about their children's development, which means this is also a key mechanism in the promotion of asymmetrical power relations between women and men and conceals the 'rela-tions of domination' they promote and sustain.[60]

> I'll be doing school collections and then we've swimming lessons and Donal, if it's fine, does soccer. And I have to drop him down there for six o'clock and then he does swimming after that, because I want him to do the lane swimming, because I just feel he's gone [so far with it]. Now I know I draw it on myself and [my husband] would often say to me, 'For

feck's sake, what are you doing that for?' . . . I just find, yeah, they are doing different things at different times and he [my husband] can't understand then why you have to have them involved in so much (June, interview).

No woman questioned the expectation that mothers should expend considerable effort in developing their children and fathers were not generally reported to be as involved as mothers in their children's acquisition of educational, social and cultural capitals. This is consistent with national data. On weekdays women spend an average of just over five hours on caring activities and household work, compared to one hour forty minutes for men.[61] It was evident in women's accounts that facilitating children's development is a normative element of the construction of motherhood in contemporary Ireland.

'Working mothers' and children's capitals

Motherhood discourses which charge women with full responsibility for their child's physical, emotional and educational development, negatively affect women who try to combine motherhood with paid work, because these discourses promote standards of achievement that are difficult for any woman to achieve, whether or not she works outside the home. Warner suggests women who work outside the home resent the constrictions of an increasingly conservative maternal role within a globalised economy in which their labour may be worth less than their childcare costs, and their children appear to face an insecure economic future unless intensively trained to be exemplary capitalist 'winners'.[62]

Child's needs discourses require women to put children first, and the discursive strains of achievement and autonomy demand the intense training of children in order to ensure their success in competitive, neo-liberal society. Women's efforts to ensure their children's acquisition of capitals therefore creates conflicts for women who also recognise the obligation to be autonomous and independent in paid work, as individualism discourses suggest. Women experience contradictory expectations and pressures. Discourses articulating a particular set of workplace opportunities and obligations are set over and against a fairly unchanged and traditional articulation of women's obligations as mothers.[63] Women who reduce their hours in paid work are privileged by being available to their children, by having more time to devote to reproduction of class position and to foster children's development, but perceive a reduction in their personal autonomy.

Walby notes it is important to retain the notion of the causal impact of gender and class as social phenomena, rather than adopt a view of interconnections so complex that causation is irrelevant.[64] Gender is a social fact and caring for children and ensuring their development is the gendered responsibility of mothers. Class is also a social fact and women who are unable to care for or develop their children experience gendered and classed inequalities, because they perceive that their children are also disadvantaged.

There are individual differences between women in this study, as well as differences between women who mother full-time in the area of the local study. Their hours of work, the nature of their occupations and whether they work in public or private sectors, as well as their positioning within dominant discourses, all influenced women's availability to develop their children's capitals.

CHAPTER 10

'Time for me is time for everybody'

That 'working mothers' experience a shortage of time is not a new issue. It is well documented that women in dual-earner couples have a significantly higher total work burden than women in male breadwinner couples, and women's recent substantial increase in paid employment has increased their total work burden.[1] Consequently, with more paid and unpaid work, women experience more time poverty and time pressure. In women's accounts, they spend time outside of paid work tending to their children, fetching and dropping children from school and social activities, spending time on their partners, their elderly parents and doing housework.

Time

Adam argues that a multitude of times exist in a single moment and suggests that the recognition of such multiplicity and complexity allows for a firm grounding of the analysis of women's experience.[2] However, frequently the complexity of women's experience in time is reduced to a dualism where feminine experience tends to be located in the level of everyday temporality understood as cyclical, reproductive and expressive and which falls in the shadow of a masculine temporality understood as progressive, standardised and instrumental.[3] Knights and Odih claim that 'female time' is relational, continuous, processual and cyclical and exists in relation to the time demands of others.[4] As this time is mediated through the needs of others, it is quite unlike decontextualised, commoditised, controlled and linear clock time. Thus, the majority of feminist research that has used time as a key concept has stayed within dualistic framings of what Davies refers to as male time and female time.[5] 'Male time' is 'a more linear, forward planning model of time' and 'female time' is 'partly cyclical . . . involving the allocation and juggling of a multiplicity of times'.[6] However, both concepts of time are combined in the ways women merge and manage working and caring, and Adam developed a timescape perspective, whereby 'phenomena, processes and events may be conceptualised as timescapes'.[7] Timescapes are analogous to landscapes because they include the temporal features of social events in a variety of socially constructed contexts. Drawing on Adam's concept of timescapes, McKie, Gregory and Bowlby developed the concept of a caringscape, which

> can be thought of as shifting and changing multi-dimensional terrain that comprises people's vision of caring possibilities and obligations; routes that are influenced by everyday scheduling, combining caring work with paid work and the paid work of carers.[8]

The caringscape concept, like the timescape, moves beyond the functional view of time, to interpretations of time and what people do with time in unique settings, as well as how time can influence people's perceptions. Women who combine motherhood with paid work navigate a caringscape that includes working time and caring time, both of which are governed by different values.

Work time

Adam contends that the project of keeping time and space explicit in social research and theory is made problematic by the complexity of social time and the difficulties of disentangling the power relations involved in the construction of conventional times in economic and industrial cultures.[9]

> Not all time is money. Not all human relations are governed by the rationalised time of the clock. Not all times are equal. That is to say, all work relations touched by clock time, are tied up with hegemony and power.[10]

Work time is not only the main way through which we order and understand time; it also provides the framework through which tasks are valued. For example, Marxist analyses of the commoditisation of time indicate its economic value and the exchange relations of labour power and profit maximisation. Monthly, weekly and hourly wages indicate how time is used as a measure of labour value. Alongside labour, capital and machinery, time becomes an economic variable and allows us to speak of a time economy. 'We spend it, waste it, invest it, budget it and save it. We equate it, in other words, with money'.[11]

> Everything is always a rush, I mean, there's always [pressure]. Your whole life really revolves around the next day and the next thing, and weekends are busy doing stuff and there's no [time]. There's a huge sense of a shortage of time, and that is the worst thing [about being a 'working mother'] (Freya, focus group).

Though there are women who have always negotiated multiple times,[12] the current dominant conception of time remains anchored in the economic sphere. For many workers, the place and time of paid work is singular and fixed and work time dominates the ways in which work is managed and ordered.[13] Brona spoke about the fixed and static nature of the shift schedule operating in the manufacturing environment and her lack of discretion over work time and space: 'I work three days a week for twelve hours, so I'm up at seven in the morning and I don't get home until half past eight at night . . . my job is only a factory job' (Brona, interview). She finds her hours of work make it difficult for her to combine motherhood with paid work: 'It's just the intensity of the three days; you don't get to see your children really. You're gone in the morning before they get up and they're hopefully in bed when you get home at night, you might go up for twenty minutes' (Brona, interview). However, as Brona has 'only a factory job', she has no discretion regarding the time she spends in paid work, with very structured work time and break times. Women who have 'jobs' as opposed to 'careers' have less choice regarding the type of work they do, have less earning power, and less discretion regarding the times and spaces of paid work. Brona's organisation culture is typical of industrial capitalism, with a regular manufacturing shift schedule. Amanda also works three twelve-hour shifts in a busy hospital where her role demands not just her presence but her full concentration on work to the exclusion of everything else:

> Once I was at work, I was at work . . . and I used to describe it as 'Stars in your Eyes'. That you just walked through that door in the morning and no matter what was happening outside, you just walked in the door, and you were at work now. And as you walked out the door, if you were in the middle of a three-day argument with your husband, as you sat into your

car, you said 'Oh shit, I've to go home now' and I would have
hardly thought of it (Amanda, interview).

Amanda and Brona's workplaces prioritise work time and space
and demand a significant commitment to work while there. Grace
also reported the expectation that work time be prioritised over all
other areas of her life, including invading home time, in her previous employment:

> In my past job now, there were no lines. They would ring you
> in the labour ward to ask you something and they really would
> 'Sorry to do this to you now, but' you know what I mean? And
> there were no lines, none whatsoever . . . Because you'd be on-
> call and you could get phone calls at any time, and they owned
> you, really at the end of the day (Grace, focus group).

The description 'they owned you' is apt for many women and
men. Deriving from neo-liberal discourses, many organisations
demand employees' permanent commitment, even when not
physically at the place of work, and assume there are no other
forms of time that impact on an individual's life:

> This socially created, artefactual resource has become so all-
> embracing that it is now related to as if it were time *per se*, as if
> there were no other times. This has the effect that even the
> embedded, lived times of work and non-work are understood
> through the mediating filter of our own creation of non-tem-
> poral time (original emphasis).[14]

As is evident in Grace's account, work time is all pervasive. Time
out of work, time not working, is not considered productive,
useful time, and with e-mail and mobile phones, employees are
expected to prioritise work over all other times, whether physically at work or not. According to Treanor, the neo-liberal ideal is
the absolutely flexible and employable employee who will always
be available.[15] It is evident in women's accounts that women identify with this discursive strain and are flexible and employable
employees, being available for work outside of working hours.
However, this flexibility of employees, being always available to
work, comes at a price for organisations, and research has shown
that employees' lose commitment to their employers[16] as a consequence of flexibility being one-way. Grace left that organisation
after the birth of her second child and moved into public-sector
employment where she initially worked full-time, and subsequently reduced her hours of work.

Kate, however, does not resent the intrusion of work into her home time and space and describes her commitment to the long-hours culture in her workplace:

> I probably spend much too much time on work, and I would probably like to rectify that, but I'm not quite sure how to pull back from work really . . . So I would be checking e-mails up till ten o'clock at night. Getting e-mails from work people and things like that, here and abroad. So I'm very attached to my work, even when I come home (Kate, interview).

Hochschild notes that information and communications technologies allow paid work responsibilities to encroach into family life and heighten expectations that employees be available around the clock.[17] To demonstrate commitment, it is expected that Kate will work whatever hours are necessary. The social relations of gender are historically and deeply embedded in complex ways in both the formal and informal workings of organisations.[18] This is often 'hidden' beneath apparently gender-neutral policies relating to targets and performance. 'The gendered substructure is hidden under a shell of rationality and neutrality:'[19]

> My employers would think nothing of organising a meeting at a quarter to five on Friday or expecting you to come in on a Saturday. And if you said anything, 'Well you know, I have children, or that's my personal time to spend with my family' or whatever. They'd say, 'Oh sure we all have families of one sort or another, it's part of your commitment, part of your responsibility' (Kate, focus group).

In Ireland, many writers have also demonstrated the power relations operating in professions that have traditionally been regarded as 'masculine'.[20] One of the ways these power relations operate is through the concept of work time. It is simply part of Kate's commitment to her profession that she be available for work whenever necessary. Job schedules continue to be predicated on outdated assumptions that workers have someone at home to tend to family responsibilities and most employers expect workers to prioritise the demands of employment ahead of family demands.[21] Long-hours cultures in some organisations are particularly difficult for those with caring responsibilities. On a forthcoming public holiday falling on a Thursday, Faye spoke of her plans:

> I think when you have a window of time, I find, I'll be thinking even a week ahead, now, like there's a couple of days coming

up, and I'm thinking, what I'll fit into nearly every minute of that time. I can tell you now exactly what I'll be doing from Wednesday night through to Friday morning when I go back to work (Faye, focus group).

It is interesting to note the work-time language Faye uses – 'a window of time', as in a little gap in work time in which to engage in non-work activities – demonstrating Faye's commitment to structured, scheduled work time and her application of it to family life. For many women, work time invades the home sphere and time out of work is subject to the same discipline as work time, with routines and schedules to be observed.

Kate spoke about the work-time culture in her organisation to the extent that she waived her statutory entitlement to maternity leave:

> Well, when I had my first three children, my immediate boss was very unsupportive and as a result I didn't take any maternity leave on my first three children. And then I went with my fourth and asked for maternity leave I was told it was going to be very disadvantageous for my colleagues and(.) But I had to for health reasons, I had to take leave. But it was very uncomfortable and very stressful . . . I induced my third child for work reasons(.) I came out of hospital, and three days after she was born I went back to work, dropped her over to my mother. (Kate, focus group).

Kate did not take maternity leave for her first three children and attributed this to her immediate supervisor's attitude. Maternity leave is a statutory entitlement, and Kate's decision to waive her entitlement on three occasions reflects the strength of the supervisor's and her own identification with the neo-liberal ideal of the flexible and available employee. While other women in that focus group discussion were surprised that Kate could leave a three-day-old baby with her mother in order to go to work, Kate claimed that it was simply expected in her profession that work time be prioritised over all other areas of life.

The degree to which the 'true' late-capitalist self is conceptualised as essentially masculine, bounded, controlled and cleanly individuated[22] is evident in hegemonic work-time cultures. While the discursive strain of 'ideal workers' who are always available is drawn on by women to explain their commitment to their employing organisations' time cultures, and their being as flexible as the organisation demands, Kate also draws on discourses of achievement and career commitment to explain her dedication to her profession. Within neo-liberalism, worker's time is a resource to which organisations see themselves as entitled. When women behave like 'ideal workers' by conforming to strong work-time cultures, they perpetuate the notion that ideal workers are always available for work, thus allowing work time to dominate all areas of people's lives.[23]

However, many women reported availing of time flexibility, contingent on their occupation and employing organisations. Freya demonstrated that the nature of the work she does makes it possible for her to have time flexibility:

> [I]'m not in a situation where people are directly dependent on me. In the sense that I'm in Finance so nothing's life or death there, whatever it is can wait until tomorrow generally, or else I'd go back in in the evening or at night, if I had to, when my husband is at home. If I had to take time off for a sick baby, I'd go back in, so, you know, pop back in for an hour or two (Freya, focus group).

Freya works full-time, but clearly can avail of unstructured flexibility on occasions and it was evident in many women's accounts of availing of flexibility, that women repaid the time and work, like Freya, by returning to work in the evening, at nights and weekends to catch up and meet targets. Jean and Colleen both work reduced hours, and both claim to achieve full-time work output in the shorter hours for which they are paid. Colleen claims 'the company sees it as a saving' (Colleen, focus group). However, as they are grateful for the opportunity to work reduced hours, both women described extremely busy work days, compressing full-time jobs into fewer hours: 'I still have to do everything I'm expected to do, but in a shorter time. I don't take any breaks' (Colleen, focus group), while Jean has considerable responsibility in her position and describes her efforts to fulfil her work obligations in less time:

> Reduced hours. I don't job share, nobody else does my work while I'm not there. And I'm supposed to work nine thirty to three. Generally I'm in like twenty minutes early, leave twenty minutes late and when needs be bring work home. I can log in from home, or occasionally I will go back to work in the evening or at the weekend if I have to . . . work though lunch, don't take coffee breaks. So generally I think I do ninety per cent of the hours that I would probably be doing if I worked full time . . . I

think you're very focused because your day is shorter and more compressed, so you have to fit in a lot more (Jean, interview).

Colleen and Jean suggest that organisations facilitate their reduced working hours as a means of facilitating women's desire to conform to gendered caring roles. However, these women increase their productivity, by producing more work in less time. It has been demonstrated that granting employees time flexibility leads to greater productivity;[24] however, this flexibility creates inequalities for these women. When women avail of reduced hours they limit their career prospects, ensuring their subordination in the workplace; their gratitude for this flexibility ensures they increase their productivity and are compliant and motivated employees.

Audrey and Amelia took parental leave when their children were small and Yolanda is taking parental leave one day a week. These women are employed in public sector organisations. Sabine also applied for parental leave: 'I tried to take my parental leave one day a week so I would have four days but I was still given a work load for five days and they made it impossible to do that. Even though they had to give me my parental leave, they made it impossible. Really' (Sabine, focus group). Sabine also works in a public sector organisation, where the immediate supervisor is significant in women's take up of the leave. Likewise Eithne found, 'My company now(.) Even though personnel say they have no problem with parental leave, my direct boss does have a big problem with it. And, I've had a lot of trouble taking some parental leave' (Eithne, focus group). However Jane claims her organisation grants employees parental leave, but does not replace staff, regarding the unpaid leave as a saving, which creates staffing problems for Jane: 'The onus is very much on the employer and they're not accepting that responsibility at all. They're just reaping the benefits and leaving the empty seats' (Jane, interview). Jane is the manager of a busy telesales department with an almost entirely female staff. The nature of telesales work requires the physical presence of staff at work in order to take calls when the business is operational. Jane appreciates the difficulties of maintaining productivity and adherence to work time while attempting to facilitate her colleagues' requests for flexibility:

> And it's very difficult. As a full-time worker and especially a full-time worker and mother . . . you are carrying the load. And at Christmas, you know, times like that, all of the people,

> you know, with children, they want Christmas off. And it's the same, there's war every year then, trying to [accommodate everyone]. And I end up having to work it [myself] (Jane, focus group).

In attempting to accommodate her staff who are 'working mothers' Jane ends up having to work herself at Christmas, even though she too is a 'working mother', and as Jane is parenting alone, this is particularly difficult. Jane is not only 'carrying the load' at home, supporting herself and her child, but she is also 'carrying the load' at work, where she is manager of the department and tries to accommodate her colleague's requests for time off. The strict work-time culture, the nature of the work and the requirements of her role as manager, mean Jane receives none of the flexibility she extends to others. As a woman in a management role, Jane supports the organisation and her colleagues by facilitating flexibility, but cannot avail of it herself. As Jane is parenting alone and responsible for providing economically for her child, she has little option but to accept the hegemonic culture at work for herself, but tries to limit its impact on her 'working mother' staff. While Jane acknowledged granting flexibility to her staff resulted in greater productivity, her employer will not engage with Jane's desire for reduced hours because of her managerial status: 'They [the company] are not willing to give me anything, any leeway with regard to time . . . I just feel that the time would be worth so much, they'd get so much more out of me if they gave me that'.

As Jane notes, women who work part-time and partnered women who work full-time experience less time pressure, whereas she is working full-time and parenting alone and is extremely time poor:

> Those women seem to be happier and more content, and I just think there's more of a balance there. Whereas maybe the people who are full-time and there's a husband and wife, or partner, they would be ok too. But it's the ones who are on their own, are the ones who are kind of stretched. Big time (Jane interview).

Thus, being in a management role, and being without the support of a partner, means the rigidity of work time is more difficult for Jane than for other 'working mothers'. One way of ensuring women do not advance to senior levels is to require that they behave as ideal workers, and women with senior positions in this research demonstrate that they do, but experience practical and emotional difficulties because they also have caring responsibilities as mothers. Employers receive greater productivity by granting employees reduced working hours, in the case of Jean and Colleen, and in Jane's case, the employer does not replace women who take unpaid parental leave. Thus these mechanisms, designed to facilitate better work/life balance, actually yield savings for these organisations.

Home time

Change in women's roles outside the family has clearly been significant, as the figures for labour force participation have shown. Within the family, however, there is not a corresponding change in gender behaviour. Despite popular belief to the contrary, gender roles within marriage have changed very little.[25] As a relationship progresses from courtship to cohabitation to marriage to parenting, gender roles in the home become increasingly traditional[26] and being a 'good wife' is still synonymous with doing an 'acceptable' amount of housework.[27] Hilliard reported that almost one-third of women in Ireland felt that they 'did much more than their fair share' of housework, while sixty-two per cent felt they did more than their fair share of household labour.[28] Coltrane found that women have slightly reduced the numbers of hours they spend on housework, while men have slightly increased their contribution.[29] Sullivan[30] also identified a trend towards greater participation of men in domestic work. However, Coltrane concluded that on average, women do three times as much housework as men. Women do more housework when they marry and become mothers, while men do less when they marry and become fathers, with 'married men creating about as much demand for household labour as they perform'.[31] McGinnity and Russell found that women with children spend the equivalent of one month more per year on committed work than their male partners[32] while Irish Social Sciences Platform data indicates that while working parents rarely go to work too tired to function well because of household tasks, a significant majority came home from work 'too tired to do chores', with women more likely than men to report this tiredness.[33] Thus, time-use data show that a traditional division of labour persists within the household, with women, even those in full-time employment, spending more time on caring and household work than men.[34]

It has been argued that women, men and families still persist as communities of interdependence and need rather than simply as expressions of individual 'choices', giving rise to 'elective relationships'.[35] However, these families exert pressure on mothers to meet the needs of other family members thereby significantly reducing the amount of choice available to women, because as Oakley argues:

> Families have, for a long time, meant different things to men and women. Men have the luxury of seeing them as havens, even when the tie of economic responsibility is broken; women know families as places of unpaid labour, caring and altruism – a moral code which is out of step with that of the wider society, and therefore largely undervalued by it.[36]

Davies illustrates how women's experiences of time when working in the home are bound up with the times of family members and others through which 'clock and process time weave complicated patterns'.[37] As Yolanda describes time in her day: 'It's all go from the minute I get up in the morning, go go go. I go to work and I come home and it's all go go go again' (Yolanda, interview).

Yolanda describes how busy she is at home the one day each week she takes parental leave, suggesting the fixed nature of clock time associated with paid work and the fluid, processual nature of time spent at home. Yolanda compares her time in work favourably to her time at home: 'Like I'm sitting down every day in work, whereas on a Wednesday [when Yolanda is at home all day], I don't sit down at all' (Yolanda, interview). Thus Yolanda demonstrates the relational nature of caring for others, doing housework and collecting and dropping family members which means her time is fractured, relational and task focused while she is caring and working in the home.

Amelia did not take extended maternity leave for her third child, even though she had done so for her first two, because of the tedious, repetitive, thankless nature of caring for small children at home:

> On my last one I ran back to work in July because I just had to get out of the house for sanity reasons really. . . . I don't know, with three children, I just found them so demanding at home, and they were all so close together, and I just had to get out of the house. And I just loved going to work to just come home

and somebody else would have all the bottles done and all the nappies done and the dinner made (Amelia).

Time spent caring for small children is repetitive and restricted in terms of space. The different values afforded to working and caring are determined not just by who does 'work' and who does 'care', but also by the location.[38] 'The economic status of women in society and their role and position in the household are formally linked by the value of time'.[39] Being 'at home' is not valued by some participants as their work caring for children is regarded as invisible, even by themselves; 'somebody else' could do the dinners, bottles and nappies.

Scott notes even where men and women in dual-earner households devote the same amount of time to their paid work, women undertake around nine hours per week more housework than men,[40] while Delphy and Leonard observe that what male partners do is described as 'helping' with the housework when their wives are in paid employment.[41] Thus, increased female employment has not led to a renegotiation of the allocation of paid and unpaid work between women and men. Women remain time-poor in comparison to men because of the disproportionate level of household tasks they undertake.[42] McGinnity and Russell found that Irish women spend more time on the physical care and supervision of children while men spend a much greater proportion of their time on social childcare such as playing.[43] 'While men do more in the home than they did in the past, women continue to do most of the domestic work and to take responsibility for organizing it.'[44]

Jean has reduced her working hours to thirty hours a week, and describes her husband's expectation that she will be the manager and organiser of their home:

> My husband says I'm the logistics manager in our house. You know if somebody has to go to a party, or somebody has to go here(.), I mean, if I say to him, 'Will you take Jill to the party?' He'll say fine, but you know, you have to figure it all out, and you have to give him the instruction then and he'll carry it all out and he wouldn't quibble with it. But, I have to work out who's collecting there, who needs to be dropped where, what clothes do they need to bring with them, who needs to bring a hurley, who needs to bring ballet clothes, whatever it is. And then he'll go off and he'll do it, but you have to do the figuring out (Jean, interview).

This suggests the gendered power structure whereby her husband bestows upon Jean the title of 'logistics manager', conferring all responsibility on Jean to continually do the managing. Reducing their working hours reinforces gendered attitudes towards women's domestic responsibilities. Often men deal only with the non-routine aspects of childcare, such as playing with children and taking them out, while mothers are left to do the housework and routine childcare. Employed women end up working very long days at the least favoured aspects of household work, 'even when they have good husbands'.[45] Chira observes that most 'working mothers' carry the double load of paid work and housework, even if male partners help.[46] 'My husband would do most of the things that I ask him to, he wouldn't think of doing it but he'd do it if I asked him' (Sabine, focus group). Other husbands do not 'help'. Regardless of Kate's commitment to full-time work and with four children, her husband refuses to have anything to do with the management of the home:

> To this day he wouldn't do housework . . . He just doesn't want to do it, [he] wasn't brought up to do it. Just doesn't want to do it. I have somebody who comes in once a week now, only since, since about a year ago. But up to then it was my responsibility. I used to do it at the weekend (Kate, focus group).

Housework reveals differences between women depending on the support of their partners. There is a juxtaposition in terms of gender. For fathers who only occasionally participate in caring work, the spaces and times involved can be relatively fixed; those who do not or cannot participate in caring may not readily appreciate the fluidity of time and space for mothers.[47] As Davies notes, 'housework is quite simply not answerable to male time'.[48] Sabine reported that when her husband cares for the children, he just cares for the children: 'He will do one thing at a time. He will mind the children and the house will be like a bomb hit it' (Sabine, focus group).

Housework is gendered and women do more housework than men and retain responsibility for organising it. Jean is the logistics manager in her home, but her husband will 'do his share' (Jean, interview). Jean attributes her husband's expectation that she should do the majority of work in the home to her reduced working hours. Kate, however, works full-time, as does her husband, yet she is the only one who does, or organises someone to do, housework. Kate has the material resources to buy in domestic support;

nevertheless management of the home is clearly Kate's responsibility. Many women find housework tedious and thankless and Yolanda and Amelia compared their structured time spent in work favourably to the 'process' time spent on housework and caring for others at home. Both work reduced hours, but both stated they would not give up paid work to stay at home. Despite their increased involvement in paid work, mothers remain responsible for doing an 'acceptable' amount of unpaid domestic work, because its performance is integral to being a 'good' wife and mother.[49]

Although everyone has twenty-four hours in a day, time is not distributed equally between men and women because women's domestic responsibilities define their time as a collective household resource subject to the demands of husbands and children, whereas men's time is more of an individual resource.[50] Thus men's time is perceived as having more value because more of it focuses on 'productive' labour.[51] Hence, men are entitled both to 'free time' and to the provision of household goods and services by women. In essence, men have more control over the use of their time but also some of women's time, even if 'working mothers' also spend time on productive labour.

Sayer argues that the time demands on parents have ratcheted upward.[52] The growth of dual-earner families means that the majority of mothers and fathers are spending time engaged in both paid work and unpaid work. Further, time pressures have expanded in both domains. Sayer, Cohen and Casper found that cultural attitudes have shifted to the point where most women and men desire and expect shared breadwinning and caregiving.[53] However, in this research, the desire and expectation of shared breadwinning and caregiving led to disappointment in reality for many women who reported being far more time poor and experiencing more time pressure than their partners, because breadwinning and caregiving are not equally shared.

Most women, whether working full-, part-time, or reduced hours maintained responsibility for the management of the home, and experienced gendered assumptions that they would. Unpaid work is not a gender-neutral bundle of chores that women perform but is instead a key aspect of the social production and reproduction of unequal power relations between women and men.[54] Women's partners were significant in the way women managed their time in the home. Some partners were involved in domestic arrangements and their partners' involvement did reduce pressure on women in terms of some household chores or some time caring for children. Partners' involvement did not lessen any woman's responsibility for managing the home.

Time for me

McGinnity and Russell found parenthood brings a reallocation of time for both men and women, leaving a more traditional division of labour in couples with children.[55] This is consistent with international gendered trends.[56] In essence, children are a 'gendered time constraint'[57] and having children increases women's unpaid workload far more than men's, regardless of women's paid working hours, with women in Ireland having one extra month of committed time per year.[58] Consequently, women have most committed time and less free time, which leads to greater time pressure, and lower life satisfaction:

> I think there is no time though, there is no time . . . Time for me doesn't exist. Time for me is time for everybody. I think it is impossible to get time, because I even think when did I try and get time, I'm thinking about them [the family]. So I don't know if there is time for me. Do you know? I don't know do you just give up on that and it's maybe it's easier just to give up on it than to actually try to work it in (Avril, focus group).

Many women, like Avril, complained of having no personal time for themselves. Forman offers a critique of the philosophical relationship between being and time, and notes that 'women do not only live in time (from birth to death), they also *give* time and that act makes a radical difference to being-in-the-world' (original emphasis).[59] Clearly Avril gives all her time to her husband and children: 'time for me is time for everybody' (Avril, focus group).

Even though Audrey described herself as having the 'career' in her home, nevertheless she retains responsibility for the management of the home and does not have the same access to personal time as her partner: 'I mean he would let everything to me on Saturdays and Sundays and he would just [leave it to me] and he does [leave it to me](.) He would take time out, I mean, he has personal time. He would take personal time' (Audrey, focus group). Audrey does not have the same access to personal time as her husband: 'I suppose I put everything I have into my family and then have very little time for outside it, for outside the family' (Audrey, interview). This is not a matter of choice, however, because Audrey's husband leaves 'everything' to Audrey at the weekends, reverting to traditional gender roles, even though she has the career Monday to Friday. While most people compromise leisure and family time due to demands of work, the compromises women make in their families tend to exceed those of their partners:

> [Fathers] can go away and do something for a few hours and not feel even remotely guilty . . . Like golf, they can play a game of golf, they can take all day Saturday, go for lunch, go for a few pints and then come home. And they're happy . . . I just don't feel they feel the same pressures and stresses (Brona, focus group).

However, with their participation in paid work, women, like men, have an expectation of personal time, while motherhood is predominantly concerned with relational time and giving time to others. It is the difficulty of integrating these times that makes women's lives so difficult: 'It's my whole life . . . there's nothing else. That it's just complete, because by the time I've done my days' work and come home, I'm just so exhausted. I don't really feel that I have any time for anything else' (Jane, interview).

Most women, like Avril and Jane, gave up on attempting to create time for themselves, while time doing housework is considered personal time by Florence: 'You just don't ever get time for you, so that's why I'm up till two in the morning, doing my ironing and watching telly, this is time out now, this is grand' (Florence, interview). Florence refers to time alone as time out, and she enjoys ironing at two in the morning, because it is the only time she has peace and quiet. Even if she is giving time to housework, she has time to herself where she is not tending to her children, her partner or her paid work.

In addition to childcare and housework, women also experience gendered expectations regarding caring for, as well as about, elderly parents. Both Anna and Jean visit their elderly mothers daily, as well as caring for their children, partners and doing housework: 'My mother is there on her own, so you're conscious that you have to call to her every day, I mean, because my father died about three years ago and she hasn't picked up outside that' (Anna, interview). Anna and Jean both work reduced hours, which Jean reckons is necessary in order for her to fulfil her obligations to her mother, as well as her children. Jean describes her role between the dependent generations: 'you are caught between parents and kids and you're in the middle trying to push, well not push, but support both sides of the sandwich' (Jean, interview). Supporting both their parents and their children is an emotional as well as a practical demand on women's time. However, women's participation in paid work under strict 'work' time, and the relational, processual nature of time at home, caring for dependent children and parents and doing housework, means women experience time pressure. The pressure to care for parents is gendered and women did not report their partners making the same efforts in relation to their own parents, but as daughters-in-law, some women reported that they were expected to support their partners' parents as well as their own. There are individual differences, of course. Some women's parents are a source of support, while other parents are more dependent and this creates additional emotional as well as time pressure for these women.

Delphy and Leonard[60] and Maushart[61] suggest that women perform less 'wifework' after the arrival of children. Many of the women in this study felt under pressure to fulfil their roles of mother and paid worker to the best of their ability which meant their relationships with their partners suffered:

> Well, at the end of the day, you have the kids, you have to go to work, you have to do the housework and then whatever time you have left for each other is very small. I end up falling asleep most nights, you're sitting down to watch the news and like half an hour later you're asleep. I've missed whatever I wanted to watch, and that's the time of the day you have to spend on each other like. We don't even have a conversation, you know. It's just the last bit of the barrel that's left (Jean, interview).

Relationships with their partners suffered because of the women's time poverty and this was also a concern for participants because, as Duncombe and Marsden[62] and Gatrell[63] also found, women felt responsible for the emotional stability of their marriages and were anxious to retain their marriages and partnerships as well as caring for their children and keeping up at work. Many women reported that the relationship with their partners suffered because of the gendered time poverty and pressure they experienced in combining motherhood with paid work:

> The worst is definitely, I think, you do compromise your relationships with your family, with your husband and with your

children. Especially the relationship with your husband as well, because you're just squeezing it in. Monday to Friday, you're just squeezing it in, you know, just a quick few words. Sometimes I wonder do we talk at all (Audrey, interview).

Time at home is given to childcare, housework and family relationships and many women manage time out of work with the same strict discipline of clock time at work. The time poverty of 'working mothers' ensures they have very little personal time and far less time for themselves than their partners:

> That many women work a second shift while their husbands work only one is deeply unfair. Our indignation obscures the fact that the difference between men and women is not that men work one shift and women two, but that women with jobs usually do not have the flexibility to decide what to do with that second shift, which is already committed.[64]

Discussions of the 'second shift' suggest that women's greater involvement in employment has simply added to their household work. However, Hochschild coined the phrase 'second shift' to describe the gender strategies in ten dual-earner households.[65] In reality, 'it is predominantly women who deal with Hochschild's third shift – noticing, understanding and coping with the emotional consequences of the compressed second shift'.[66] However, there are differences between women depending on the number of children, whether women work full- or part-time and the level of support from partners.

'Working mothers' and time

All women in this research experienced degrees of time pressure and time poverty. Many women found it difficult to reconcile gendered expectations both at work and at home and many women failed to combine motherhood with paid work in a satisfying way. Their individual coping strategies include better management, cutting back on employment demands through reduced working hours, multi-tasking and outsourcing housework. These strategies are not optimal, however, because they maintain the gendered order of caring.

Many women reduce their hours of work, work shifts, job share or work part-time in order to care for their children and to facilitate their children's social and cultural development. Women do not see this privilege as perpetuating gender inequalities for themselves by limiting their earning power, career prospects and maintaining them in a subordinate position in the workplace. Women who reduced their hours in paid work claimed to have achieved better balance between caring and working time, but at the expense of greater domestic responsibility and career compromise.

The time-impoverishment of 'working mothers' increases women's stress. Some try to shape their paths through time and space so as to realise particular aims and goals. But, for many, their mothering activities are taken for granted or restricted by the availability of time, resources and income; for others, their working activities are restricted by their domestic responsibilities. There are obvious differences in the life chances of participants, the ways women differentially use their time and differentially value time. Women with partners, women with professions and women with greater economic resources are privileged in that they have more choice in the ways they manage time. Benn[67] suggests material resources can ameliorate some of the difficulties of combining motherhood with paid work. However, material conditions did not reduce participants' frustration and exhaustion which came from attempting to spend time working and caring, in situations governed by quite different temporal values. A culture of time that values speed and efficiency combined with an intensifying work ethic that places higher priority on paid work rather than on family, means women's time budgets are stretched to the maximum, women sacrifice expectations of personal time, and women's individual solutions alone are unable to remedy their time poverty.

Many of the women in this study subscribe to the view that their better management of time is critical to combining motherhood with paid work, which maintains their time poverty and pressure as their own private issue to resolve. Women describe being time poor, rushed and busy because they attempt to provide the same level of care for their children as full-time stay-at-home mothers in the area. There is no absolute lack of time per se; it is the way time is socially constructed and ordered to fit gendered concepts of what motherhood and employment is and ought to be that influences the way women and men spend their time. The time pressure and time poverty of 'Working Mothers' is caused by and causes multiple intersecting inequalities for them at the intersection of gender and class with family, workplace and society. There are gendered pressures on women in paid work to spend time performing like 'ideal workers', unencumbered by caring responsibilities. There are gendered pressures on women in families to spend time caring for children, doing housework and spending time with their elderly parents and their partners. Consequently, all women experienced gendered inequalities in relation to demands on their time. Nilsen and Brannen suggest that life chances underpin the choices available to individuals, and stress the importance of class in terms of economic and political resources and prestige.[68] However, gender is probably the significant factor in determining one's life chances. As Nowotny notes, empirical studies of time in relation to gender have superseded those of time in respect of social class.[69] However, in this research, both class and gender influence the ways women merge and manage caring and working time.

Examining women's caringscapes demonstrates that families promote traditional gender hierarchies with women undertaking taking greater domestic responsibilities than their partners. In this research one partner is taking parental leave one day a week, another regularly collects children from school, and many women described their partners as 'helping'. Nevertheless the management of the home invariably fell to women. Although changes in families and workplaces are similar across industrialised countries, and there is legislation granting 'equality' and promoting work-life balance, generally 'working mothers' handle work and family time pressures without significant social or institutional support; their time budgets are stretched to the limit and women's time is 'time for everybody'.

CHAPTER 11

A new gender regime

That women find it difficult to reconcile work and family life is not surprising; that women tolerate the situation, blaming themselves and other women is remarkable. Having it all means doing it all and these accounts by 'working mothers' reveal they really are on a treadmill. As already noted, gender is probably the significant factor in determining one's life chances. Gender inequality is a system of oppression in its own right, but gender relations are intertwined in complex ways with other forms of social inequality. Gender, combined with motherhood and employment, demonstrates a new complex form of inequality for 'working mothers'. This intersectional analysis was significant in revealing the diversity and difference within the group of 'working mothers', which led to different degrees of privilege and penalty, and also revealed the ways that intersecting inequalities depend upon and mutually construct each other and work together to shape outcomes. The inequalities women experience are constructed as private troubles, and their privileges are constructed as the outcome of their freely made choices, which is why women appear to accept a situation which is patently unfair. 'Working mothers' occupy troubled subject positions[1] at the intersection of multiple intersecting inequalities. As Oakley argues, power operating through social values, customs and relations is experienced as the constant fracturing of personal identity by those who are powerless.[2] Women experience powerless responsibility, and because they are seduced by the illusion of choice, they do not see the operation of power, but accept their inequalities as personal troubles. These troubles are 'ignored, redescribed as enjoyment or justified as freely chosen, deserved, or inevitable'.[3]

The heroic efforts women make in combining motherhood with paid work, as if they are 'ideal workers' in the workplace and full-time-in-the-home mothers, reveals the difficulty and futility of making super-human efforts, because motherhood and employment are irreconcilable as currently constructed in Irish society. Whatever women do, the elusive 'right way' of combining motherhood with paid work will not be realised by women's efforts alone. By making significant efforts to sustain motherhood with paid work, women demonstrate they are acutely aware of the limitations on their freedom to be 'workers' and 'mothers' and many women resist and transfigure these categories in their daily enactment. Women are challenging traditional gender roles and all women describe their participation in paid work as well as their motherhood as important components in their reflexive biographies.

Current ideas about 'ideal mothers' and 'ideal workers', promoted in social institutions, are force fields operating to oppress women. These ideas are promoted in dominant discourses, taken up by institutions and by women themselves, revealing the depth and extent of the opposition to women's progress. Women are divided and conquered, because women are silenced and ignored. By privileging some women sometimes, enduring inequalities are created for all women.

This research reaches out from the experiences of women to reveal the ways dominant discourses conflict and compete, and are 'oriented to produce certain political outcomes'.[4] These outcomes are the multiple, complex inequalities 'working mothers' experience as well as the ways in which these inequalities are maintained as women's own individual problems to address in their own individual ways, thus maintaining women in subordinate roles in public and private spheres. The privatisation of the difficulties women experience allows partners, employers, society and the state to abdicate responsibility for gender equality, childcare and childminders.

This research considers the discursive and political construction of the social institutions of family, workplace and society. It draws attention away from the different identities of 'worker' and 'mother' and focuses more intently on the contextual processes and conditions in which women's representations of themselves as 'mothers' and 'workers' are allowed to be produced, governed and socially organised. Thus gender and class are processes which take on different meanings for individuals in family, workplace and society; discourse is the political process which gives meaning to 'mother' and 'worker' in different institutions and social locations.

Dominant discourses are productive as well as dominating and are interdependent and work together to create and maintain intersecting inequalities and privileges for 'working mothers'.

The Irish state has 'consistently prioritised the needs of the economy over social objectives',[5] and the state has favoured market forces to the detriment of social well-being.[6] In 2011, the President of Ireland, Michael D. Higgins, wrote: 'We need a discourse that is capable of handling all the connections between economy, society and the State. This cannot simply be a discourse for experts; it must be a publicly informed discourse with real participation.[7] We need a new discourse that values community, caring and equality for all.

According to Fairclough, changes in orders of discourse are a precondition for wider processes of social change.[8] In contemporary Ireland we need a discourse that supports a society, not just an economy, and we need social change which leads to an Irish society in which it is possible to engage in paid work and to parent without guilt or conflict, and where all parents and children are equally valued.

Gender regimes are interconnected systems, through which paid work is connected to unpaid work, state services and benefits are delivered to individuals or households, costs are allocated and time is shared between men and women within households and between households and employment.[9] In Ireland as elsewhere, changes in the male breadwinner model, with women's participation in paid work, have not been matched by changes in society, polity and economy to support gender equality. It can no longer be assumed that fatherhood means providing, particularly in times of austerity or after relationship breakdown. Policies for supporting unpaid care work are undeveloped compared with labour market activation measures. The most fundamental shift needs to occur in the way men, women and the state regard the centrally important issue of care and caring work. Pascall and Lewis argue that to achieve gender equality, a dual-earner/dual-carer model is required in which paid work and unpaid care work are equally valued and equally shared between men and women, and which are underpinned by social rights.[10]

The gender system has to change. By shifting the focus to power and to the gender system which creates and sustains this complex inequality, we can create a discourse of community, caring and equality for all, which will lead to a new gender regime. This regime will ensure equality for men and women across the five domains of paid work, care work, income, time and voice.

Paid work

Systems of inequality exist at the intersection of gender with paid work where women are either maintained in a subordinate position by reducing their commitment to paid work, or are required to behave as 'ideal workers'. Gender relations persist in the economy with women earning less than their male counterparts.[11] Class intersects with paid work to reveal women's limited employment options and limited discretion over time spent in paid work. At the intersection of class with household work, women with fewer resources are less able to buy in domestic supports, and because these women also have less discretion over their time spent in paid work, they experience more powerless responsibility, time pressure and guilt than other 'working mothers'. In Irish society, legislation has been enacted to provide employment equality, but as is evident in women's accounts, workplaces have not changed their shape or organisation to accommodate 'working mothers' and continue to promote the 'ideal worker', long-hours cultures that make combining paid work with motherhood very difficult. In Ireland changes in the polity with equality legislation have caused little corresponding change in employing organisations. The system produces women as 'ideal workers', who behave as 'ideal workers', i.e. men, adopting liberal-individualist attitudes, which perpetrate the gender order and position other women in structures of disadvantage.

Paid work is important to women's independence, whether women are in relationships or not. Gender equality in paid work means equal access to quality jobs with equality of labour market attachment. Equal pay legislation is already in place, but there is still a gender pay gap, vertical and horizontal segregation, and part-time workers are mainly women. To balance paid work with care work, men and women need equal access and involvement in paid work and care work. Women have entered the workforce in greater numbers, but gender equality is only available to a minority: those who have good resources, or have no caring responsibilities.

Recent census analysis reveals a growing number of younger couples in Ireland where the woman has the higher qualifications and higher occupational classification.[12] This means that for many couples, it is the woman who has higher earning power. This fundamentally changes the financial consequences of decisions to balance work and family following childbirth. Where women reduce their working hours, there are likely to be greater financial consequences for individual families and larger economy wide effects in terms of under utilised human capital. Furthermore, unemployment statistics suggest that women are now the main earners in many households in this age of austerity. This evidence points to the necessity of increasing the flexibility of working arrangements for fathers as well as mothers, so that economic impacts on careers can be less concentrated on women, and economic impacts of women's detachment from the workforce have less impact on families.

Denmark has a high degree of gender equality in the labour market, with seventy-nine per cent of mothers of children under six in employment. A significant contributing factor is that high numbers of men and women both work part-time, within the context of a shorter standard working week. Women work on average thirty-two hours per week, while men work an average of thirty-seven, compared to the thirty-eight and forty-four EU averages.[13] In Ireland the average working week is thirty-nine hours, excluding breaks (with breaks, this brings the average time spent at work to forty-six hours). However, the Organisation of Working Time Act 1997,[14] prohibits employees working more than an average of forty-eight hours in a week, excluding breaks. In a recent survey of 600 professionals in Ireland, sixty per cent of those surveyed reported that they worked in excess of forty hours every week.[15]

In these austere times, employers (including the state) are demanding more work for less compensation and employees are working longer hours for less pay. Currently, flexibility is the preserve of employers. However, if the working week was shortened, as in Denmark, this would generate employment for a greater number of people who would work fewer hours. If part-time employment was a right, not a privilege granted by few employers, more men and women would work fewer hours, increasing the overall employment rate, improving gender balance and encouraging balance between work and family life for men and women. This would bring greater gender equality in employment, emphasising equal access to jobs in quality and quantity, whereby both men and women would have a three-quarter job model, rather than men and some women having one job, and the majority of women having a half-job. This is what Pascall and Lewis call a 'two x three quarter earner model instead of one and a half'.[16] Shortening the working week and introducing entitlements to part-time work may seem radical, worker-centred measures, which employers would be expected to resist. However, it has been demonstrated in this research and elsewhere that increasing flexibility improves productivity.

Care work

A system of inequality exists at the intersection of gender with household work, where women demonstrate they undertake a greater proportion of domestic work than their partners, and retain responsibility for the management of the home, regardless of their time contribution to paid work. At the intersection of gender with culture, there is a system of inequality with the persistence of the gendered order of caring: this is maintained at the intersection of gender with the state, where women are charged with caring as a personal and social duty; in civil society with schools having an expectation of a full-time mother in the home and all childminders being women, performing work which is undervalued and under rewarded. To facilitate the women who are 'ideal workers', the system also produces childcare workers in hierarchical relationships to 'working mothers', which maintains gender systems and systems of inequality.

Children need to be seen as a public good, needing to be socially supported, to avoid non-parents' free-riding on parents,[17] through policies for parental leave, regulating working hours, and quality social care for children. Currently there is no statutory entitlement to paid paternity leave in Ireland and employers offer leave at their own discretion, with many not offering leave at all. The Early Years Strategy has recommended the introduction of two weeks' paid paternity leave around the birth of a child.[18] In Denmark, fathers are entitled to take up to two weeks paid leave after the birth of the child, and according to the European Platform for Investing in Children (EPIC),[19] nearly all fathers make use of paternity leave. According to a Eurobarometer survey, Danes are the happiest in Europe with their family life. Denmark has introduced many measures aimed at supporting families, including flexible working hours, universal childcare coverage, extensive leave entitlements and generous individual benefits.

Similar structural change could happen in Ireland, and the state could implement new policies in the areas of paternity leave, maternity leave and parental leave. The Early Years Strategy has recommended that Irish society must value and support parents/guardians, families and everyone who promotes the well-being, learning and development of young children.[20] Ways of working that are reasonable and flexible and which facilitate parents' involvement in care, would be one tangible way to value and support families.

Ireland has a shameful history regarding the welfare of children in its care.[21] Currently childcare is privatised and costly, education cutbacks are severe and only those with the resources can make significant investments in the care and education of their children. In contrast with other countries that regard children as a public good and care services as essential, with individual and societal benefits, Ireland regards children as the personal responsibility of families, not the state. The average financial cost of raising a child up to the age of eighteen has been estimated to be €200,000,[22] and raising a child to university completion can be as high as €250,000.[23] However, the investment parents make in time, domestic labour and emotion is also considerable. Some social analysts would assert that having children is a private decision made by rational individuals, who would only choose to do so if, costs notwithstanding, they deem it to be in their own interests. As a consequence, any costs associated with children should be wholly borne by parents.[24] This view is flawed. Parents who raise children are performing a public service, because their investment in children benefits society and the economy, and far exceeds the private benefit to their parents. Economic gains are reflected in the higher salaries that the children earn later in life, the greater economic contribution to society that these salaries tend to reflect, and the higher resulting tax payments, including those that contribute towards an increasing pension bill.[25] Following a review of international studies, Start Strong concluded that 'the economic argument alone is such that there is a strong and unambiguous case for government investment in children's early care and education in Ireland'.[26] Thus, the state has an obligation to contribute to the costs of caring for children, regarding childcare as a public good.

The notion of universalism in childcare provision has been called for by many social and voluntary organisations in Ireland,[27] who argue that universal access to quality and affordable childcare for all children provides social and economic benefits to society as a whole. Many Irish, EU and OECD reports recommend that the Irish state makes greater investment in early childhood care and education, because it is crucial for the future social, education and health development of children and also because it is a key economic consideration in that it facilitates parents, mainly mothers, to remain in and take up employment.[28] When compared to other EU and OECD countries, Ireland's public spending on childcare and early education is amongst the lowest in the OECD.[29] This means childcare costs in Ireland are prohibitive. The OECD estimates the childcare cost in Ireland is twenty-nine per cent of family net income, more than double the OECD average of thirteen per cent and the third most expensive behind the UK and Switzerland.[30] It is clear that the low levels of current provision in Ireland do not facilitate women combining work and family life and children have uneven access to childcare and education resources.

NESC in its model of the 'Developmental Welfare State' identifies childcare as one of an essential set of services which can play a significant role in achieving social cohesion, social inclusion and good economic performance. NESC recommends an approach to access – 'tailored universalism' – which is tailored to an individual's specific circumstances, including their ability to pay.[31] Denmark has such a system. Childcare provision includes family- and centre-based day care for children from six months to six years. Approximately seventy per cent of facilities are operated by public, community services with the remainder provided by independent, non-profit providers, thereby offering parents a choice of service. Fees are capped at twenty-five per cent of the running costs, with those on lower incomes using services free of charge or at reduced rates. This universal system ensures all children have equal access to the same quality care. In Ireland primary school begins at a younger age than in other countries. In Ireland, although education is not compulsory until age six, approximately forty per cent of four-year-olds and almost all five-year-olds are in publicly-funded provision in the infant classes of primary schools.[32] Children start school at age six in France and Germany, while in Denmark and Sweden, children start school at age seven.[33]

The Free Pre-School Year has reduced the cost in the year immediately prior to school entry (for three- to four-year-olds or four- to five-year-olds), but outside these age bands and weekly hours covered by these supports, most childcare receives no subsidy. OECD figures indicate that costs in Ireland as a proportion of family income are among the highest internationally, and for lone parents are the highest in the OECD.[34] For many families, particularly families on low incomes or experiencing poverty, the cost is a significant barrier to participation. A similar system of universal care to that available in Denmark, could be provided in Ireland, including a second year of the Aistear/Siolta pre-school curriculum, which is currently provided for one year.

The neo-liberal state, combined with individualism, has contributed to the competitive practices women engage in when developing educational, social and cultural capitals in their children. Families with better resources are better able to care for and educate their children. If the state treated all children equally and properly resourced education, children would be regarded as a public good. Removing the privatisation of rearing and caring for children would counteract the pressures on women, and all children would have the opportunity to develop equally. Properly resourcing education is also a necessary part of the care infrastructure, and would establish children as assets and investments for the future of the society and economy. Therefore, cuts to education budgets of previous years could be reversed, with the aim of public expenditure on education reaching thirteen per cent, similar to other EU and OECD countries.

After-school care is also seriously under-resourced and the state could provide subsidised, extended, out-of-school-hours care for five- to fourteen-year-olds. This could be delivered through the existing primary and secondary school infrastructure, which would make it accessible for all parents. Barnardos has also called for the development of a public subsidised model of ECCE which must also include after-school services, thus creating a comprehensive child-centred system, comparable to that of Scandinavian countries. Such a system would meet the dual purpose of being directly beneficial to the child but also enabling parents to re-enter or remain in the labour market.[35] With the introduction of a shorter working week and a statutory entitlement to part-time work, more carers would be employed in the system to provide this after school care for school-going children.

The teaching profession in Ireland is largely feminised, as teaching hours facilitate balancing work and family life. With the introduction of the shorter working week (the 2 x ¾ model), this would bring other workers' working time in line with teachers' current hours during the working week. Harmonising teaching hours with other occupations would attract men to teaching, which would in turn provide equality of access to quality jobs for both men and women.

Providing universal care and education for children, shortening the working week, and introducing a statutory entitlement to part-time working, as well as introducing paternity leave and enhancing parental leave provisions, would require the employment of more people, working shorter working weeks. The provision of after-school care would assist with the development of children's educational, social and cultural capital, thus eliminating the pressure on parents to engage in intense, competitive practices. The provision of universal childcare ensures all children's capitals are developed and facilitates all working parents to better balance work and home. These initiatives would ensure standardised universal education and care for all children, greater employment for more people for fewer hours each week, and better balance between working and caring for all 'working parents'.

Income

Women, as well as men, now tend to be seen as both primary carers and as individuals responsible for earning for themselves, their children and for their own pensions. Women need equal opportunities to earn, a fairer share of quality work and fair pensions. Caring work, predominantly performed by women, needs to be fairly rewarded and valued. Ireland's adoption of neo-liberal policies, combined with the rise of individualism has resulted in Ireland being among the developed world's most unequal societies. TASC found that Ireland is first in the EU-15 in terms of income inequality.[36] CORI claims that Ireland is characterised by a widening gap between rich and poor and that absolute inequality has increased.[37]

It seems extraordinary that the people who do the important work of caring for children and vulnerable others, are not recognised or rewarded in Irish social policy. Providing credits for women in the home who leave paid work to care for children, disabled, and older adults, and paying decent rates of pay to those who do caring work in the economy would indicate that caring work has value, regardless of whether done by family or by paid carers. Social insurance systems should recognise care work as a civic duty equally with paid employment, and recompense care with contributory benefits. In Ireland, the homemakers' credit, which was supposed to offset the inequality in pensions, because many women were forced to leave employment because of the marriage bar, was abandoned in 2012 due to expense.[38] This decision could be reversed and the homemakers credit reinstated, while women and men who leave paid work to care for children and vulnerable others could receive contributory benefits. These measures would recognise care as work in social policy.

In a review of the National Childminding Initiative (which was developed following the National Childcare Strategy Report) for Waterford City and County, Daly commented that 'an integrated, regulated and resourced childcare and education service (including childminding settings) is needed in order to ensure that services provided to children are safe, and are of high quality.[39] Similar to the professionalisation of nursing,[40] establishing recognised qualifications for childminding, associated with membership of a childminding professional body with which all childminders are required to register and engage in continuous professional development would be necessary. The current FETAC Level 5 Certificate in Childcare should be the recognised training programme for childminders and similar to nursing, the qualification should be a requirement to be admitted to the professional body. Regulation should be mandatory, similar to the Scottish system, whereby anybody who looks after one or more children under sixteen years for reward must register if they do so for more than two hours a day on six days or more a year.[41] Registration requirements should include personal references, Garda checks on the potential childminder and every other adult in their household, inspection of their home to ensure it is safe and suitable, and public liability insurance. Regular inspections of registered childminders ought to take place at least once every six months. Childminders who work in employing households could also be registered with the HSE, have Garda clearance and be insured. Professionalising and registering childminders would enhance childminders' professional standing while regulation would give families real choice for their children's early care and education, with regulated services available in both home-based and centre-based settings.

In this research, childminders were 'backstage actors', but accounts of 'working mothers' present a clear picture of the demand for safe, affordable childcare and the uneven supply and uneven treatment of childcare workers and children. As Lynch and Lyons argue 'To have good public services, including caring services, a state must invest in them'.[42] Childminders should be recognised and supported with training, education and support networks, and should be paid fairly for their efforts. Social Justice Ireland has long called for the state to increase Ireland's tax take in an equitable way that taxes all citizens in a proportionate manner. It has also called for reversing recent budget cuts which have disproportionately affected lower income earners and those who are dependent on welfare.[43] Childminders should only be required to pay tax on the portion of their earnings in excess of €18,000, which is the equivalent tax-free allowance of PAYE workers, and parents should receive tax relief on receipted childminding expenses with registered childminders.

Time

As this research has shown, caring time is gendered, with women performing more caring work and housework than men, so having less leisure time and greater time pressure and stress. Men's greater involvement in care in the home will de-gender and value caring work. Ways of increasing flexibility could include paid parental leave and apportioning parental leave in equal measure or in shared portions between fathers and mothers. Ireland could introduce a system, similar to the Icelandic model, which would encourage fathers' involvement in their children's care, and which would eliminate economic hardship for families who wish to take leave when their children are small. In Iceland, since 2000, nine months' paid parental leave has been granted to parents, apportioned with three months to the mother, three months to the father and three months' joint entitlements. This leave is paid at eighty per cent of the parents' previous wages, and could be used until the child is aged eighteen months. Following the economic crisis in 2008, the ceiling on payment was reduced to seventy-five per cent. However, since 2012 new legislation has been enacted with paid parental leave gradually being extended, so that by 2016, parents will be entitled to twelve months' paid parental leave, with five months to the mother, five to the father and two months of joint entitlement.[44] Parents who do not use their entitlement to parental leave forfeit it. Iceland resources paid parental leave with tax revenues. The Early Years Strategy has also recommended longer paid leave for parents, increasing incrementally each year. The aim is that paid parental leave would be available at the end of the present period of paid maternity leave, so that within five years, parents may avail of one year's paid leave after the birth of each child.[45] Apportioning this leave between parents, similar to the Icelandic model, would support and encourage fathers' involvement in their children's care.

In the public sector, a shorter-working-year scheme is available, which provides any civil servant the opportunity to take up to three continuous blocks of 2, 4, 6, 8, 10 or 13 weeks (to a maximum of thirteen weeks) unpaid leave for any reason at any time during the year. Staff may apply for more than one period in any year subject to a maximum of thirteen weeks in that year.[46] Staff may also apply for administrative arrangements, spreading their salary over the full year, to ensure they receive part of their basic salary during the leave period. Typically, the scheme is largely utilised by women, but this scheme could be extended to all workers.

Standardising the school day and the school calendar would also facilitate working parents to balance work and care. The current requirement of 183 days (thirty-six weeks) at primary level and 167 days (thirty-three weeks) at second level should be lengthened, similar to the UK, which has a school year of 195 days (thirty-nine weeks). This recommendation may, however, lengthen the teachers' working year. This recommendation reveals that contradictory effects can emanate from policy change. Those who are currently teaching, mainly women, may perceive a loss of privilege, as their working year would be longer. However, the purpose is not to reduce individual privilege, but to shift the focus from individualism to universalism and to make recommendations that improve the situation for all those who combine work and care. Teachers' perceived loss of privilege would be offset by the availability of universal care for all children, greater maternity, paternity and parental leave entitlements, and the availability of the shorter working year scheme.

Extending the shorter working year scheme to all employers, making mandatory a shorter working week and entitlement to part-time work, introducing paid paternity and parental leave, with parental leave apportioned between fathers and mothers, and providing universal child and after-school care, together with a longer school year, would support men and women in achieving a better balance of time working and caring.

Voice

This research reveals women's lack of awareness of the ways other women combine paid work with motherhood, which suggests, apart from mothers' websites,[47] there are no fora for debating and discussing issues regarding ways of combining working and mothering, or campaigning for better conditions for balancing work and care for families.

'Working mothers' are a silent majority, managing working and caring with little social support. This research suggests that women are too stretched in terms of time and other pressures to organise, and seek changes to social policy which would underpin, recognise and support caring work and facilitate better balance between men and women, caring and employment. Individualism and neo-liberal discourses have silenced individuals and effectively prevented collective action.

Moving forward requires changing the discourse. Motherhood discourses require women to sublimate their own needs to those of their children, and to develop children who are disciplined and high-achieving. Neo-liberalism and individualism discourses foster atomistic and individualistic behaviours in pursuit of independence and autonomy. We need a new discourse which values community, caring and equality and we need a new voice which demands this change.

There are many organisations that publicly campaign for gender equality, for care to be recognised in social policy and for income equality and social justice.[48] These organisations are doing important work in calling for social justice and equality, but they are not giving voice to the women who every day are affected by the lack of social policy that would support caring work for those in paid employment. This research demonstrates that women who combine motherhood with paid work are voiceless. The state's neo-liberal agenda, combined with individualism and an allegiance to traditional maternal roles, has created a society where women cannot voice the difficulties and inequalities they experience as these are constructed as personal failures. In fact, these are symptoms of the failure of the state. This research demonstrates the importance of empirical research with and for women, which demonstrates the extent of women's isolation and lack of voice.

Feminism and feminist discourses have received much criticism and for many women, feminism seems to have abandoned them, particularly once they become mothers. In reality, feminisms do seek equality for women, however much contemporary theorising has little relevance in women's daily lives. This research demonstrates the necessity of feminism. Despite small gains, women are far from achieving equality and the women in this research demonstrate how this complex inequality serves to divide, silence and conquer women. Currently women navigate their own routes between working and caring, attributing success to 'luck' and failure to their own poor choices. Caring is not simply the responsibility of each individual woman in each individual household. Caring is a public good and requires social support. Feminist writers have suggested that women need a voice for caring issues in formal, informal, national and international contexts.[49]

A feminist discourse of equality is needed more than ever now, one which promotes a balance of needs, and which regards children and childcare as public goods, regards workers as people and recognises that families need to see and spend time with each other. We also need structural changes in the areas of gender-equal parenting, valuing children, care and care workers. The only way something approximating equality will be achieved is through social policy, flexible employment practices and a public attitude that supports and rewards men's, as well as women's, involvement in care and caring work.

As citizens, we need to speak up, demand changes in social policy and a fair and just society for all our children and those who are vulnerable, as well as those who provide paid and unpaid care – carers, parents and guardians. Changing the discourse requires us to 'trouble women',[50] by asking them to consider their own discourses in order to highlight and avoid women participating in perpetuating further gender inequalities. Remaining silent is being complicit with the status quo.

Conclusion

It has been successfully demonstrated in Iceland and Denmark that it is possible to integrate employment and family life, that men as well as women are rejecting the 'ideal worker' model and desire to spend time caring as well as working, and that this can be achieved simultaneously with economic growth.

It will of course, be argued that the Irish state cannot implement any of these proposed measures leading to greater equality between men and women. It will be argued that the state cannot afford to reduce the working week, offer part-time employment, or fund parental and paternity leave. It will be argued that the cost of introducing universal childcare and a regulation system for childminders is too costly and too complex. It will be argued by employers that the administrative burden is too great to shorten the working week, extend the shorter-working-year scheme, and facilitate part-time employment. Employers will resist paternity and parental leave provisions. It will also be argued that the state cannot afford to reverse cuts to pensions and cuts to lone parents and other marginalised groups, invest in the childcare infrastructure and extend the school year. These arguments draw on neo-liberal ideals and reflect the values of those in positions of privilege.

Changing the way work is organised and structured requires a fundamental shift away from the traditional male breadwinner/female caregiver model. In reality families are more diverse, and many women are engaged in paid work outside the home. Families are currently combining working and caring in many different ways, but with little social support. In reality, the traditional model no longer reflects dominant practice, yet the myth and the imagery of mum, dad, two kids, the dog and a white picket fence persists in the popular imagination. It is high time this traditional, outdated image was abandoned.

Legal framework – employment equality in Ireland

1973: *The Civil Service (Employment and Married Women) Act 1973* was passed, which removed the marriage ban in the Civil Service, Local Authorities and Health Boards.

1974: *The Anti-Discrimination (Pay) Act* was passed, which guaranteed 'like pay' for 'like work' by the same or an associated employer.

1977: *The Employment Equality Act* was passed which resulted in the establishment of the Employment Equality Agency.

1994: *The Maternity Protection of Employees Act* was introduced, granting women maternity leave to have their babies, then fourteen weeks, a guarantee of their position at the same level on return from leave and state benefit for the period of the leave. Improvements to the provisions were introduced in 2000, increasing the leave to eighteen weeks, and in 2006, increasing the leave period to twenty six weeks, with an entitlement to a further sixteen consecutive weeks unpaid maternity leave beginning immediately after the end of the twenty-six weeks. Maternity benefit is paid by the state, and in 2013, this benefit became liable for income tax.

1981: *The Unfair Dismissals Act 1977* was amended to include maternity as an automatically unfair ground for dismissal.

1991: *The Child Care Act 1991* was introduced which was primarily focused on children in the care of the state. Until the 1991 Act was implemented, child care policy had been regulated by the 1908 Children Act. The 1991 Act provides the legislative basis for dealing with children in need of care and protection. One small section of the act (Part VII – Supervision of Pre-school services) deals with pre-school care and child minders.

1998: *The Parental Leave Act 1998* was introduced, and entitles employees to avail of fourteen weeks' unpaid leave from employment to enable them to care for their children aged under eight years. Under the Parental Leave Act, provision was also made for force majeure leave, which is three days paid leave in a five year period to enable employees to have leave from work to deal with family emergencies resulting from the injury or illness of certain family members. Since

8 March 2013 the amount of parental leave available amounts to a total of eighteen working weeks per child. Where an employee has more than one child, parental leave is limited to eighteen weeks in a twelve month period. This can be longer if the employer agrees. Both parents have an equal separate entitlement to parental leave.

1998: *The Employment Equality Act, 1998–2011* was introduced and outlaws discrimination in recruitment and promotion, pay, working conditions; training, dismissal and harassment including sexual harassment on the grounds of gender, marital status, age, disability, race, religion, sexual orientation, family status or membership of the travelling community. The provisions of the Act were improved and extended with the introduction of the Equal Status Acts 1998 and 2004 which outlaw discrimination outside the workplace, in particular in the provision of goods and services, selling, renting or leasing property and certain aspects of education.

2000: *The National Minimum Wage Act* was introduced, which guaranteed a minimum wage of €7.00 per hour. The provisions of the act were increased in 2005 to €7.65 per hour, and the rate was increased to €8.30 from 1 January 2007, and is €8.65 in 2014.

2001: *The Carer's Leave Act 2001* was introduced, granting leave to employees to provide full-time care for one relative. Leave period is a minimum of thirteen weeks and a maximum of 104 weeks. Employers can refuse to grant leave which is less than thirteen weeks in duration. Carer's leave from employment is unpaid but the Carer's Leave Act ensures that those who propose to avail of carer's leave will have their jobs kept open for them for the duration of the leave. A carer's benefit is payable by the state for those with sufficient PRSI contributions; alternatively a means-tested Carer's Allowance may be paid. Carer's leave is available regardless of whether the person qualifies for either payment.

Participant biographies (Interview)

(All names are pseudonyms)

AGATHA is married with two children aged seven and eleven years. Agatha works full-time as an international travel consultant, working thirty-two hours a week. Agatha's husband works full-time. Agatha is aged forty-one to forty-five years, and her husband and her sister provide childcare. Agatha participated in a focus group discussion, but not an interview.

AISLING is married with four children, aged two to nine years. Aisling works full-time as a teacher at post-leaving certificate-level, working thirty hours a week. Aisling is aged thirty-six to forty years, and she engages a childminder in the childminder's home. Her husband works full-time. Aisling participated in both a focus group discussion and an interview.

AMANDA is married with two children aged twelve and fourteen years. Amanda works as a clinic nurse manager, working full-time at thirty-nine hours a week. She is aged forty-one to forty-five years, and her childcare is provided by a childminder who comes to Amanda's home. Her husband works full-ime. Amanda participated in a focus group discussion and an interview.

AMELIA is married and has three children aged two to seven years, with a husband who works full-time on a shift pattern. Amelia works as a nurse, working part-time at twenty hours a week. Amelia is thirty-one to thirty-five years, and has a childminder who comes into Amelia's home. At the time of interview, Amelia had changed to working as a nurse in the private sector, part-time. Amelia participated in both a focus group discussion and an interview.

AMY is married with two children aged seven to ten years. Amy works part-time as a midwife. Amy is aged forty-one to forty-five years and at the time of the focus group she engaged a childminder in the childminder's home, but subsequently engaged a childminder who comes to Amy's home. Amy participated in both a focus group discussion and an interview.

ANASTASIA is married with two children aged ten years and eighteen years. Anastasia works part-time at twenty-nine hours a week, as a personal care assistant. Anastasia is aged forty-one to forty-five years and childcare is provided when necessary by Anastasia's husband and her sister. Her husband works full-time on a night shift. Anastasia participated in a focus group discussion, but not an interview.

ANGELA is married with three children who range from nine to fifteen years of age. Her husband works full-time. Angela works as a respite carer, working fourteen hours a week. These hours are irregular based on clients' needs. Angela is aged forty-one to forty-five years, and her childcare is provided by a neighbour. Angela participated in both a focus group discussion and an interview.

ANITA is married with two children, aged eleven and twelve years. Anita is aged forty-one to forty-five years. She works as a nurse, working part-time at fifteen hours a week and does not need childcare, as she works mornings when the children are in school. Anita's husband works full-time, and Anita participated in a focus group discussion, but not an interview.

ANNA is married with three children, aged four to eleven years. Anna works part-time as a civil servant, working eighteen hours a week. Anna is aged thirty-six to forty years, and engaged a childminder in the childminder's home at the time of the focus group. However, Anna subsequently changed her work pattern and eliminated child-minding altogether. Anna's husband works full-time. Anna participated in both a focus group discussion and an interview.

AUDREY is married and has three children aged between eight and fifteen years. Audrey works full-time as a director of nursing, and works thirty-nine hours a week. Audrey is aged forty-one to forty-five years, and her husband works full-time. Audrey participated in both a focus group discussion and an interview.

AVRIL is married and has five children aged from newborn to fifteen years. Avril works as a physiotherapist, working reduced hours at twenty-eight hours a week. Avril is aged thirty-six to forty years and engages a childminder in Avril's own home. Avril participated in both a focus group discussion and an interview.

BRONA is married with three children aged three to seven years. Brona works as a general operator in a manufacturing company, working full-time at thirty-six hours a week on a twelve-hour, three-shift pattern. Brona is aged thirty-six to forty years, and her childcare is provided by a childminder who comes to Brona's home. Her husband works full-time. Brona participated in both a focus group discussion and an interview.

CINDY is married with two children aged four and nine. Cindy works as a retail sales assistant, working twenty hours a week. She is aged thirty-six to forty years, and her childcare is provided by her parents who collect her children from primary school. Cindy participated in a focus group discussion, but not an interview.

COLLEEN was in the process of separating at the time of the focus group discussion. Colleen is aged thirty-six to forty years. Colleen has a seven-year-old child and works reduced hours as a quality specialist in a manufacturing company, working thirty-two hours a week. Colleen engaged a childminder in the childminder's home. Colleen participated in both a focus group discussion and an interview. At the time of the interview, Colleen had separated and had changed her childminding arrangements to an after-school club.

COLLETTE is married with two children aged one and seven years. Her husband works full time. Collette works full-time as a software manager, working thirty-eight hours a week. Collette is aged twenty-six to thirty years and engages a childminder in the childminder's home. Collette participated in a focus group discussion, but not an interview as she had moved away from the local area.

EITHNE is married with two children aged three and five years. Eithne works full-time, as a product development executive, working thirty-five hours a week. Her husband works full-time, working a shift pattern. Eithne is aged forty-one to forty-five years and uses a combination of crèche care and her husband. Eithne participated in both a focus group discussion and an interview.

FAYE is married with two children aged four and seven years. Faye works full-time, working forty-five hours a week as a company director. She is aged thirty-six to forty years. Faye engages a childminder four days a week, while Faye's husband takes parental leave one day a week to mind the children on the fifth day. Faye participated in both a focus group discussion and an interview.

FLORENCE is married with three children aged from one to ten years. Florence works part-time as a nurse, working two days a week. Florence is aged thirty-six to forty years and employs a child-minder who comes to Florence's home. Her husband works full-time. Florence participated in both a focus group discussion and an interview.

FREYA is married and has three children aged newborn to eight years. Freya is aged thirty-one to thirty-five years. Freya works full time as an accountant in a manufacturing company working thirty-eight hours a week. Freya engages an au pair for her older two children, while the baby attends a crèche. Freya's husband works full-time. Freya participated in a focus group discussion, but not an interview.

GINA is married with two children, aged three and six years. Gina is aged thirty-six to forty years. Gina works as a bank official and job shares, working one week on, one week off. During the week Gina is at work, her children are minded by a childminder, who comes to Gina's home. Gina's husband works full-time. Gina participated in both a focus group discussion and an interview.

GRACE is married with two children, aged five and nine years and a husband who works full-time. Grace works as an inspector for a statutory agency and is aged thirty-six to forty years. Grace worked full-time at the time of the focus group discussion, working thirty-nine hours a week, but had just negotiated reduced working hours. At the time of the interview, Grace had been working reduced hours for almost a year. Grace engages a childminder in the child-minder's home. Grace participated in both a focus group discussion and an interview.

JANE is divorced with one child, aged nine years. Jane works as an advertising manager, working full-time at thirty-six hours a week. Jane is aged thirty-six to forty years, and uses a combination of grandparents and a childminder in the childminder's home. Jane participated in both a focus group discussion and an interview.

JASMINE is married with two children, aged ten and thirteen years. Jasmine works full-time as a school principal, working thirty-plus hours a week. Jasmine is aged forty-one to forty-five years, and childcare is provided by a combination of after-school club and Jasmine's husband, who works a night shift. Jasmine participated in both a focus group discussion and an interview.

JEAN is married with three children aged five to nine years. Jean works as a chartered accountant with a manufacturing company, working reduced hours at thirty hours a week. Jean is aged thirty-six to forty years, and her childcare is provided by a combination of parents and childminder. Jean's older child is minded by her mother, while the younger two children go to a childminder in the childminder's home. Her husband works full-time. Jean participated in both a focus group discussion and an interview.

JOY is married and has three children aged three to eight years. Joy works part-time between eight and sixteen hours a week doing market research, which she does at evenings and weekends when her husband is available to mind the children. Joy is aged thirty-one to thirty-five years and her husband works full-time. Joy participated in both a focus group discussion and an interview. At the time of the interview, Joy had become pregnant with her fourth child.

JUNE is married with three children, aged one to eight years. June works part time as a midwife, working eighteen hours a week. June is aged thirty-six to forty years and engages a childminder in the childminder's home. June's husband works full-time and June participated in both a focus group discussion and an interview.

KATE is married with four children, aged six to twelve years. Kate works as a lecturer, working full-time at forty-plus hours a week. Kate is aged thirty-six to forty years and her childcare is provided by her sister. Her husband works full-time. Kate participated in both a focus group discussion and an interview.

SABINE was married at the time of the focus group discussion. Sabine is aged thirty-six to forty years and has two children, aged five and eight years. At the time of the focus group, Sabine worked part-time as an accounts assistant, working 17.5 hours a week and with parents-in-law providing childcare when necessary. Sabine participated in both a focus group discussion and an interview. By the time of the interview, Sabine had separated and her childcare was provided by an au pair. Sabine had also changed job to a full-time accounts assistant role in the private sector.

TAMSIN is divorced and remarried. She has one child aged twelve. Tamsin is aged thirty-six to forty years, and engages a childminder in the childminders' home. Tamsin works full-time as a shipping clerk, working thirty-nine hours a week. Tamsin's husband works full-time. Tamsin participated in both a focus group discussion and an interview.

YOLANDA is married with two children aged three and six years. Yolanda works as an accounts assistant, taking one day of parental leave a week. Yolanda is aged thirty-six to forty years and she engages a childminder for two days and her parents provide childcare for two days. Yolanda works thirty-two hours per week. Her husband works full-time. Yolanda participated in both a focus group discussion and an interview.

Bibliography

Abrams, R., *Three Shoes, One Sock and No Hairbrush; Everything You Need to Know about Having Your Second Child* (London: Cassell, 2001)
——, *Time and Social Theory* (Cambridge: Polity Press, 1990)
——, *Timewatch: The Social Analysis of Time* (Cambridge: Polity Press, 1995)
——, *Timescapes of Modernity. The Environment and Invisible Hazards* (London and New York: Routledge, 1998)
——, 'The Temporal Gaze: The Challenge for Social Theory in the Context of GM Food', *British Journal of Sociology* 51.1 (2000), pp. 125–142
——, *Time* (Cambridge, UK and Malden, MA: Polity, 2004)
Adkins, L., *Revisions: Gender and Sexuality in Late Modernity* (Buckingham: Open University Press, 2002)
Anthias, F., 'Theorizing identity, difference and social divisions' in M. O'Brien, S. Penna and C. Hay (eds), *Theorizing Modernity: Reflexivity, Environment and Identity in Giddens' Social Theory* (London: Longman, 1999), pp. 156–178
Archer, M.S., *Structure, Agency and the Internal Conversation* (Cambridge: Cambridge University Press, 2004)
Armstrong, A., *Foucault and Feminism* (online: http://www.iep.utm.edu/f/foucfem.htm, 2003) [accessed 28/04/05]
Ashcraft, K., 'Managing Maternity Leave: A Qualitative Analysis of Temporary Executive Succession', *Administrative Science Quarterly* 44 (June 1999), pp. 240–280
Asher, R., *Shattered: Modern Motherhood and the Illusion of Equality* (London: Random House, 2011)
Ask about Money – thread: 'Paying somebody cash' (online:http://www.askaboutmoney.com/showthread.php?t=183663, 2012)
——, thread: 'Childminding and Social Welfare Payments' (online: http://www.askaboutmoney.com/showthread.php?t=175168, 2013)
Bacik, I., *Kicking and Screaming: Dragging Ireland into the 21st Century* (Dublin: The O'Brien Press, 2004)
Badgett, M., Lee, V. and Folbre, N., 'Assigning Care: Gender Norms and Economic Outcomes', *International Labour Review* 138.3 (1999), pp. 311–326
Badinter, E., *The Conflict: How Modern Motherhood Undermines the Status of Women* (New York: Henry Holt, 2011)

Baker, J., Lynch, K., Cantillon, S. and Walsh, J (eds), *Equality: From Theory to Action* (London: Palgrave Macmillan, 2004)

Barker, P. and Monks, K., *Career Progression of Chartered Accountants* (Dublin: Dublin City Business School, 1994)

Barnardos, *Analysis of Budget 2012 from a Children and Families Perspective* (online: http://www.barnardos.ie/assets/files/Advocacy/Analysis%20of%20Budget%202012%20from%20a%20Children%20and%20Families%20Perspective.pdf)

——, *Childrens' Budget 2013*, (online: http://www.barnardos.ie/assets/files/Advocacy/2013ChildrensBudget.pdf

Barry, U., *Lifting the Lid* (Dublin: Attic Press, 1986)

——, 'Changing Economic and Social Worlds of Irish Women' in U. Barry (ed.), *Where Are We Now?: New Feminist Perspectives on Women in Contemporary Ireland* (Dublin: TASC at New Island, 2008), pp. 1–29

Bateson, M.C., *Composing a Life* (New York: Grove Press, 1989)

Bauman, Z., *Thinking Sociologically* (Oxford: Blackwell, 1990)

——, *Liquid Modernity* (Cambridge: Polity Press, 2000)

Beck, U., *Risk Society: Towards a New Modernity* (London: Sage, 1992)

——, 'The Reinvention of Politics: Towards a Theory of Reflexive Modernization' in U. Beck, A. Giddens and S. Lash (eds), *Reflexive Modernization: Politics, Tradition and Aesthetics in the Modern Social Order* (Cambridge: Polity Press, 1994), pp. 1–55

Beck, U. and Beck-Gernsheim, E., *Individualization* (London: Sage, 2001)

Becker, G., *A Treatise on the Family* (Cambridge, MA: Harvard University Press, 1991)

Beck-Gernsheim, E., *Reinventing the Family: In Search of New Lifestyles* (Cambridge: Polity Press, 2002)

Beechley, V and Perkins, T., *A Matter of Hours: Women, Part Time Work and the Labour Market* (Oxford: Polity Press, 1997)

Benn, M., *Madonna and Child: Towards a New Politics of Motherhood* (London: Jonathan Cape, 1998)

Bennett, A., *Popular Music and Youth Culture* (Basingstoke: Macmillan, 2000)

Bennett, J., 'ECEC financing in Ireland', paper presented at the *'A Decade of Reflection', Early Childhood Education and Care in Ireland 1996–2006* (Dublin: DIT, 2006)

Bennetts, L., *The Feminine Mistake: Are We Giving Up Too Much?* (New York: Hyperion, 2007)

Berk, S.F., *The Gender Factory: the Apportionment of Work in American Households* (New York: Plenum Press, 1985)

Berlant, L., *The Queen of America Goes to Washington City: Essays on Sex and Citizenship* (Durham NC: Duke University Press, 1997)

Bernard, J., *The Future of Marriage* (London: Souvenir Press, 1973)

Best Place to Work Institute, *Mission and Values* (online: www.greatplacetowork.ie/gptw/mission.php, 2008)

Bianchi, S., Milkie, M., Sayer, L. and Robinson, J., 'Is Anyone Doing the Housework? Trends in the Gender Division of Household Labour', *Social Forces* 79 (2000), pp. 191–228

Biddulph, S., *Raising Babies: Why Your Love is Best: Should Under 3s Go to Nursery?* (London: Harper Thorsons, 2006)

Bjornberg, U., 'Parenting in transition: an introduction and summary' in U. Bjornberg (ed.), *European Parents in the 1990s: Contradictions and Comparisons* (New Brunswick: Transaction Publishers, 1992), pp. 1–41

Blackmore, J., *Troubling Women: Feminism, Leadership and Educational Change* (UK: Open University Press, 1999)

Blair-Loy, M., 'Cultural constructions of family schemas: The case of women finance executives', *Gender and Society* 15 (2001), pp. 687–709

——, *Competing Devotions: Career and Family Among Women Executives* (Harvard: Harvard University Press, 2003)

Boards.ie, thread 'How much to pay a childminder?' (online: http://www.boards.ie/vbulletin/showthread.php?p=61254920, 2013)

Boh, K., 'European family life patterns – a reappraisal' in K. Boh, M. Bak, C. Clason, M Pankratova, J., Qvortrup, G.B. Sgritta and K. Waerness (eds), *Changing Patterns of European Family Life: A Comparative Analysis of Fourteen European Countries* (London: Routledge, 1989), pp. 265–298

Boniolla-Silva, E., 'Rethinking racism: toward a structural interpretation', *American Sociological Review* 62.3 (1997), pp. 465–480

Bordo, S., *Unbearable Weight: Feminism, Western Culture, and the Body* (Berkeley: University of California Press, 1993)

Boucher, G. and Collins, G., 'Having one's cake and being eaten too: Irish Neoliberalcorporatism', *Review of Social Economy*, vol. lxi.3 (2003), pp. 295–316

Bourdieu, P., *Outline of a Theory of Practice*, translated by R. Nice (Cambridge and New York: Cambridge University Press, 1977)

——, *Distinctions: A Social Critique of the Judgment of Taste*, translated by R. Nice (Cambridge MA: Harvard University Press, 1984)

——, *Masculine Domination*, translated by R. Nice (Cambridge: Polity Press, 2001)

Bourdieu, P. and Wacquant, L., *An Invitation to Reflexive Sociology* (Cambridge: Polity, 2002)

Brah, A., *Cartographies of Diaspora: Contesting Identities* (London: Routledge, 1996)

Brah, A. and Phoenix, A., 'Ain't I a Woman?: Revisiting Intersectionality', *Journal of International Women's Studies* 5.3 (2004), pp. 75–87

Brines, J., 'Economic Dependency, Gender, and the Division of Labor at Home', *American Journal of Sociology* 100.3 (1994), pp. 652–688

Broom, G. and Dozier, D., *Using Research in Public Relations: Application to Programme Management* (New Jersey: Prentice Hall, 1990)

Bubeck, D.E., *Care, Gender and Justice* (Oxford: Oxford University Press, 1995)

Buchner, P., 'Growing up in the 1980s: Changes in the Social Biography of Childhood in the FRG' in L. Chisholm, P. Buchner, H.H. Kruger and P. Brown (eds), *Childhood, Youth and Social Change: A Comparative Perspective* (London: Falmer Press, 1990), pp. 941–958

Buxton, J., *Ending the Mother War: Starting the Workplace Revolution* (London: Macmillan, 1998)

Buzzanell, P. and Liu, M., 'It's "give and take": maternity leave as a conflict management process', *Human Relations* 60 (2007), pp. 383–495

Cantillon, S., Corrigan, C., Kirby, P. and O'Flynn, J. (eds), *Rich and Poor: Perspectives on Tackling Inequality in Ireland* (Dublin: Oak Tree Press, 2001)

Chartered Institute of Personnel and Development. *Flexibility Vital for Workplace Productivity* (online: www.cipd.co.uk/ireland, 2009)

Chira, S., *A Mother's Place: Choosing Work and Family without Guilt or Blame* (New York: Harper Perennial, 1998)

Chodorow, N., *The Reproduction of Mothering: Psychoanalysis and the Sociology of Gender* (Berkley and Los Angeles: University of California Press, 1978)

Citizens Information Board, *Income Tax Bands* (online: http://www. citizensinformation.ie.http://www.citizensinformation.ie/en/money_and_tax/tax/income_tax/how_your_tax_is_calculated.html, 2014)

Coakley, A., 'Gendered Citizenship: The Social Construction of Mothers in Ireland' in A. Byrne and M. Leonard (eds), *Women and Irish Society: A Sociological Reader* (Belfast : Beyond the Pale, 1997), pp. 181–195

——, *Mothers, Welfare and Labour Market Activation*, Working Paper 05/04 (Dublin: Combat Poverty Agency, 2005)

Cockburn, C., 'Resisting Equal Opportunities' in S. Jackson and S. Scott (eds), *Gender: A Sociological Reader* (London and New York: Routledge, 2002), pp. 180–191

Cohen, L., Manion, L. and Morrison, K., *Research Methods in Education*, 5th edition (London: Routledge-Falmer: 2000)

Cole, E.R., 'Intersectionality and Research in Psychology', *American Psychologist* 6.3 (2009), pp. 170–180

Collins, G. and Wickham, J., *What Childcare Crisis? Irish Mothers Entering the Labour Force.* ERC Labour Market Observatory (Dublin: Trinity College, 2001)

Collins, P., Hill *Fighting Words: Black Women and the Search for Justice* (Minneapolis: University of Minnesota Press, 1998)

——, *Black Feminist Thought: Knowledge, Consciousness and the Politics of Empowerment*, 2nd edition (New York: Routledge, 2000)

Coltrane, S., 'Research on Household Labor: Modeling and Measuring the Social Embeddedness of Routine Family Work', *Journal of Marriage and the Family* 62.4 (2000), pp. 1208–1233

Combat Poverty Agency, *Submission to NESF of Improving the Delivery and Quality of Public Services* (Dublin: Combat Poverty Agency, 2006)

——, *Developing a Local Anti-Poverty and Social Inclusion Strategy: a Guide* (Dublin: Combat Poverty Agency, 2008)

Connell, R.W., *Gender and Power: Society, the Person and Sexual Politics* (Cambridge: Polity Press, 1987)

——, *Masculinities* (Cambridge: Polity Press, 1995)

——, 'Making Gendered People' in M. Marx Ferree, J. Lorber and B. Hess (eds), *Revisioning Gender* (London: Sage, 1999), pp. 449–471

Conner, L., *Wedlocked Women* (London: Feminist Books Ltd, 1974)

Connolly, L. and O'Toole, T., *Documenting Irish Feminisms: The Second Wave* (Dublin: Woodfield Press, 2005)

Cooper, P., Diamond, I. and High, S., 'Choosing and using contraceptives: Integrating qualitative and quantitative methods in family planning', *Journal of the Market Research Society* 35(4) (1993), pp. 325–339

CORI, *Income Distribution: Pre-budget Submission* (Dublin: CORI and Dominican Publications, 2004)

Council of the European Union, *Council Conclusions on the European Pact for Gender Equality for the Period 2011–2020* (3073th Employment, Social Policy, Health and Consumer Affairs Council meeting Brussels, 7 March 2011)

Coveney, E., Murphy-Lawless, J. and Sheridan, S., *Women, Work and Family Responsibilities* (Dublin: Larkin Unemployed Centre, 1998)

Coward, R., *Our Treacherous Hearts: Why Women Let Men Get Their way* (London: Faber and Faber, 1992)

Cradden, J., 'Raising children can be extremely expensive' 10/02/2009 (online: http://www.independent.ie/business/personal-finance/ latest-news/raising-children-can-be-extremely-expensive-26514758.html.)

Crenshaw, K.W., 'Demarginalizing the Intersection of Race and Sex: A Black Feminist Critique of Antidiscrimination Doctrine, Feminist Theory and Antiracist Politics', *University of Chicago Legal Forum* 139 (1989), pp. 139–167

——, 'Mapping the margins: intersectionality, identity politics and violence against women of colour', *Standford Law Review* 43.6 (1991), pp. 1241–1299

——, 'Mapping the margins: intersectionality, identity politics and violence against women of color' in K. Crenshaw, N. Gotanda, G. Peller and K. Thomas (eds), *Critical Race Theory: The Key Writings That Informed the Movement* (New York: New York Press, 1995), pp. 357–383

Crittenden, A., *The Price of Motherhood: Why the Most Important Job in the World is Still the Least Valued* (New York: Henry Holt, 2001)

Crompton, R., *Employment and the Family: The Reconfiguration of Work and Family Life in Contemporary Societies* (Cambridge: Cambridge University Press, 2006)

CSO, *Socio Economic Groupings, Census of Population 1996* (Cork: Central Statistics Office, 1996)

——, *Quarterly National Household Survey Childcare Fourth Quarter 2002* (online: http://www.cso.ie/en/media/csoie/releasespublications/ documents/labourmarket/2002/qnhs_moduleonchildcareqtr 42002.pdf. 2003)

——, *Census of Population 2006* (Cork: Central Statistics Office, 2006)

——, *Census 2006. Volume 8: Occupations.* (online: http://www.cso.ie/en/ media/csoie/census/census2006results/volume8/volume_8_occu pations_entire_volume.pdf. 2006).

——, *Quarterly National Household Survey Childcare Quarter 4 2007* (online:

http://www.cso.ie/en/media/csoie/releasespublications/docu ments/labourmarket/2007/childcareq42007.pdf

——, *Quarterly National Household Survey, Q1 2009: Married Women's Participation Rates* (online: http://www.cso.ie/en/media/csoie/ releasespublications/documents/labourmarket/2009/qnhs_q12 009.pdf).

——, *Women and Men in Ireland 2009* (Cork: Central Statistics Office, 2010)

——, *Women and Men in Ireland 2011* (Cork: Central Statistics Office, 2012)

——, *Statistical Yearbook of Ireland 2013* (Cork: CSO, 2014)

——, *Quarterly National Household Survey, Parental Involvement in Children's Education Q2 2012* (Cork, Central Statistics Office, 2014)

Cusk, R., *A Life's Work: On Becoming a Mother* (London: Harper Collins, 2001)

Daly, M. (ed.), *Care Work: The Quest for Security* (Geneva: International Labour Office, 2001)

——, *Families and Family Life in Ireland: Challenges for the Future.* Report of the Public Consultation Fora (Dublin: Department of Social and Family Affairs, 2004)

——, *An Evaluation of the Impact of the National Childminding Initiative on the Quality of Childminding in Waterford City and County* (Waterford City and County Childcare Committees and HSE South, 2010)

Daly, M. and Rake, K., *Gender and the Welfare State: Care, Work and Welfare in Europe and the USA* (London: Polity, 2003)

Davies, B., 'The concept of agency: a feminist poststructuralist analysis', *Social Analysis* 300 (1991), pp. 42–53

Davies, K., *Women, Time and the Weaving of the Strands of Everyday Life* (Aldershot, England: Gower, 1990)

Delphy, C. and Leonard, D., *Familiar Exploitation: A New Analysis of Marriage in Contemporary Western Societies* (Oxford: Polity Press and Blackwell Publishers, 1992)

Department of Social Protection, *Subsidised after-school child care scheme* (online: http://www.welfare.ie/en/pressoffice/pdf/SW135, 2013)

Devine, D., Nic Ghiolla Phádraig, M. and Deegan, J., *Time for Children – Time for Change? Children's Rights and Welfare in Ireland During a Period of Economic Growth* (Dublin: Report to The COST Network, 2004)

Dhamoon, R., 'Considerations in Mainstreaming Intersectionality as an Analytic Approach', paper delivered at 2008 Annual Meeting of the Western Political Science Association, San Diego (20–22 March 2008)

Dietz, M.G., 'Citizenship with a Feminist Face: The Problem with Maternal Thinking', *Political Theory* 13.1 (1985), pp. 19–39

Dillaway, H. and Paré, E., 'Locating Mothers: How cultural debates about stay-at-home versus working mothers define women and home', *Journal of Family Issue* 29.4 (2008), pp. 437–464

DiQuinzio, P., *The Impossibility of Mothering: Feminism, Individualism and the Problem of Mothering* (New York and London: Routledge, 1999)

Douglas, S. and Michaels, M., *The Idealization of Motherhood and How it has Undermined All Women* (New York and London: Free Press, 2004)

Drew, E., 'Part-Time Working in Ireland: Meeting the Flexibility Needs of

Women Workers or Employers?' *Canadian Journal of Irish Studies* 18.1 (1992), pp. 95–109

Drew, E and Daverth, G., Living to Work . . . or Working to Live? The Role of Managers in Creating Work-life balance in Ireland , Dublin, Irish Congress of Trade Unions, January, 2009, 1(27) (online: http://www.ictu.ie/download/pdf/20090113104912.pdf)

Duncan, P., 'Most Primary Pupils get homework help', *The Irish Times* (Friday 3 January 2014)

Duncan, S., *Mothers, Care and Employment: Values and Theories.* Working Paper No. 1 (CAVA and University of Bradford. London: ESRC, 2003)

——, 'Mothering, Class and Rationality', *The Sociological Review* 53.2 (2005), pp. 50–76

Duncan, S. and Edwards, R., *Lone Mothers, Paid Work and Gendered Moral Rationalities* (Houndsmill: Macmillan Press,1999)

Duncombe, J. and Marsden, D., 'Whose Orgasm is this Anyway? "Sex Work" in Long-term Heterosexual couple relationships' in S. Jackson and S. Scott (eds), *Gender: a Sociological Reader* (London: Routledge, 2002), pp. 231–237

Dyck, I., 'Integrating Home and Wage Workplace: Women's Daily Lives in a Canadian suburb', *The Canadian Geographer* 33, Winter (1989), pp. 329–341

Eagly, A. and Wood, W., 'The origins of sex differences in human behaviour: Evolved dispositions versus social roles', *American Psychologist* 54.6 (1999), pp. 408–423

EAPN, *Ireland Benchmarking Paper on Childcare* (online: http://www.eapn.ie/eapn/wp-content/uploads/2009/10/childcare-benchmarking-paper.pdf, 2007)

Earle, S. and Letherby, G., 'Conceiving Time? Women who do or do not conceive', *Sociology of Health and Illness* 29.2. (2007), pp. 233–250

Early Childhood Ireland, *Early Childhood Ireland Salary Survey 2012* (online: http://www.earlychildhoodireland.ie/policy-advocacy-and-research/surveys/salary-survey-2012/ 2012)

Ehrenreich. B., *Fear of Falling: The Inner Life of the Middle Class* (New York: Perennial,1990)

Ehrenreich, B. and Hochschild, A., *Global Woman: Nannies, Maids, and Sex Workers in the New Economy* (New York: Henry Holt, 2003).

Eisenstein, Z., *The Radical Future of Liberal Feminism* (Boston: Northeastern University Press, 1993)

Emirbayer, M., 'Manifest for a Relational Sociology', *The American Journal of Sociology* 10.3 (1987), pp. 281–317

Enright, A., *Making Babies: Stumbling into Motherhood* (London: Jonathan Cape, 2004)

Ermath, E., 'The solitude of women and social time' in E. Forman and C. Sowton (eds), *Taking our Time: Feminist Perspectives on Temporality* (Oxford: Pergamon Press, 1989), pp. 37–46

Esping-Andersen, G., *The Three Worlds of Welfare Capitalism* (Cambridge: Polity Press & Princeton: Princeton University Press, 1990)

——, *The Social Foundations of Postindustrial Economies* (Oxford University Press, 1999)

European Anti-Poverty Network, *Access to Affordable Childcare for Low Income Families* November 2007 (online: http://www.eapn.ie/eapn/wp-content/uploads/2009/10/access-to-affordable-childcare-for-low-income-families.pdf, 2007)

European Commission, *Rationale of Motherhood Choices: Influence of Employment Conditions and Public Policies* (Brussels: European Commission, 2004)

European Community Household Panel, *Ireland Wave, Irish Social Science Data Archive* (online: www.ucd.ie/issda/dataset. 2001)

European Platform for Investing in Children, Denmark: Towards ideal conditions for balancing family and work (online: http://europa.eu/epic/countries/Denmark/index_en.htm 2013)

Fairclough, N., 'Critical Discourse Analysis', *Marges Linguistiques* 9 (2005), pp. 76–94

Family Support Unit, *Government Discussion Paper: Proposals for Supporting Lone Parents* (Dublin: Department of Social and Family Affairs, 2006)

Farough, S.D., 'Believing is Seeing: the matrix of vision and white masculinities', *Journal of Contemporary Ethnography* 35.1 (2006), pp. 51–83

Fellows, M.L. and Razack, S., 'The Race to Innocence: Confronting Hierarchical Relations among Women', *Journal of Gender, Race and Justice* 1.2 (1998), pp. 335–352

Felski, R., *The Gender of Modernity* (Cambridge MA: Harvard University Press, 1995)

Fennell, N. and Arnold, M., *Irish Women Agenda for Practical Action: A Fair Deal for Women, December 1982–1987, Four Years of Achievement.* Department of Women's Affairs and Family Law Reform (Dublin: Government Publications, 1987)

Ferguson, J., 'The uses of Neo-Liberalism', *Antipode* 41, S1. (2009), pp. 166–184

Fernandes, L., *Producing Workers: the Politics of Gender, Class and Culture in the Calcutta Jute Mills* (Philadelphia: University of Pennsylvania Press, 1997)

Ferree, M. Marx, 'Introduction' in M. Marx Ferree and A.M. Tripp (eds), *Globalization and Feminism: Opportunities and Obstacles for Activism in the Global Arena* (New York: New York University Press, 2006), pp. 4–23

——, 'Inequality, Intersectionality and the Politics of Discourse: Framing Feminist Alliances' in E. Lombardo, P. Meier, M. Verloo (eds), *The Discursive Politics of Gender Equality: Stretching, Bending and Policy-Making* (New York: Routledge, 2009), pp. 84–101

Figes, K., *Life after Birth* (London: Penguin, 1998)

——, 'A Distress Not to be Borne', *The Guardian* (24 June 2002)

Finch, J. and Groves, D., *A Labour of Love: Women, Work and Caring* (London: Routledge, 1983)

Fine Davis, M., 'Fathers and Mothers: Dilemmas of the Work Life Balance',

Work Life Balance Conference Proceedings (University of Dublin, Trinity College, 2002), pp. 11–13

——, *Childcare in Ireland Today*. Social Attitude and Policy Research Group (Dublin: Trinity College, 2007)

Flax, J., 'What is the subject? Review Essay on Psychoanalysis and Feminism in Postcolonial Time', *Signs* 29(3) (2004), pp. 905–923

Folbre, N., *Who Pays for the Kids?: Gender and the Structures of Constraint* (London: Routledge, 1994)

——, 'A theory of the misallocation of time' in N. Folbre and M. Bittman (eds), *Family Time: the Social Organisation of Care* (New York: Routledge, 2004), pp. 7–24

Folbre, N. and Nelson, J.A., 'For love or money – or both?' *Journal of Economic Perspectives* 14.4 (2000), pp. 123–140

Forman, F., 'Feminizing Time: An Introduction' in E. Forman and C. Sowton (eds), *Taking our Time: Feminist Perspectives on Temporality* (Oxford: Pergamon Press, 1989), pp. 1–9

Foucault, M., *Discipline and Punish: the Birth of the Prison*, translated by A. Sheridan (New York: Pantheon Books, 1977)

——, *Power/Knowledge: Selected Interviews and Other Writings, 1972–1977* (Brighton: Harvester, 1980)

——, *The History of Sexuality, vol. I* (Harmondsworth: Penguin, 1981)

——, 'The subject and power', *Critical Inquiry* 8.4 (1982), pp. 777–795

——, *Politics, Philosophy, Culture: Interviews and Other Writings 1977–1984* (New York: Routledge, 1990)

Franklin, S., Lury, C. and Stacey, J., 'Units of Genealogy' in S. Franklin, C. Lury and J. Stacey (eds), *Global Culture, Global Nature* (London: Sage, 2000), pp. 68–93

Fraser, N. and Gordon, L., 'A Genealogy of "Dependency": Tracing a Keyword of the U.S. Welfare State' in N. Fraser (ed.), *Justice Interruptus* (New York: Routledge, 1997), pp. 121–149

Freund, P. and Maguire, M., *Health, Illness and the Social Body: A Critical Introduction*, 3rd edition (London: Prentice Hall, 1999)

Friedman, M., *Capitalism and Freedom* (Chicago: University of Chicago Press, 1962)

——, *Free to Choose* (New York: Harcourt Brace Jovanovich, 1980)

Garey, A., 'Constructing motherhood on the night shift: "Working mothers" as "stay-at-home moms" in K.V. Hansen and A.I. Garey (eds), *Families in the U.S.: Kinship and Domestic Policies* (Philadelphia: Temple University Press, 1998), pp. 709–726

Garvey, E., Murphy, E. and Osikoya, P., *Estimates of the Cost of a Child in Ireland* (Dublin: Combat Poverty Agency, Working Paper Series 11/0, August 2011)

Gatrell, C., *Hard Labour: The Sociology of Parenthood* (Berkshire: Open University Press, 2005)

——, 'Managing the Maternal Body: A Comprehensive Review and Transdisciplinary Analysis', *International Journal of Management Reviews* 13 (2011), pp. 97–112

——, 'Maternal Body work: How Women Managers and professionals negotiate pregnancy and new motherhood at work', *Human Relations* 66.5 (2013), pp. 621–664

Gelles, R., *Contemporary Families: A Sociological Review* (Thousand Oaks, California: Sage, 1995)

Giddens, A., *The Constitution of Society: Outline of the Theory of Structuration* (Cambridge: Polity Press, 1984)

——, *The Consequences of Modernity* (Cambridge: Polity Press, 1990)

——, *Modernity and Self-Identity: Self and Society in the Late Modern Age* (Cambridge: Polity Press, 1991)

——, 'Foreword' in C. Hakim *Work-Lifestyle Choices in the 21st Century* (Oxford : Oxford University Press, 2000), pp. i–xiii

Gill, R.T. and Gill, T.G., 'A New Plan for the Family', *Public Interest* 111 (Spring 1993), pp. 86–94

Gilligan, C. Hearing the difference: theorizing connection', *Hypatia*, 20.2 (1995), pp. 119–134

Glenn, E. Nanako, 'From Servitude to Service Work: Historical Continuities in the Racial Division of Paid Reproductive Labor', *Signs* 18.1 (1992), pp. 1–43

——, *Unequal Labour: How Race and Gender Shaped American Citizenship and Labor* (Cambridge: Harvard University Press, 2002)

Glucksman, M.A., '"What a difference a day makes": A theoretical and historical exploration of temporality and gender', *Sociology* 32.2 (1998), pp. 239–258

Goodbody Economic Consultants, *Children 2020: Cost-Benefit Analysis* (Dublin: Goodbody Consultants, 2011)

Gornick, J.C. and Meyers, M.K., *Families that Work: Policies for Reconciling Parenthood and Employment* (New York: Russell Sage Foundation, 2003)

Government of Iceland, *Althingi (n.d.) Pingskjol* – Parliamentary documents (online: www.althingi.is., 2013)

Government of Ireland, *Bunreach na h-Eireann. [Constitution of Ireland]* (Dublin: Government Publications, 1937)

——, *Civil Service (Employment of Married Women) Act 1973* (Dublin: Government Publications, 1973)

——, *Anti-Discrimination (Pay) Act* (Dublin: Government Publications, 1974)

——, *Social Welfare Act 1974* (Dublin: Government Publications, 1974b)

——, *The Health (Family Planning) Act 1979* (Dublin: Government Publications, 1979)

——, *Child Care Act 1991* (Dublin: Government Publications, 1991)

——, *The Family Law (Divorce) Act, 1996* (Dublin: Government Publications, 1996)

——, *Organisation of Working Time Act (1997)* (Dublin: Government Publications, 1997)

——, *National Childcare Strategy Report of the Partnership 2000 Expert Working Group on Childcare* (Dublin: Department of Justice Equality and Law Reform. Government Publications, 1999)

——, *Budget 2000* (Dublin: Department of Finance, Government Publications, 2000)

——, *National Development Plan 2000–2006* (Dublin: Government Publications, 2000)

——, *Childcare Regulations* (Dublin: Department of Health and Children. Government Publications, 2006)

——, *Budget 2006* (Dublin: Department of Finance, 2006)

——, *National Action Plan for Social Inclusion 2007–2016* (Dublin: Government Publications, 2007)

——, *National Childcare Strategy 2006–2010. Guidelines for Childminders, Revised Edition, August 2008* (Dublin: Department of Health and Children, Government Publications, 2008)

——, *Budget 2009* (Dublin: Department of Finance, 2009)

——, *Circular 14 of 2009 Shorter Working Year Scheme* (online: http://hr.per.gov.ie/family-friendly-policies) [accessed 31/07/14]

——, Department of Finance, *Budget 2010* (Dublin: Department of Finance, Government Publications, 2010)

——, *Early Childhood Care and Education Scheme* (Dublin: Department of Children and Youth Affairs, Government Publications, 2010)

——, Department of Finance, *Budget 2011* (Dublin: Department of Finance, Government Publications, 2011)

——, Department of Finance, *Budget 2012* (Dublin: Department of Finance, Government Publications, 2012)

——, *Pathways to Work: Government Policy Statement on Labour Market Activation* (Dublin: Department of An Taoiseach, Government Publications, 2012)

——, *Protection of Life During Pregnancy Act 2013* (Dublin: Government Publications, 2013)

——, *Budget 2013* (Dublin: Department of Finance, Government Publications, 2013)

——, *Child and Family Agency Bill 2013* (Dublin: Government Publications, 2013)

——, *Public Service Stability Agreement 2013–2016 'Haddington Road Agreement'* (Dublin: Government Publications, 2013)

——, *Right from the Start: Report of the Expert Advisory Group on the Early Years Strategy* (Dublin: Department of Children and Youth Affairs, Government Publications, 2013)

——, Department of Social Protection. *Job Path* (online: http://www.welfare.ie/en/Pages/JobPath.aspx, 2014)

Gray, B., *Women and the Irish Diaspora* (London and New York, Routledge, 2004)

Grewal, I. and Kaplan, C., 'Introduction: Transnational Feminist Practices and Questions of Postmodernity' in I. Grewal and C. Kaplan (eds), *Scattered Hegemonies: Postmodernity and Transnational Feminist Perspectives* (Minneapolis: University of Minnesota Press, 1994)

Growing up in Ireland, *Child Cohort, Key findings: 9 year olds. no. 3: The Education of Nine-Year Olds, November 2009* (online: http://www.

growingup.ie/fileadmin/user_upload/documents/Update_Key_Fin
dings/Key_Findings_3.pdf, 2009)

Growing up in Ireland, *The Lives of 9-Year-Olds* (online: http://www.
growingup.ie/fileadmin/user_upload/documents/1st_Report/
Barcode_Growing_Up_in_Ireland_-_The_Lives_of_9-Year-Olds_
Main_Report.pdf, 2012)

Hadfield, G.K., 'The Dilemma of Choice: A Feminist Perspective on "The
Limits of Freedom of Contract"', *Osgoode Hall Law Journal* 33(2),
(1995), pp. 338–351

Hagerstrand, T., 'Survival and Arena: On the Life Histories of Individuals
in Relation to their Geographical Environment' in T. Carlstein, D.
Parkes, and N. Thrift (eds), *Timing Space and Spacing Time* (London:
Edward Arnold Ltd 1978), vol. 2, pp.122–145

Hakim, C., *Work-Lifestyle Choices in the 21st Century* (Oxford: Oxford
University Press, 2000)

——, 'A new approach to explaining fertility patterns: preference theory',
Population and Development Review 29.3 (2003), pp. 349–374

——, *Key Issues in Women's Work* (London: Glasshouse Press, 2004)

Halford, S., Savage, M. and Witz, A., *Gender, Careers and Organisations*
(London: Macmillan, 1997)

Hall, E.T., *The Dance of Life: The Other Dimension of Time* (Garden City, NY:
Anchor Press/Doubleday, 1983)

Halpenny, A.M., Nixon, E. and Watson, D., *Parent's Perspectives on
Parenting Styles and Disciplining Children* (Dublin: Office of the
Minister for Children and Youth Affairs, 2010)

Hancock, A.M., 'Intersectionality as a normative and empirical paradigm',
Politics and Gender 3 (2007), pp. 248–254

——, 'When Multiplication Doesn't Equal Quick Addition: Examining
Intersectionality as a Research Paradigm', *Perspectives on Politics* 5.1
(2007), pp. 63–79

Hardie, V. 'The world became a more dangerous place' in K. Gieve (ed.),
Balancing Acts: On Being a Mother (London: Virago, 1989)

Hardiman, N., 'From Conflict to Coordination: Economic Governance and
Political Innovation in Ireland', *West European Politics* 25(4) (2004), pp.
1–25

Harding, S., 'Rethinking Standpoint Epistemology: What is "Strong
Objectivity"?' in S. Harding (ed.), *The Feminist Standpoint Theory
Reader: Intellectual & Political Controversies* (New York and London:
Routledge, 1993), pp. 127–140

Harney, M., 'Remarks by Tánaiste, Mary Harney at a meeting of the
American Bar Association', at the Law Society of Ireland, Blackhall
Place, Dublin (21 July, 2000)

Harris, A., '"I've given them the best start" Donna May, stay-at-home
mother of three', *The Herald* (21 June, 2013)

Hartmann, H., 'The family as a locus of gender, class and political
struggle: the example of housework', *Signs* 6.3 (1981), pp. 366–394

Hartsock, N., 'The Feminist Standpoint: developing the ground for a specifically feminist historical materialism' in S. Harding (ed.), *Feminism and Methodology* (Bloomington: University of Indiana Press, 1987), pp. 157–180

——, 'The feminist standpoint: developing the ground for a specifically feminist historical materialism' in D. Meyers (ed.), *Feminist Social Thought: A Reader* (New York: Routledge, 1997), pp. 462–483

Harvey, D., *A Brief History of Neo-liberalism* (London: Oxford, 2005)

Hattery, A., *Women, Work and Family: Balancing and Weaving* (Thousand Oaks, London and New Delhi: Sage, 2001)

Hawkesworth, M., *Feminist Inquiry: From Political Conviction to Methodological Innovation* (New Jersey: Rutgers University Press, 2006)

Hayek, F., *Law, Legislation and Liberty: A New Statement of the Liberal Principles and Policital Economy, Volume 1: Rules and Order* (London, Routledge, 1973)

Hayles, N.K., *Chaos and Order: Complex Dynamics in Literature and Science* (Chicago: University of Chicago Press, 1991)

Hays, S., *The Cultural Contradictions of Motherhood* (New Haven: Yale University Press, 1996)

Hearne, J., 'Ratios and regulations: how crèches are controlled' (online: http://www.independent.ie/life/family/mothers-babies/ratios-and-regulations-how-crches-are-controlled-26884899.html 2012).

Herbert, S., 'I've had a baby too', *Sunday Telegraph* (9 September 2001

Higgins, M.D., *Renewing the Republic* (Dublin: Liberties Press, 2011)

Hilliard, B., 'Changing gender roles in intimate relationships' in J. Garry, N. Hardiman and D. Payne (eds), *Irish Social and Political Attitudes* (Liverpool: University of Liverpool Press, 2006), pp. 33–42

——, 'Family', in S. O'Sullivan (ed.), *Contemporary Ireland: A Sociological Map* (Dublin: University of Dublin Press, 2007), pp. 83–100

Hobson, A (ed.), *Gender and Citizenship in Transition* (Basingstoke: Macmillan, 2000)

Hochschild, A., *The Managed Heart: Commercialization of Human Feeling* (Berkeley: University of California Press, 1989)

——, *The Second Shift: Working Parents and the Revolution at Home* (London: Piatkus, 1990)

——, *The Time Bind: When Work Becomes Home and Home Becomes Work* (New York: Metropolitan Books, Henry Holt, 1997)

Holloway, S. 'Local Childcare Cultures: Moral geographies of mothering and the social organisation of pre-school education', *Gender, Place & Culture: A Journal of Feminist Geography* 5.1 (1998), pp. 29–53

——, 'Reproducing Motherhood' in N. Laurie, C. Dwyer, S. Holloway and F. Smith (eds), *Geographies of New Femininities* (London: Longman, 1999), pp. 91–112

Hooks, b., *Killing Rage: Ending Racism* (New York: Henry Holt, 1996)

Hoy, D., *Critical Resistance from Poststructuralism to Postcritique* (Massachusetts: Massachusetts Institute of Technology, 2004)

Hughes, C., *Key Concepts in Feminist Theory and Research* (London: Sage, 2002)

Inglis,T., *Moral Monopoly: The Rise and Fall of the Catholic Church in Modern Ireland* (Dublin: UCD Press, 1987)

——, *Truth, Power and Lies: Irish Society and the Case of the Kerry Babies* (Dublin: UCD Press, 2003)

——, *Global Ireland Same Difference* (New York and London: Taylor and Francis, 2008)

Irish National Teachers Organisation, 'Irish Spending on Education Falls Sharply'. Press Release (Tuesday 25 June 2013)

——, 'Overcrowded Classes: The Facts', *In Touch September 2013* (online: http://www.into.ie/ROI/ProtectingPrimaryEducation/ClassSizeSupplement.pdf, 2013)

Jackson, S. and Scott, S., 'Paid and Unpaid Work Introduction' in S. Jackson and S. Scott (eds), *Gender: A Sociological Reader* (London and New York: Routledge, 2002), pp. 151–153

Jaggar, A. *Feminist Politics and Human Nature* (U.K: Harvester Press, 1983)

Johnston, D. and Swanson, D., 'Moms hating moms: The internalization of mother war rhetoric', *Sex Roles* 51 (2004), pp. 497–510

Jones, A., 'Teaching post-structuralist feminist theory in education: student resistances', *Gender and Education* 9.3 (1997), pp. 261–270

Jones, B., *Women Who Opt Out: The Debate Over Working Mothers and Work Family Balance* (New York: NYU Press, 2012)

Jones, C., Tepperman, L. and Wilson, S., *The Futures of the Family* (New Jersey: Prentice Hall, 1995)

Jurczyk, K., 'Time in women's everyday lives: Between self-determination and conflicting demands', *Time and Society* 7.2–3 (1998), pp. 283–308

Kaplan, E.A., *Motherhood and Representation: The Mother in Popular Culture and Melodrama* (London: Routledge, 1992)

Kennedy, F., *Cottage to Crèche: Family Change in Ireland* (Dublin: IPA, 2001)

Kennedy, P., *Motherhood in Ireland: Creation and Context* (Cork: Mercier Press, 2004)

Keohane, K. and Kuhling, C., *Collision Culture: Transformations of Everyday Life in Ireland* (Dublin: Liffey Press, 2004)

Kiely, G., 'The Value of Unpaid Work in the Home', International Year of the Family + 10: Working for the Family Conference. University College Dublin (21 October 2004)

Kirby, P., *The Celtic Tiger in Distress* (London: Pluto Press, 2002)

——, 'Introduction' in D. Jacobsen, P. Kirby and D. O'Broin (eds), *Taming the Tiger: Social Exclusion in a Globalised Ireland* (Dublin: New Ireland Press, 2006), pp. 13–23

Kittay, E., *Love's, Labor: Essays on Women, Equality and Dependency* (New York and London: Routledge, 1999)

Knapp, G.A., 'Race, Class, Gender: Reclaiming Baggage in Fast-Travelling Theories', *European Journal of Women's Studies* 12.3 (2005), pp. 249–265

Knight, I., 'Who are they trying to Kid?', *Sunday Times* (9 September 2001)

Knights, A and Odih, P., '"It's about time!" The significance of gendered time for financial services consumption', *Time and Society* 4.2 (1995), pp. 205–231

Kuriloff, P. and Reichert, M., 'Boys of class: boys of colour: Negotiating the academic and social geography of an elite independent school', *Journal of Social Issues* 59.4 (2003), pp. 751–769

Land, H., 'The changing worlds of work and families' in S. Watson and L. Doyal (eds), *Engendering Social Policy* (Buckingham: Open University Press, 1999), pp. vii–xii

Lareau, A., 'Invisible Inequality: Social Class and Childrearing in Black Families and White Families', *American Sociological Review* 67.5 (2002), pp. 747–776

Latour, B., *Science in Action: How to Follow Scientists and Engineers Through Society* (Cambridge: Harvard University Press, 1987)

Lash, S., 'Reflexivity and its Doubles: Structure, Aesthetics, Community' in U. Beck, A. Giddens and S. Lash (eds), *Reflexive Modernization: Politics, Tradition and Aesthetics in the Modern Social Order* (Cambridge: Polity Press, 1994), pp. 110–173

——, 'Foreword: Individualization in a non-linear mode' in U. Beck and E. Beck-Gernsheim, *Individualization* (London: Sage, 2002), pp. vii–xiii

Lather, P., *Getting Smart: Feminist Research and Pedagogy With/in the Postmodern* (New York: Routledge, 1991)

Lawler, S., *Mothering the Self: Mothers, Daughters, Subjects* (New York: Routledge, 2000)

——, 'Symbolic Violence' in D. Southerton (ed.), *Encyclopedia of Consumer Culture* (Thousand Oaks, CA: Sage, 2011), pp. 1423–1425

Lenz, I., 'Varieties of Gender Regimes and Regulating Gender Equality at Work in the Global Context' in S. Walby, H. Gottfried, K. Gottschall and M. Osawa (eds), *Gendering the Knowledge Economy: Comparative Perspectives* (London and New York: Palgrave Macmillan, 2007), pp. 109–139

Leonard, M., 'Women Caring and Sharing in Belfast' in A. Byrne and M. Leonard (eds), *Women and Irish Society: A Sociological Reader* (Belfast. Beyond the Pale Publications, 1997), pp. 111–126;

Letherby, G., 'Other than mother and mother as others: the experience of motherhood and non-motherhood in relation to "infertility" and "involuntary childlessness"', *Women's Studies International Forum* 22.3 (1999), pp. 359–372

——, 'Challenging Dominant Discourses: identity and change and the experience of "infertility" and "involuntary childlessness", *Journal of Gender Studies* 11.3 (2002), pp. 277–288

——, *Feminist Research in Theory and Practice* (Buckingham: Open University Press, 2003)

Letherby, G. and Williams, C., 'Non-motherhood: ambivalent autobiographies', *Feminist Studies* 25.3, (1999), pp. 719–728

Levine, J., *Sisters: The Personal Story of an Irish Feminist* (Dublin: Ward River Press, 1982)

Lewis, J., 'Gender and the development of welfare regime', *Journal of European Social Policy* 2.3 (1992), pp. 159–173

Lister, R., *Citizenship: Feminist Perspectives* (London: Macmillan, 1997)

Looney, F., *Misadventures in Motherhood: Life with the Small Girl, the Boy and the Toddler* (Dublin: O'Brien Press, 2005)

Lorber, J., 'The Variety of Feminisms and their Contribution to Gender Equality' in M. Marx Ferree, J. Lorber and B. Hess (eds), *Revisioning Gender* (London: Sage, 1999), pp. 7–43

Lott, B., 'Cognitive and behavioural distancing from the poor', *American Psychologist* 57 (2004), pp. 100–110

Lunn, P. and Fahey, T., *Households and Family Structures in Ireland* (Dublin: Family Support Agency, 2011)

Lynch, K. 'Solidary Labour: Its Nature and Marginalisation', *The Sociological Review* 37.1 (1989), pp. 1–14

——, 'Love labour as a distinct and non-commodifiable form of Care Labour', *Sociological Review* 54.3 (2007), pp. 550–570

——, 'A Care-Full model of Citizenship: Challenging the Rational Economic Actor (REA) Model', paper presented to Connecting with Family Carers International Conference (University College Cork) (4 September 2008)

Lynch, K. and Baker, J., *Affective Equality: Who Cares?* (London: Palgrave Macmillan, 2008)

Lynch, K. and Lyons, M., 'The Gendered Order of Caring' in U. Barry (ed.), *Where Are We Now?: New Feminist Perspectives on Women in Contemporary Ireland* (Dublin: TASC at New Island Press, 2008), pp. 163–183

Lynch, K. and McLaughlin E., 'Caring Labour and Love Labour' in P. Clancy, S. Drucy, K. Lynch and L. O'Dowd (eds), *Irish Society: Sociological Perspectives* (Dublin: IPA, 1995)

Lynch, K. and O'Dowd, L. (eds), *Irish Society: Sociological Perspectives* (Dublin: IPA, 1995), pp. 250–292;

Macdonald, C.L., 'Manufacturing motherhood: the shadow work of nannies and au pairs', *Qualitative Sociology* 21.1 (1998), pp. 25–48

MacEwan, A., 'Early childhood education as an essential component of economic development' (Political Economy Research Institute, University of Massachusetts. January 2013) (online: http://www.peri. umass.edu/fileadmin/pdf/published_study/ECE_MacEwan_PERI_ Jan8.pdf, 2013)

MacLean, L., 'Intersectionality, social locations of privilege and conceptions of women's oppression', paper prepared for the CPSA meeting, May 2009, Carleton University, Ottowa, Canada (online:http://www. cpsa-acsp.ca/papers-2009/MacLean.pdf, 2009)

Macleod, T., 'The Truth about Motherhood – If You're an Angst Ridden Novelist, That Is', *Evening Standard* (2 September 2001)

Magic Mum, thread, 'Thinking about getting a nanny: Issues/advice? (online: http://www.magicmum.com/phpBB/viewtopic.php?f=117&t=566863, 2013)

Maher, M., 'Women's Liberation', *The Irish Times* (9 March 1971)

Mahon, E., 'Equal Opportunities in the Irish Civil Service – Interim Review', *Women in Public Service Equal Opportunities International* 10.2 (1991), pp. 2–10

——, 'Changing Gender Roles, State, Work and Family Lives' in E. Drew,

R. Emerek, and E. Mahon (eds), *Women, Work and the Family in Europe* (London: Routledge, 1998), pp. 153–158

——, 'Class, Mothers and Equal Opportunities to Work' in E. Drew, R. Emerek and E. Mahon (eds), *Women, Work and the Family in Europe* (London and New York: Routledge, 1998), pp. 170–181

——, 'Reconciling Work and Family Lives', paper presented to Irish Social Policy Association Conference (Dublin: 17 September 2004)

Martinez, E., 'Beyond Black/White: The Racisms of Our Times', *Social Justice* 20 (1993), pp. 1–2

Martinez, E. and Garcia, A., *What is 'Neo-Liberalism'? A Brief Definition* (online: http:www.globalexchange.org/campaigns. 2000)

Maushart, S., *The Mask of Motherhood: How Becoming a Mother Changes our Lives and Why We Never Talk About It* (London: Penguin, 1997)

——, *Wifework* (New York: Bloomsbury, 2001)

Mauthner, N. and Doucet, A., 'Reflections on a Voice-Centred Relational Method: Analysing Maternal and Domestic Voices' in J. Ribbens and R. Edwards (eds), *Feminist Dilemmas in Qualitative Research: Public Knowledge and Private Lives* (London: Sage, 1998), pp. 119–146

Maynard, M., 'Feminists' knowledge and the knowledge of feminisms: epistemology, theory, methodology and method' in T. May and M. Williams (eds), *Knowing the Social World* (Buckingham: Open University Press. 1998), pp. 120–137

Mayo, M. and Weir, A., 'The future for feminist social policy?' in R. Page and J. Baldock (eds), *Social Policy Review* 5 (1993), pp. 35–57

McCafferty, N., *A Woman to Blame* (Dubin: Attic Press, 1985)

McCall, L., *Complex Inequality: Gender Class and Race in the New Economy* (New York: Blackwell, 2001)

——, 'The Complexity of Intersectionality', *Signs* 30(3) (2005), pp. 1771–1800

McCarty, M. and Higgins, A., 'Moving to an all graduate profession: preparing preceptors for their role', *Nurse Education Today* 23(2) (2003), pp. 89–95

McCashin, A., *Lone Mothers in Ireland: A Local Study* (Dublin: Combat Poverty Agency, 1996)

McGibney, T., cited in S. Ryan, 'Can't really afford to quit work to look after your child? . . . think again' (online: http://www.herald.ie/lifestyle/cant-really-afford-to-quit-work-to-look-after-your-child-think-again-29357887.html) Herald.ie (19 June 2013)

McGinnity, F. and Russell, H., *Gender Inequalities in Time Use: the Distribution of Caring, Housework and Employment among Women and Men in Ireland* (Dublin: Equality Authority, 2008)

McGinnity, F., Russell, H. and Smyth, E., 'Gender, Work-Life Balance and Quality of Life' in T. Fahey, H. Russell and C.T., Whelan (eds), *Best of Times? The Social Impact of the Celtic Tiger* (Dublin: IPA, 2005), pp. 199–216

McGinnity, F., Russell, H., Williams, J. and Blackwell, S., *Time Use in Ireland 2005* (Dublin: ESRI, 2005)

McGinnity, F., Russell, H. and O'Connell, P., 'The Impact of Flexible

Working Arrangements on Work-life Conflict and Work Pressure in Ireland', *Gender Work and Organisation* 16.1 (2009), pp. 73–97

McKay, F., 'Women Politicians and the Ethic of Care', *Gender and Scottish Society: Polities, Policies and Participation* (Edinburgh: Unit for the Study of Government in Scotland, University of Edinburgh, 1998)

McKie, L., Biese, I., and Jyrkinen, M., '"The Best Time is Now!" The temporal and spatial dynamics of women opting in to self employment', *Gender Work and Organisation* 20 (2013), pp. 184–196

McKie, L., Gregory, S. and Bowlby, S., 'Caringscapes: Experiences of Caring and Working', Centre for Research on Families and Relationships, The University of Edinburgh, Research Briefing No. 13 (February, 2004)

——, 'Shadow Times: The Temporal and Spatial Frameworks and Experiences of Caring and Working', *Sociology* 36.4 (2002), pp. 897–924

McKinnon, A., 'Girls, School and Society: a generation of change?' (Clare Burton Memorial Lecture: University of South Australia, 2005)

McLaughlin, E., 'Ireland: Catholic Corporatism' in A. Cochrane and J. Clarke (eds), *Social Policy in Ireland: Principles, Practice and Problems* (Dublin: Oak Tree Press, 1993), pp. 297–328

——, *Social Security and Community Care: The Case of the Invalid Care Allowance.* Department of Social Security Research Report No. 4 (London: Stationery Office, 2001)

McRae, S., 'Choice and constraints in mothers' employment careers: McRae replies to Hakim', *British Journal of Sociology* 54.4 (2003), pp. 585–592

Meagher, G., 'Is it wrong to pay for housework?', *Hypatia* 17.2 (2002), pp. 52–66.

Miller, T., *Making Sense of Motherhood: A Narrative Approach* (Cambridge: University Press, 2005)

Mohanty, C.T., '"Under Western Eyes" Revisited: Feminist Solidarity through Anticapitalist Struggles', *Signs* 28(2) (2002), pp. 499–535

Mooney, B., 'The Scientific PROOF that sending mothers out to work harms children', Mail online/femail (online: http://www.daily mail.co.uk/femail/article-2296567)20 March 2013

Mooney-Simmie, G., 'The Pied Piper of Neo-liberalism Calls the Tune in the Republic of Ireland: An analysis of Education Policy Text from 2000–2012', *Journal for Critical Education Policy Studies* 10.2 (2012), pp. 485–514

Moran, J., 'From Catholic Church dominance to social partnership promise and now economic crisis, little changes in Irish social policy', *Irish Journal of Public Policy* (online: http://publish.ucc.ie/ijpp/2010/01/moran/01/en, 2009)

Moran, M., 'Social inclusion and the limits of pragmatic liberalism: The Irish case', *Irish Political Studies* 21.2 (2006), pp. 181–201

——, 'Wealth, poverty and redistribution in Ireland', paper presented at *Poverty and Wealth – Wealth concentration and increasing poverty: current trends, root causes and strategies to address them.* Thesis papers of the seminar (Athens, 18–21 April 2013)

Morgan, D., *Focus Groups as Qualitative Research* (London: Sage, 1988)

Morgan, D.H.J., *Family Connections* (Cambridge: Polity Press, 1996)

Murphy-Lawless, J (2000), 'Changing Women's Lives: Child Care Policy in Ireland', *Feminist Economics* 6(1) (2000), pp. 89–94

Murray, D., 'The Soul of Europe', *The Furrow* 49.1 (1998)

Murray, M., 'The polluter pays? Individualising Ireland's Waste Problem' in M. Corcoran and M. Peillon (eds), *Uncertain Ireland* (Dublin: Institute for Public Administration) (2006), pp. 103–114

Murray, S., Tapson, J., Turnbull, L., McCallum, J. and Little, A., 'Listening to local voices: Adapting rapid appraisal to assess health and social needs in general practice', *British Medical Journal* 308 (no. 6930) (1994), pp. 698–700

Narayan, U., 'The Project of a Feminist Epistemology: Perspectives from a Nonwestern Feminist' in S. Harding (ed.), *The Feminist Standpoint Theory Reader: Intellectual & Political Controversies 2004* (New York and London: Routledge), pp. 213–224

National Foundation for Education Research, 'Compulsory age of starting school in European countries'. (online: http://www.nfer.ac.uk/nfer/index.cfm?9B1C0068-C29E-AD4D-0AEC-8B4F43F54A28, 2014)

Nedelsky. J., *Law, Autonomy and the Relational Self: A Feminist Revisioning of the Foundations of Law* (Oxford: Oxford University Press, 2005)

NESC, *The Developmental Welfare State.* Report 113 (Dublin: National Economic and Social Council, 2005)

NESF, *Early Childhood and Education Report 31* (Dublin: NESF, 2005)

Nilsen, A. and Brannen, J., 'Theorising the individual-structure dynamic' in J. Brannen, S. Lewis, A. Nilsen and J. Smithson (eds), *Young Europeans, Work and Family: Futures in Transition* (London: Routledge, 2002), pp. 30–48

Nowotny, H., 'Time and social theory: towards a social theory of time' *Time and Society* 1.3 (1992), pp. 421–454

Nussbaum, M.C., 'Emotions and Women's Capabilities' in M.C. Nussbaum and J. Glover (eds), *Women, Culture and Development: A Study of Human Capabilities* (Oxford: Oxford University Press, 1995) pp. 360–395

——, 'Human Capabilties, Female Human Beings' in M.C. Nussbaum and J. Glover (eds), *Women, Culture and Development: A Study of Human Capabilities* (Oxford: Oxford University Press, 1995), pp. 61–104

——, *Women and Human Development: The Capabilities Approach* (Cambridge: Cambridge University Press, 2000)

NWCI, *Valuing Care Work* (online: http://www.nwci.ie/index.php/learn/publication/valuing_care_work 2003)

——, *A Woman's Model for Social Welfare Reform* (online: http://www.nwci.ie/index.php/learn/publication/a_womans_model_for_social_welfare_reform, 2005)

——, *An Accessible Childcare Model* (online: http://www.nwci.ie/index.php/learn/publication/an_accessible_childcare_model, 2005)

——, *Who Cares?: Challenging the myths about gender and care in Ireland* (online: http://www.nwci.ie/index.php/learn/publication/who_cares 2009)

——, *Budget 2014: Submission* (Dublin: NWCI, August 2013)

O'Brien, C., 'Most childminders not declaring income', *The Irish Times* (4 July 2009)

——, 'Creche Crisis: The Staff Speak', *Weekend Review, The Irish Times* (Saturday 1st June 2013)

O'Brien, M., 'Mothers as Educational Workers': Mothers Emotional Work at the Children's Transfer to Second Level Education' *Irish Educational Studies* 24.2–3 (2005), pp. 223–242

——, 'Mothers' Emotional Care Work in Education and its Moral Imperative', *Gender and Education* 19.2. (2007), pp. 139–157

O'Connor, O. and Murphy, M., 'Women and Social Welfare' in U. Barry (ed.), *Where Are We Now? New Feminist Perspectives on Women in Contemporary Ireland* (Dublin: TASC at New Island, 2008), pp. 30–52

O'Connor, P. *Emerging Voices: Women in Contemporary Irish Society* (Dublin: IPA, 1998)

——, 'Ireland: A Man's world?' *The Economic and Social Review* 31.1 (2000), pp. 81–102

——, 'A bird's eye view . . . Resistance in Academia', *Irish Journal of Sociology* 10.2 (2001), pp. 86–104

——, 'The Patriarchal State: Continuity and Change' in M. Adshead, P. Kirby, M. Millar (eds), *Contesting the State* (Manchester: Manchester University Press, 2008), pp. 143–164.

——, *Irish Children and Teenagers in a Changing World* (Manchester University Press, 2008)

O'Connor, P., Smithson, J. and des Dores Goerreiro, M., 'Young People's Awareness of Gendered Realities' in J. Brannen, S. Lewis and A. Nielsen (eds), *Young Europeans: Work and Family* (London: Routledge, 2002), pp. 89–115

O'Donnell, R., 'The Celtic Tiger', Presentation to Re-Imagining Ireland Conference (University of Virginia: May 2003)

O'Hagan, C., 'Ideologies of Motherhood and Single Mothers' in M.C. Ramblado-Minero and A. Pérez-Vides (eds), *Single Motherhood in Twentieth Century Ireland: Cultural, Historical and Social Essays* (London and New York: The Edwin Mellen Press, 2006), pp. 65–82

——, 'Working and mothering: interlocking locations in the caringscape', *Families Relationships and Societies* 3(2) (2014), pp. 201–218

——, 'Broadening the intersectional path: revealing organizational practices through "working mothers" narratives about time', *Gender Work and Organisation* (online: http://onlinelibrary.wiley.com/doi/10.1111/gwao.12056/full.23 June 2014)

O'Reilly, A. (ed.), *Mother Outlaws: Theories and Practices of Empowered Mothering* (Toronto: Women's Press, 2004)

O'Sullivan, C., 'Government fails to clamp down on black market childminders', *Irish Examiner* (Monday, 18 October 2010)

O'Sullivan, S., 'Gender and the Workforce' in S. O'Sullivan (ed.), *Contemporary Ireland: A Sociological Map* (Dublin: University College Dublin Press, 2007), pp. 265–282

Oakley, A., *Housewife* (Harmondsworth: Penguin, 1974)

——, *Gender on Planet Earth* (London and New York: Polity Press, 2002)

OECD, *Employment Outlook Study* (Paris: OECD, 1990)

——, *Thematic Review of Early Childhood Education and Care: Background Report. Ireland* (online: www.oecd.org/\els\social\family\database, 2002)

——, *Early Childhood Education and Care – Country Note for Ireland* (online: http://www.oecd.org/dataoecd/51/18/3445332.pdf, 2004)

——, *Thematic Review of Early Childhood Education and Care Policy in Ireland* (Paris: OECD, 2004)

——, *Country Profiles: An Overview of Early Childhood Education and Care Systems in Participating Countries – Ireland* (Paris: OECD, 2006)

——, *Babies and Bosses: Reconciling Work and Family Life, A Synthesis of Findings for OECD Countries* (Paris: OECD, 2007)

——, *Growing Unequal? Income Distribution and Poverty in OECD Countries* (Paris: OECD, 2008)

——, *Trends in the income position of different household types* (online: www.oecd.org/\els\social\family\database, 2009)

——, *Gender Brief.* Prepared by the OECD Social Policy Division (online: www.oecd.org/els/social Version: March 2010)

——, *Doing Better for Families* (Paris: OECD, 2011)

——, *Closing the Gender Gap: Act Now* (Paris: OECD Publishing, 2012)

——, *Going for Growth :Economic Policy Reforms* (Paris: OECD, 2012)

——, *Education at a Glance 2013. OECD Indicators – A Country Profile for Ireland June 2013* (Paris: OECD, 2014)

One Parent Family Agency, *Pre-Budget submission 2014* (online: http://www. onefamily.ie/wp-content/uploads/One-Family_Pre-Budget-Submission-2014_10-Solutions.pdf. 2014)

Pacholok, S and Gauthier, A.H., 'A Tale of Dual-Earner Families in Four Countries' in N. Folbre and M. Bittman (eds), *Family Time: The Social Organisation of Care* (London: Routledge, 2004) pp. 197–223

Pascall, G. and Lewis, J., 'Emerging Gender Regimes and Policies for Gender Equality in a Wider Europe', *Journal of Social Policy* 33.3 (2004), pp. 373–394

Pearson, A., *I Don't Know How She Does It* (London: Anchor Books, 2003)

Petchesky, R.P., 'Foetal Images: The power of visual culture in the politics of reproduction' in M. Stanworth (ed.), *Reproductive Technologies: Gender, Motherhood and Medicine* (Cambridge: Polity, 1980), pp. 59–80

Phoenix, A., 'Centring marginality? Otherness, difference and the "Psychology of Women" British Psychological Association Conference 2006 Proceedings 14.1 (February 2006)

Phoenix, A. and Pattynama, P., 'Editorial: Intersectionality', *European Journal of Women's Studies* 13.3 (2006), pp. 187–192

Pitt, K., 'Being a New Capitalist Mother', *Discourse and Society* 13.2 (2002), pp. 251–267

Plummer, K., 'Intimate Choices' in G. Browning, A. Halcli and F. Webster (eds), *Understanding Contemporary Society: Theories of the Present* (London: Sage, 2000), pp. 432–44

Pobal, *Annual Survey of the Early Years Sector 2012* (Dublin: Pobal, 2013)

Prasad, M., *The Politics of Free Markets: The Rise of Neoliberal Economic Policies in Britain, France, Germany, & The United States* (Chicago: University of Chicago Press, 2006)

Quiney, R., 'Confessions of the New Capitalist Mother: Twenty-first-century Writing on Motherhood as Trauma', *Women: A Cultural Review* 18.1 (2007), pp. 19–40.

Raftery, M. and O'Sullivan, E., *Suffer the Little Children* (Dublin: New Island Books, 1999)

Reay, D., *Class Work: Mother's Involvement in Their Children's Primary Schooling* (London: RoutledgeFalmer, 1998)

——, 'Doing the dirty work of social class? Mothers' work in support of their children's schooling' in M. Glucksmann, L. Pettinger, J. Parry and R. Taylor (eds), *A New Sociology of Work* (London: Blackwell, 2005), pp. 104–118

Reid, P.T., 'Poor women in psychological research: Shut up and shut out', *Psychology of Women Quarterly* 17.2 (1993), pp. 133–150

Ribbens, J., *Mothers and their Children: A Feminist Sociology of Childrearing* (London: Sage, 1994)

Rich, A., *Of Woman Born: Motherhood as Experience and Institution* (USA: Virago Press, 1977)

Richardson, D., *Women, Motherhood and Childrearing* (London: Macmillan, 1993)

Riggs, J.M., 'Mandates for Mothers and Fathers: Perceptions of Breadwinners and Care Givers', *Sex Roles* 37 (October 1997), pp. 565–580

Riley, D., *'Am I that name?' Feminism and the Category of 'Women' in History* (Basingstoke: Macmillan, 1988)

Risman, B.J., 'Gender as a social structure: Theory wrestling with activism', *Gender and Society* 18.4 (2004), pp. 429–450

Robert, Walters, Ireland Employee Insights Survey (online:http://www.robertwalters.ie/wwwmedialibrary/files/Ire%20Content/employee-insight-survey-ireland-2012.pdf. 2012)

Roche, W., 'Pay Determination and the Politics of Industrial Relations' in T.V. Murphy and W.K. Roche (eds), *Irish Industrial Relations in Practice* (Dublin: Oak Tree Press, 1997), pp. 145–226

Rollercoaster, (online discussion: http://www.rollercoaster.ie/Discussions/tabid/119/ForumThread/141392186/Default.aspx, 2013)

Rose, D., *Revisiting Feminist Research Methodologies – A Working Paper*, Status of Women (online: www.swc-cfc.gc/pubs, 2001)

Rose, N., *Governing the Soul* (London: Routledge, 1989)

——, 'Governing the enterprising self' in P. Heelas and P. Morris (eds), *The Values of the Enterprise Culture: The Moral Debate* (London: Routledge, 1992), pp. 141–164

——, 'Preface to the Second Edition', *Governing the Soul. The Shaping of the Private Self* (London: Free Association Books, 1999), pp. vii–xxvii

——, *Powers of Freedom: Reframing Political Thought* (Cambridge: Cambridge University Press, 1999)

——, 'The death of the social? Re-figuring the territory of government', *Economy and Society* (25)3 (2006), pp. 327–356

RTE, 'Breach of Trust' *Prime Time* (Tuesday, 28 May 2013)

Rubery, J., Smith, M. and Fagan, C., 'National Working Time Regimes and Equal Opportunities', *Feminist Economics* 4.1 (1998), pp. 71–101

Rubin, L., *Families on the Fault Line* (New York: Harper Collins, 1994)

Russell, H. and Corcoran, M., *The Experiences of those Claiming the One-Parent Family Payment: A Qualitative Study* (Dublin: Department of Social and Family Affairs, 2000)

Russell, H., McGinnity, F., Callan, T., and Keane, C., *A Woman's Place: Female Participation in the Irish Labour Market* (Dublin: Equality Authority, 2009)

Ryan, A., 'Contemporary discourses of working, earning and spending: acceptance, critique and the bigger picture' in C. Coulter and S. Coleman (eds), *The End of Irish History?: Critical Reflections on the Celtic Tiger* (Manchester: Manchester University Press, 2003)

Ryan, C., 'Women disproportionately hit by contributory pension scheme cuts', *Irish Examiner* (22 April 2014)

Sarantinos, V., Flexibility in the workplace: What happens to commitment? *Business and Public Affairs* vol. 1.2 (2007), pp. 1–10

Sayer, L.C., 'Gender differences in the relationships between long employee hours and multitasking' in T. Van der Lippe and P. Peters (eds), *Time Competition: Disturbed Balances and New Options in Work and Care* (New York: Edward Elgar, 2007), pp. 403–435

Sayer, L.C., Cohen, P.N. and Casper, L.M., *Women, Men, and Work* (Washington, DC: Russell Sage Foundation and Population Reference Bureau, 2004)

Schlessinger, L., *In Praise of Stay-at-Home-Moms* (New York: Harper Collins, 2009)

Schooldays.ie., Homework: how much time should your child spend on it? (online:http://www.schooldays.ie/articles/Homework-how-much-time, 2013)

Schwartz, B., 'The Tyranny of Choice', *Scientific American* 290.4 (2004), pp. 70–75

Scott, J., 'The Evidence of Experience' in H. Abelore, M. Barade and D.M. Halpenn (eds), *The Lesbian and Gay Studies Reader* (New York: Routledge, 1993) pp. 397–415

——, 'Family change: revolution or backlash?' in S. McRae (ed.), *Changing Britain, Families and Households in the 1990s* (Oxford: Oxford University Press, 1999), pp. 98–119

Scott, J., *Social Network Analysis: A Handbook* (London: Sage, 2000)

Scottish Commission for the Regulation of Care, *Improving the Quality of Care in Scotland: An Overview of Care Commission findings, 2002 to 2010* (Scotland: SCRC, 2011)

Sevenhuijsen, S., *Citizenship and the Ethics of Care: Feminist Considerations on Justice, Morality and Politics* (London: Routledge, 1998)

Siim, B., *Gender and Citizenship* (Cambridge: Cambridge University Press, 2000)

Siltanen, J., 'Equality, diversity, and the politics of scale: The Canadian public policy experience', paper presented at ESRC seminar: 'Public Policy, Equality and Diversity in the Context of Devolution' (University of Edinburgh, 10 June 2005)

Sirianni, C. and Negrey, C., 'Working Time as Gendered Time', *Feminist Economics* 6.1 (2000), pp. 59–76

Skeggs, B., *Formations of Class and Gender: Becoming Respectable* (London: Sage, 1997)

——, *Class, Self, Culture* (London and New York: Routledge, 2004)

Smith, D., 'Women's Perspective as a Radical Critique of Sociology' in S. Harding (ed.), *The Feminist Standpoint Theory Reader: Intellectual & Political Controversies* 2004 (New York and London: Routledge) pp. 21–33

——, *The Everyday World as Problematic: A Feminist Sociology* (Boston: Northeastern University Press, 1987)

Smyth, L., *The Demands of Motherhood* (Basingstoke: Palgrave Macmillan, 2012)

Social Justice Ireland, *Analysis and Critique of Budget 2013* (online: www.socialjustice.ie/sites/default/files/file/Budget/Budget%20201 3%20Analysis%20and%20Critique.pdf 2013) [accessed 17/11/13]

——, *Policy Briefing 2012 Poverty and Income Distribution* (online: http://www.socialjustice.ie/sites/default/files/file/Budget/2012/2011–12-07%20-%20Budget%202012%20Analysis%20and%20Critique.pdf. 2013)

Spelman, E.V., *Inessential Woman* (Boston: Beacon Press, 1988)

Sprague, J., 'Comment on Walby's "Against Epistemological chasms: the science question in feminism revisited": structured knowledge and strategic methodology', *Signs* 26(2) (2001), pp. 527–536

Standard Occupational Classification. 2nd edition (London: Her Majesty's Stationery Office, 1995)

Stanford Internet Encyclopedia of Philosophy. 'Feminist Standpoint Theory' (online:http://www.iep.utm.edu/fem-stan/ 2014)

Stanley, L. and Wise, S., 'Method, methodology and epistemology in feminist research processes' in L. Stanley (ed.), *Feminist Praxis: Research, Theory and Epistemology in Feminist Sociology* (London: Routledge, 1990) pp. 20–60

——, *Breaking Out Again: Feminist Ontology and Epistemology* (London: Routledge, 1993)

Start Strong, *Children 2020 Planning Now, for the Future, Children's Early Care and Education in Ireland, November 2010* (Dublin: Start Strong, 2010)

——, *Childminding: Regulation and Recognition. Policy Brief 12* (Dublin: Start Strong, 2012)

——, *The Economics of Children's Early Years Early Care and Education in Ireland: Costs and Benefits* (online http://www.startstrong.ie/files/Economics_of_Childrens_Early_Years.pdf.) [accessed 31/07/14]

Stone, P., *Opting Out?: Why Women Really Quit Careers and Head Home* (California: University of California Press, 2008)

Sue, D.W., 'Whiteness and ethnocentric monoculturalism: Making the "invisible" visible', *American Psychologist* 59.8 (2004), pp. 761–769

Sullivan, O., 'The Division of Domestic Labour: Twenty Years of Change?' *Sociology* 34.3 (2000), pp. 437–456

TASC, *The Solidarity Factor: Public Responses to Economic Inequality in Ireland* (Dublin: TASC at New Island, 2009)

Teague, P., 'Pay Determination in the Republic of Ireland: Toward Social Corporatism?' *British Journal of Industrial Relations* 33.2 (1995) pp. 253–273

Temple, B., '"Collegiate accountability" and bias: the solution to the problem?' *Sociological Reseach Online* 2.4 (1997) (online: www/socre sonline/org.uk/socresonline/2/4/8,1997)

Tertia, *The Cutthroat World of Motherhood* (online: Parenting Issues. http://www.tertia.org/, 2006)

Thompson, J.B., *Ideology and Modern Culture* (Oxford: Polity Press, 1990)

Thompson, L. and Walker, A.J., 'The Place of Feminism in Family Studies', *Journal of Marriage and the Family* 57.4 (1995), pp. 847–865

Thorsen, D.E. and Lie, A., 'What is Neo-liberalism?' Department of Political Science, Oslo University (online: http://folk.uio.no/daget/What%20is%20Neo-Liberalism%20FINAL.pdf, 2013)

Treanor, P., *Neoliberalism: Origins, Theory, Definition* (online: http://web.inter.nl.net/users/Paul.Treanor/neoliberalism.html, 2007)

Treoir, *Babies and Bosses* Newsletter (November/December 2003) (online: www.treoir.ie, 2003)

Tronto, J., *Moral Boundaries: A Political Argument for an Ethic of Care* (London: Routledge, 1993)

——, 'Gender and Care' in *International Encyclopedia of the Social and Behavioral Sciences* (London: Elsevier, 2002)

TV3, 'Back To School: Homework' (online: http://www.tv3.ie/ireland_am_article.php?locID=1.901.983&article=111668, 2013)

Ungerson, B., 'The Commodification of Care: Current Policies and Future Politics' in B. Hobson (ed.), *Gender and Citizenship in Transition* (Basingstoke: Macmillan, 2000), pp. 173–200

Vincent, C. and Ball, S., *Childcare, Choice and Class Practices: Middle Class Parents and their Children* (Oxon and New York, 2006), p. 163

Voet, R., *Feminism and Citizenship* (London: Sage, 1998)

Walby, S., *Theorizing Patriarchy* (Oxford: Blackwell, 1990)

——, *Gender Transformations* (London and New York: Routledge, 1997)

——, 'The European Union and Gender Equality: Emergent Varieties of Gender Regime', *Social Politics* 11.1 (2004), pp. 4–19

——, 'Complexity Theory, Systems Theory, and Multiple Intersecting Social Inequalities', *Philosophy of the Social Sciences* 37.4 (2007), pp. 449–470

——, 'Introduction: Theorizing the Gendering of the Knowledge Economy: Comparative Perspectives' in S. Walby, H. Gottfried, K. Gottschall and M. Osawa (eds), *Gendering the Knowledge Economy: Comparative Perspectives* (London and New York: Palgrave Macmillan, 2007), pp. 3–50

——, *Globalization and Inequalities: Complexity and Contested Modernities* (London: Sage, 2009)

Warner, J., 'The Mommy Madness Generation', *Newsweek* (21 February, 2005), pp. 42–49

——, *Perfect Madness: Motherhood in the Age of Anxiety* (London: Vermillon, 2006)

——, 'The Motherhood Religion' in A. O'Reilly (ed.), *Maternal Theory: Essential Readings* (Toronto: Demeter Press, 2007), pp. 705–725

Webb, J., 'Organisations, Self-Identities and the New Economy', *Sociology* 38(4) (2004), pp. 719–738

Weber, L. and Parra-Medina, D., 'Intersectionality and Women's Health: Charting a path to eliminating health disparities' in V. Demos and M.T. Segal (eds), *Advances in Gender Research: Gender Perspectives on Health and Medicine* (Amsterdam: Elsevier, 2003), pp. 181–230

Weedon, C., *Feminist Practice and Poststructuralist Theory.* 2nd edition (Oxford: Blackwell, 1997)

West, C. and Zimmerman, D.H., 'Doing Gender', *Gender & Society* 1.2 (1987), pp. 125–151

Wetherell, M. 'Positioning and interpretative repertoires: conversation analysis and poststructuralism in dialogue', *Discourse & Society* 9.3 (1998), pp. 387–412

Wheelock, J. and Jones, K., 'Grandparents are the next best thing: informal childcare for working parents in urban Britain', *Journal of Social Policy* 31.3 (2002), pp. 441–463

Whipp, R., 'A time to be concerned; A position paper on time and management', *Time and Society* 3 (1994), pp. 99–116

White, V., *Mother Ireland: Why Ireland Hates Mothers* (Dublin: Londubh Books, 2010)

——, 'Our children don't need corporate creches — all they need is love', *Irish Examiner* (Thursday, 30 May 2013)

——, 'We shouldn't make it hard for parents to stay home and care for their children' *Irish Examiner* (Thursday 6 June 2013)

Wickham, J., 'Technological and Organisational Choice', Policy Paper (Dublin: Employment Research Centre, University of Dublin, Trinity College, 2004)

Wilkinson, S., 'Focus group methodology: a review', *International Journal of Social Research Methodology* 1.3 (1998), pp. 181–203

Williams, F., 'Time to Care, Time not to Care'. ESRC 4th National Social Science Conference (London: 28 November 2000)

——, 'Changing Families – Changing Values?' ESRC Research Group on Care, Values and the Future of Welfare (London: 22 October 2001)

——, *Rethinking Families* (London: Calouste Gulbenkian Foundation, 2004)

——, *Unbending Gender: Why Family and Work Conflict and What to Do About It* (Oxford and New York: Oxford University Press, 2000)

WIN–Gallup, *International Global Index of Religiosity and Atheism* (online: http://www.scribd.com/doc/136318147/Win-gallup-International-Global-Index-of-Religiosity-and-Atheism-2012, 2012)

Wolf, N., *Misconceptions: Truth, Lies and the Unexpected on the Journey to Motherhood* (London: Chatto and Windus, 2001)

Women's Health Council, *Women's Mental Health: Promoting a Gendered Approach to Policy and Service Provision* (Dublin: The Women's Health Council, 2004)

Wright Mills, C., *The Sociological Imagination* (New York: Oxford University Press, 1959)

Zinn, M.B. and Thornton Dill, B., 'Theorizing Difference from Multiracial Feminism', *Feminist Studies* 22.2 (1996) pp. 321–331

Notes and References

INTRODUCTION

1 I use the term 'working mother' to mean women with children who engage in paid work. The term 'working mother' is taken in common parlance to mean women with children who engage in paid work outside the home. I acknowledge that the term could be read to imply that women with children who work full-time in the home do not work. Women who mother full-time in the home work very hard indeed and also experience inequalities. However these are different from the inequalities experienced by women who combine motherhood with paid work. This research is only concerned with exploring the complex inequality experienced by women who combine motherhood with paid work outside the home and I use the term 'working mother' in single quotation marks to highlight this problem of definition with the word 'work'.

2 F. McGinnity and H. Russell, *Gender Inequalities in Time Use: The Distribution of Caring, Housework and Employment Among Women and Men in Ireland* (Dublin: Equality Authority, 2008).

3 R. Asher, *Shattered: Modern Motherhood and the Illusion of Equality* (London: Random House, 2011); P. DiQuinzio, *The Impossibility of Mothering: Feminism, Individualism and the Problem of Mothering* (New York and London: Routledge, 1999); E. Badinter, *The Conflict: How Modern Motherhood Undermines the Status of Women* (New York: Henry Holt, 2011).

4 L. Bennetts, The Feminine Mistake: Are we giving up too much? (New York: Hyperion, 2007); M. Benn, *Madonna and Child: Towards a New Politics of Motherhood* (London: Jonathan Cape, 1998); R. Cusk, *A Life's Work: On Becoming a Mother* (London: Harper Collins, 2001); K. Figes, *Life after Birth* (London: Penguin, 1998).

5 M. Blair-Loy, 'Cultural constructions of family schemas: The case of women finance executives', *Gender and Society* 15 (2001) pp. 687–709; M. Blair-Loy, *Competing Devotions: Career and Family among Women Executives* (Harvard: Harvard University Press, 2003); P. Stone, *Opting Out?: Why Women Really Quit Careers and Head Home* (California: University of California Press, 2008); B. Jones, *Women Who Opt Out: The Debate Over Working Mothers and Work Family Balance* (New York: NYU Press, 2012); L. McKie, I. Biese and M. Jyrkinen, '"The Best Time is Now!": The temporal and spatial dynamics of women opting in to self employment', *Gender Work and Organisation* 20 (2013), pp. 184–196.

6 J. Warner, *Perfect Madness: Motherhood in the age of Anxiety* (London: Vermilion, 2006); A. Crittenden, *The Price of Motherhood: Why the Most*

233

Important Job in the World is Still the Least Valued (New York: Henry Holt, 2001); S. Douglas and M. Michaels, *The Idealization of Motherhood and How it Has Undermined All Women* (New York and London: Free Press, 2004).

7   S. Hays, *The Cultural Contradictions of Motherhood* (New Haven: Yale University Press, 1996).

8   C. Gatrell, *Hard Labour: The Sociology of Parenthood* (Berkshire: Open University Press, 2005).

9   C. Gatrell, 'Managing the Maternal Body: A Comprehensive Review and Transdisciplinary Analysis', *International Journal of Management Reviews* 13 (2011), pp. 97–112.

10 T. Miller, *Making Sense of Motherhood: A Narrative Approach* (Cambridge: University Press, 2005).

11 D. Reay, *Class Work: Mothers' Involvement in Their Children's Primary Schooling* (London: Routledge Falmer, 1998).

12 L. Smyth, *The Demands of Motherhood* (Basingstoke: Palgrave Macmillan, 2012).

13 P. Kennedy, *Motherhood in Ireland: Creation and Context* (Cork: Mercier Press, 2004).

14 V. White, *Mother Ireland: Why Ireland Hates Motherhood* (Dublin: Londubh Books, 2010).

15 Government of Ireland, *Civil Service (Employment of Married Women) Act 1973* (Dublin: Government Publications, 1973).

16 CSO, *Quarterly National Household Survey, Q1 2009: Married Women's Participation Rates* (online: *www.cso.ie*, 2009) [accessed 30/3/10].

17 A. Hochschild, *The Second Shift: Working Parents and the Revolution at Home* (London: Piatkus, 1990); M.C. Bateson, *Composing a Life* (New York: Grove Press, 1989); K. Boh, 'European family life patterns – a reappraisal' in K. Boh, M. Bak, C. Clason, M. Pankratova, J. Qvortrup, G.B. Sgritta and K. Waerness (eds), *Changing Patterns of European Family Life: A Comparative Analysis of Fourteen European Countries* (London: Routledge, 1989), pp. 265–298; U. Bjornberg, 'Parenting in transition: an introduction and summary' in U. Bjornberg (ed.), *European Parents in the 1990s: Contradictions and Comparisons* (New Brunswick: Transaction Publishers, 1992), pp. 1–41; P. O'Connor, *Emerging Voices: Women in Contemporary Irish Society* (Dublin: IPA, 1998); J. Murphy-Lawless, 'Changing Women's Lives: Child Care Policy in Ireland', *Feminist Economics* 6(1) (2000), pp. 89–94; E. Drew, *Uptake of Family Friendly Workplace Arrangements* (online: *www.siptu.ie/information*, 2009) [accessed 30/01/15]; E. Mahon, 'Reconciling Work and Family Lives', paper presented to Irish Social Policy Association Conference (Dublin: 17 September 2004); A. Coakley, *Mothers, Welfare and Labour Market Activation*, Working Paper 05/04 (Dublin: Combat Poverty Agency, 2005); U. Barry, 'Changing Economic and Social Worlds of Irish Women' in U. Barry (ed.) *Where Are We Now?: New Feminist Perspectives on Women in Contemporary Ireland* (Dublin: TASC at New Island, 2008), pp. 1–29.

18 K. Lynch and M. Lyons, 'The Gendered Order of Caring' in U. Barry (ed.) *Where Are We Now?: New Feminist Perspectives on Women in Contemporary Ireland* (Dublin: Tasc at New Island Press, 2008), pp. 163–183, p. 174.

19 K. Lynch and M. Lyons, op. cit., p. 174.

20 European Community Household Panel, *Ireland Wave. Irish Social Science Data Archive* (online: *www.ucd.ie/issda/dataset*, 2001) [accessed 14/06/06].

21 C. Jones, L. Tepperman and S. Wilson, *The Futures of the Family* (New Jersey: Prentice Hall, 1995), p. 110.

22 T. Hagerstrand, 'Survival and Arena: On the Life Histories of Individuals in Relation to their Geographical Environment' in T. Carlstein, D. Parkes, and N. Thrift (eds), *Timing Space and Spacing Time* (London: Edward Arnold Ltd, 1978), volume 2, pp. 122–145.

23 K. Davies, *Women, Time and the Weaving of the Strands of Everyday Life* (Aldershot, England: Gower, 1990); H. Nowotny, 'Time and social theory: towards a social theory of time', *Time and Society* 1(3) (1992), pp. 421–454; D. Knights and P. Odih, '"It's about time!" The significance of gendered time for financial services consumption', *Time and Society* 4(2) (1995), pp. 205–231; A. Lareau, 'Invisible Inequality: Social Class and Childrearing in Black Families and White Families', *American Sociological Review* 67(5) (2002), pp. 747–776; L. McKie, S. Gregory and S. Bowlby, 'Shadow Times: The Temporal and Spatial Frameworks and Experiences of Caring and Working', *Sociology* 36(4) (2002), pp. 897–924.

24 B. Adam, *Time and Social Theory* (Cambridge: Polity Press, 1990); K. Davies, op. cit.

25 F. Williams, 'Time to Care, Time not to Care', ESRC 4th National Social Science Conference (London: 28 November 2000).

26 P. O'Connor, 'The Patriarchal State: Continuity and Change' in M. Adshead, P. Kirby, M. Millar, (eds) *Contesting the State* (Manchester: Manchester University Press, 2008), pp. 143–164.

27 J. Williams, *Unbending Gender: Why Family and Work Conflict and What to Do About It* (Oxford and New York: Oxford University Press, 2000).

28 S. O'Sullivan, 'Gender and the Workforce' in S. O'Sullivan (ed.), *Contemporary Ireland: A Sociological Map* (Dublin: University College Dublin Press 2007), pp. 265–282, p. 271.

29 N. Fairclough, 'Critical Discourse Analysis', *Marges Linguistiques* 9 (2005), pp. 76–94, p. 80.

30 Ibid.

31 B. Skeggs, *Formations of Class and Gender: Becoming Respectable* (London: Sage, 1997), p. 12.

32 G. Letherby, 'Challenging Dominant Discourses: Identity and Change and the Experience of Infertility and Involuntary Childlessness', *Journal of Gender Studies* 11(3) (2002), pp. 277–288, p. 286.

33 K.W. Crenshaw, 'Demarginalizing the Intersection of Race and Sex: A Black Feminist Critique of Antidiscrimination Doctrine, Feminist Theory and Antiracist Politics', *University of Chicago Legal Forum* 139 (1989), pp. 139–167.

34 H. Dillaway and E. Paré, 'Locating Mothers: How cultural debates about stay-at-home versus working mothers define women and home', *Journal of Family Issues* 29(4) (2008), pp. 437–464.

35 L. McCall, 'The Complexity of Intersectionality', *Signs* 30(3) (2005), pp. 1771–1800.

36 J. Lorber, 'The Variety of Feminisms and their Contribution to Gender Equality' in M. Marx Ferree, J. Lorber and B. Hess (eds), *Revisioning Gender* (London: Sage, 1999), pp. 7–43.

37 Ibid.

38 Ibid.

39 Ibid.
40 Ibid., pp. 25–26.
41 L. McCall, *Complex Inequality: Gender Class and Race in the New Economy* (New York: Blackwell, 2001).
42 M. Marx Ferree, 'Inequality, Intersectionality and the Politics of Discourse: Framing Feminist Alliances, in E. Lombardo, P. Meier, M. Verloo (eds), *The Discursive Politics of Gender Equality: Stretching, Bending and Policy-Making* (New York: Routledge, 2009), pp. 84–101.
43 P. Bourdieu, *Distinctions: A Social Critique of the Judgment of Taste,* translated by R. Nice (Cambridge MA: Harvard University Press, 1984).
44 Ibid.
45 NWCI, *Who Cares?: Challenging the Myths About Gender and Care in Ireland* (online: *www.nwci.ie,* 2009) [accessed 23/3/10].
46 S. Walby, 'Complexity Theory, Systems Theory, and Multiple Intersecting Social Inequalities', *Philosophy of the Social Sciences* 37(4) (2007), pp. 449–470.
47 M. Marx Ferree (2009), op. cit.
48 M. Foucault, *Discipline and Punish: the Birth of the Prison,* translated by A. Sheridan (New York: Pantheon Books, 1977).
49 A. Oakley, *Housewife* (Harmondsworth: Penguin, 1974).
50 P. Bourdieu, *Outline of a Theory of Practice,* translated by R. Nice (Cambridge and New York: Cambridge University Press, 1977).
51 J. Warner (2006), op. cit.
52 G. Pascall and J. Lewis, 'Emerging Gender Regimes and Policies for Gender Equality in a Wider Europe', *Journal of Social Policy* 33.3 (2004), pp. 373–394.

1. No country for 'working mothers'

1 M. Friedman, *Capitalism and Freedom* (Chicago: University of Chicago Press, 1962); M. Friedman, *Free to Choose* (New York: Harcourt Brace Jovanovich, 1980); F. Hayek, *Law, Legislation and Liberty: A New Statement of the Liberal Principles and Political Economy, Volume 1: Rules and Order* (London, Routledge, 1973); D.E. Thorsen and A. Lie, 'What is Neo-liberalism?' Department of Political Science, Oslo University (online: http://folk.uio.no/daget/What%20is%20Neo Liberalism%20FINAL.pdf) [accessed 14/06/14].
2 J. Ferguson, 'The uses of Neo-Liberalism', *Antipode* 41.S1 (2009).
3 D. Harvey, *A Brief History of Neo-liberalism* (London: Oxford, 2005).
4 J. Ferguson, op. cit.
5 P. Treanor, *Neoliberalism: Origins, Theory, Definition* (online: http://web.inter.nl.net/users/Paul.Treanor/neoliberalism.html, 2007) [accessed 28/07/10].
6 M. Harney, 'Remarks by Tánaiste, Mary Harney at a meeting of the American Bar Association' at the Law Society of Ireland, Blackhall Place, Dublin (21 July, 2000).
7 Ibid.
8 E. McLaughlin, 'Ireland: Catholic Corporatism' in A. Cochrane and J. Clarke (eds), *Social Policy in Ireland: Principles, Practice and Problems* (Dublin: Oak Tree Press, 1993), pp. 297–328, p. 305.
9 P. Teague, 'Pay Determination in the Republic of Ireland: Toward Social Corporatism?' *British Journal of Industrial Relations* 33.2 (1995), pp. 253–273; W. Roche, 'Pay Determination and the Politics of Industrial Relations' in T.V.

Murphy and W.K. Roche (eds), *Irish Industrial Relations in Practice* (Dublin: Oak Tree Press, 1997), pp. 145–226; N. Hardiman, 'From Conflict to Coordination: Economic Governance and Political Innovation in Ireland', *West European Politics* 25.4 (2004), pp. 1–25.

10 R. O'Donnell, 'The Celtic Tiger', Presentation to Re-Imagining Ireland Conference, University of Virginia (May 2003).

11 G. Boucher and G. Collins, 'Having one's cake and being eaten too: Irish Neoliberalcorporatism', *Review of Social Economy*, vol. lxi (3) (2003), pp. 295–316.

12 M. Prasad, *The Politics of Free Markets: The Rise of Neoliberal Economic Policies in Britain, France, Germany & The United States* (Chicago: University of Chicago Press, 2006).

13 J. Ferguson, op. cit.

14 T. Inglis, *Global Ireland Same Difference* (New York and London: Taylor and Francis, 2008), p. 28.

15 M. Moran, 'Wealth, poverty and redistribution in Ireland'; paper presented at *Poverty and Wealth – Wealth concentration and increasing poverty: current trends, root causes and strategies to address them*. Thesis papers of the seminar in Athens (18–21 April 2013), p. 27.

16 Ibid.

17 D. Harvey, op. cit.

18 M. Prasad, op. cit.

19 E. Martinez and A. Garcia, *What is 'Neo-Liberalism'? A Brief Definition* (online: http:www.globalexchange.org/campaigns, 2000) [accessed 28/07/2010]; I. Lenz, 'Varieties of Gender Regimes and Regulating Gender Equality at Work in the Global Context' in S.H. Gottfried, K. Gottschall and M. Osawa (eds), *Gendering the Knowledge Economy: Comparative Perspectives* (London and New York: Palgrave Macmillan, 2007), pp. 109–139; S. Walby, 'Introduction: Theorizing the Gendering of the Knowledge Economy: Comparative Perspectives' in S. Walby, H. Gottfried, K. Gottschall and M. Osawa (eds), *Gendering the Knowledge Economy: Comparative Perspectives* (London and New York: Palgrave Macmillan, 2007), pp. 3–50.

20 P. Bourdieu, 1984, op. cit.

21 D. Harvey, op. cit.

22 J. Ferguson, op. cit.

23 G. Esping-Andersen, *The Three Worlds of Welfare Capitalism* (Cambridge: Polity Press & Princeton: Princeton University Press, 1990); G. Esping-Andersen, *The Social Foundations of Postindustrial Economies* (Oxford University Press, 1999).

24 H. Russell, F. McGinnity, T. Callan, C. Keane, *A Woman's Place: Female Participation in the Irish Labour Market* (Dublin: Equality Authority, 2009); J. Lewis, 'Gender and the development of welfare regime', *Journal of European Social Policy* 2(3) (1992), pp. 159–173; F. McGinnity, H. Russell and P. O'Connell, 'The Impact of Flexible Working Arrangements on Work-life Conflict and Work Pressure in Ireland', *Gender Work and Organisation* 16 (1) (2009), pp. 73–97.

25 D. Harvey, op. cit.,

26 Government of Ireland, *Budget 2000* (Dublin: Department of Finance, Government Publications, 2000).

27 P. Kennedy, op. cit.

28 A nationwide consultation process on 'The future of the family' was con-
ducted in 2004, with public meetings taking place in several major centres.
The findings of the 'Family Fora' reveal public attitudes to family life in
Ireland and were published in 2004. M. Daly, *Families and Family Life in Ireland:
Challenges for the Future*. Report of the Public Consultation Fora (Dublin:
Department of Social and Family Affairs, 2004).

29 E. Mahon, 2004. op. cit.

30 E. Mahon, 'Changing Gender Roles, State, Work and Family Lives' in E. Drew,
R. Emerek and E. Mahon (eds), *Women, Work and the Family in Europe* (London:
Routledge, 1998), pp. 153–158; C. O'Hagan, 'Ideologies of Motherhood and
Single Mothers' in M.C. Ramblado-Minero and A. Pérez-Vides (eds), *Single
Motherhood in Twentieth Century Ireland: Cultural, Historical and Social Essays*
(London and New York: The Edwin Mellen Press, 2006), pp. 65–82.

31 TASC, *The Solidarity Factor: Public Responses to Economic Inequality in Ireland*
(Dublin: TASC at New Ireland, 2009), p. 2.

32 CORI, *Income Distribution: Pre-budget Submission* (Dublin: CORI and
Dominican Publications, 2004).

33 S. Cantillon, C. Corrigan, P. Kirby and J. O'Flynn (eds), *Rich and Poor:
Perspectives on Tackling Inequality in Ireland* (Dublin: Oak Tree Press, 2001). p.
304.

34 P. Kirby, *The Celtic Tiger in Distress* (London: Pluto Press, 2002), p. 5.

35 D. Murray, 'The Soul of Europe', *The Furrow* 49.1 (1998), p. 5.

36 P. Treanor, op. cit.

37 M. Murray, 'The polluter pays? Individualising Ireland's Waste Problem' in
M. Corcoran and M. Peillon (eds), *Uncertain Ireland* (Dublin: Institute for
Public Administration, 2006), pp. 103–114.

38 J. Webb, 'Organisations, Self-Identities and the New Economy', *Sociology* 38(4)
(2004), pp. 719–738.

39 T. Inglis (2008), op. cit.

40 Ibid.

41 P. O'Connor, *Irish Children and Teenagers in a Changing World* (Manchester
University Press, 2008).

42 T. Inglis (2008), op. cit.

43 Ibid.

44 T. Inglis, *Truth, Power and Lies: Irish Society and the Case of the Kerry Babies*
(Dublin: UCD Press, 2003), p. 137.

45 Government of Ireland, *Bunreacht na h'Eireann [Constitution of Ireland]*
(Dublin: Government Publications, 1937). The Irish Constitution (Article
41.2) states 'The state recognises that by her life within the home, woman
gives to the state the support without which the common good cannot be
achieved. The state shall, therefore, endeavour to ensure that mothers shall
not be obliged by economic necessity to engage in labour to the neglect of
their duties within the home.'

46 J. Moran, 'From Catholic Church dominance to social partnership promise
and now economic crisis, little changes in Irish social policy', *Irish Journal of
Public Policy* (online: http://publish.ucc.ie/ijpp/2010/01/moran/01/en,
2009) [accessed 21/01/14].

47 Government of Ireland, *The Health (Family Planning) Act 1979* (Dublin:
Government Publications, 1979). This act legalised contraceptives (condoms
and the pill).

48 Government of Ireland, *The Family Law (Divorce) Act, 1996* (Dublin: Government Publications, 1996). This act introduced divorce in circumstances where the couple had been living apart for five years.

49 Government of Ireland, *Protection of Life During Pregnancy Act 2013* (Dublin: Government Publications, 2013). This act provides for lawful access to abortion where a pregnant woman's life is at risk.

50 T. Inglis, *Moral Monopoly: The Rise and Fall of the Catholic Church in Modern Ireland* (Dublin: UCD Press, 1987), p. 253.

51 Ibid., p. 138

52 N. Rose, *Governing the Soul* (London: Routledge, 1989); N. Rose, 'Preface to the second edition', *Governing the Soul. The Shaping of the Private Self* (London: Free Association Books, 1999), pp. vii–xxvii.

53 A. Giddens (1991), op. cit., p. 32.

54 S. Lash, 'Reflexivity and its Doubles: Structure, Aesthetics, Community' in U. Beck, A. Giddens and S. Lash (eds), *Reflexive Modernization: Politics, Tradition and Aesthetics in the Modern Social Order* (Cambridge: Polity Press, 1994), pp. 110–173, p. 120.

55 F. Anthias, 'Theorizing identity, difference and social divisions' in M. O'Brien, S. Penna and C. Hay (eds), *Theorizing Modernity: Reflexivity, Environment and Identity in Giddens' Social Theory* (London: Longman, 1999), pp. 156–178.

56 L. Adkins, *Revisions: Gender and Sexuality in Late Modernity* (Buckingham: Open University Press, 2002).

57 S. Franklin, C. Lury and J. Stacey, 'Units of Genealogy' in S. Franklin, C. Lury and J. Stacey (eds), *Global Culture, Global Nature* (London: Sage, 2000), pp. 68–93, p. 75.

58 B. Gray, *Women and the Irish Diaspora* (London and New York: Routledge, 2004), p. 158.

59 B. Hilliard, 'Family' in S. O'Sullivan (ed.), *Contemporary Ireland: A Sociological Map* (Dublin: University of Dublin Press, 2007), pp. 83–100.

60 B. Skeggs, *Class, Self, Culture* (London and New York: Routledge, 2004).

61 G.K. Hadfield, 'The Dilemma of Choice: A Feminist Perspective on "The Limits of Freedom of Contract"', *Osgoode Hall Law Journal* 33.2 (1995), pp. 338–351.

62 P. DiQuinzio, op. cit.

63 G. Becker, *A Treatise on the Family* (Cambridge, MA: Harvard University Press, 1991); G.K. Hadfield, op. cit.

64 A. McKinnon, 'Girls, School and Society: a generation of change?', Clare Burton Memorial Lecture (University of South Australia, 2005).

65 A. Oakley, *Gender on Planet Earth* (London and New York: Polity Press, 2002), p. 121.

66 G. Pascall and J. Lewis, op. cit.

67 E. Beck-Gernsheim, *Reinventing the Family: In Search of New Lifestyles* (Cambridge: Polity Press, 2002).

68 Ibid.

69 J. Williams, op. cit., p. 5.

70 T. Inglis (2008), op. cit., p. 160.

71 P. Bourdieu (1984), op. cit.

72 A. Giddens (1991), op. cit.; N. Rose, 'Governing the enterprising self' in P. Heelas and P. Morris (eds), *The Values of the Enterprise Culture: The Moral*

Debate (London: Routledge, 1992), pp. 141–164; Z. Bauman, *Liquid Modernity* (Cambridge: Polity Press, 2000).

73 L. Connolly and T. O'Toole, *Documenting Irish Feminisms: The Second Wave* (Dublin: Woodfield Press, 2005), p. 90.

74 Central Statistics Office, *Women and Men in Ireland 2009* (Cork: Central Statistics Office, 2010).

75 Government of Ireland, 1973, op. cit.

76 Government of Ireland, *Anti-Discrimination (Pay) Act* (Dublin: Government Publications, 1974).

77 Government of Ireland, *Social Welfare Act 1974* (Dublin: Government Publications, 1974).

78 Government of Ireland, *Anti-Discrimination Act* (1974), op. cit.

79 M. Mayo and A. Weir, 'The future for feminist social policy?' in R. Page and J. Baldock (eds), *Social Policy Review* 5 (1993), pp. 35–57.

80 I. Bacik, *Kicking and Screaming: Dragging Ireland into the 21st Century* (Dublin: The O'Brien Press, 2004).

81 M. Maher, 'Women's Liberation', *The Irish Times* (9 March 1971); J. Levine, *Sisters: The Personal Story of an Irish Feminist* (Dublin: Ward River Press, 1982); N. McCafferty, *A Woman to Blame* (Dubin: Attic Press, 1985); U. Barry, *Lifting the Lid* (Dublin: Attic Press, 1986); N. Fennell and M. Arnold, *Irish Women Agenda for Practical Action: A Fair Deal for Women, December 1982–1987, Four Years of Achievement,* Department of Women's Affairs and Family Law Reform (Dublin: Government Publications, 1987); M. Daly (ed.), *Care Work: The Quest for Security* (Geneva: International Labour Office, 2001); E. Drew, 'Part-Time Working in Ireland: Meeting the Flexibility Needs of Women Workers or Employers?' *Canadian Journal of Irish Studies* 18(1) (1992), pp. 95–109; E. Mahon, 'Equal Opportunities in the Irish Civil Service – Interim Review', *Women in Public Service Equal Opportunities International* 10.2 (1991), pp. 2–10; E. Mahon, 'Class, Mothers and Equal Opportunities to Work' in E. Drew, R. Emerek and E. Mahon (eds), *Women, Work and the Family in Europe* (London and New York: Routledge, 1998), pp. 170–181.

82 L. Connolly and T. O'Toole, op. cit., p. 90.

83 H. Dillaway and E. Paré, 'Locating Mothers: How cultural debates about stay-at-home versus working mothers define women and home', *Journal of Family Issues* 29(4) (2008), pp. 436–464.

84 B. Gray, op. cit.

85 J. Murphy-Lawless, op. cit., p. 93.

86 P. DiQuinzio, op. cit.

87 E.A. Kaplan, *Motherhood and Representation: The Mother in Popular Culture and Melodrama* (London: Routledge, 1992).

88 J. Buxton, *Ending the Mother War: Starting the Workplace Revolution* (London: Macmillan, 1998), p. 1.

89 V. White, op. cit. *For reactions to Mother Ireland: Why Ireland Hates Mothers.* On the website MagicMum: see http://www.magicmum.com/phpBB/view-topic.php?f=182&t=286654&start=24&view=print

90 R. Quiney, 'Confessions of the New Capitalist Mother: Twenty-first-century Writing on Motherhood as Trauma', *Women: A Cultural Review* 18.1 (2007), pp. 19–40.

91 J. Warner, op. cit., p. 67.

92 S. Hays, op. cit.; A. O'Reilly (ed.), *Mother Outlaws: Theories and Practices of Empowered Mothering* (Toronto: Women's Press, 2004); C. Gatrell, 2005, op. cit.; S. Maushart, *The Mask of Motherhood: How Becoming a Mother Changes Our Lives and Why We Never Talk About It* (London: Penguin, 1997); A. Hattery, *Women, Work and Family: Balancing and Weaving* (Thousand Oaks, London and New Delhi: Sage, 2001); S. Douglas and M. Michaels, op. cit.

93 T. Miller, op. cit.

94 S. Duncan and R. Edwards, *Lone Mothers, Paid Work and Gendered Moral Rationalities* (Houndsmill: Macmillan Press 1999).

95 J. Baker, K. Lynch, S. Cantillon and J. Walsh (eds), *Equality: From Theory to Action* (London: Palgrave Macmillan, 2004).

96 K. Lynch and M. Lyons, op. cit.

97 D. Richardson, *Women, Motherhood and Childrearing* (London: Macmillan, 1993); C. Gilligan, 'Hearing the difference: theorizing connection', *Hypatia* 20.2 (1995), pp. 119–134;

98 M.C. Nussbaum (1995), op. cit.; M.C. Nussbaum (1995), op. cit.

99 E. Kittay, op. cit.

100 J. Tronto (2002), op. cit.

101 K. Lynch (2007), op. cit.; K. Lynch, 'A Care-Full Model of Citizenship: Challenging the Rational Economic Actor (REA) Model', paper presented to Connecting with Family Carers International Conference (University College Cork, 4 September 2008).

102 K. Lynch and J. Baker *Affective Equality: Who Cares?* (London: Palgrave Macmillan, 2008).

103 K. Lynch, 'Solidary Labour: Its Nature and Marginalisation', *The Sociological Review* 37(1) (1989), pp. 1–14.

104 K. Lynch and E. McLaughlin, 'Caring Labour and Love Labour' in P. Clancy, S. Drury, K. Lynch and L. O'Dowd (eds), *Irish Society: Sociological Perspectives* (Dublin: IPA, 1995); K. Lynch and L. O'Dowd (eds), *Irish Society: Sociological Perspectives* (Dublin: IPA, 1995), pp. 250–292; M.C. Nussbaum (2000), op. cit.; K. Lynch (2008), op. cit.; K. Lynch and J. Baker (2008), op. cit.; R. Crompton, *Employment and the Family: The Reconfiguration of Work and Family Life in Contemporary Societies* (Cambridge: Cambridge University Press, 2006), p. 191.

105 K. Lynch and E. McLaughlin, op. cit.

106 K. Lynch and M. Lyons, op. cit.; J. Baker, K. Lynch, S. Cantillon and J. Walsh (2004), op. cit.

107 K. Lynch and M. Lyons, op. cit.

108 E. Mahon (1998), op. cit.

109 McGinnity et al (2008), op. cit.

110 CSO, *Women and Men in Ireland 2011* (Cork: Central Statistics Office, 2012), p. 11.

111 A. McCashin, *Lone Mothers in Ireland: A Local Study* (Dublin: Combat Poverty Agency, 1996); V. Beechley and T. Perkins, *A Matter of Hours: Women, Part Time Work and the Labour Market* (Oxford: Polity Press, 1997); E. Coveney, J. Murphy-Lawless and S. Sheridan, *Women, Work and Family Responsibilities* (Dublin: Larkin Unemployed Centre, 1998), p. 11.

112 CSO (2012), op. cit., p. 21

113 CSO, *Statistical Yearbook of Ireland 2013* (Cork: CSO, 2014).

114 A. Coakley, 'Gendered Citizenship: The Social Construction of Mothers in Ireland' in A. Byrne and M. Leonard (eds), *Women and Irish Society: A Sociological Reader* (Belfast: Beyond the Pale, 1997), pp. 181–195, p. 185.

115 M. Moran, 'Social inclusion and the limits of pragmatic liberalism: The Irish case', *Irish Political Studies* 21(2) (2006), pp. 181–201.

116 B. Adam (1990), op. cit.; B. Adam (1995), op. cit.

117 K. Davies, op. cit.

118 D.E. Bubeck, *Care, Gender and Justice* (Oxford: Oxford University Press, 1995); M. O'Brien, 'Mothers as Educational Workers': Mothers' Emotional Work at the Children's Transfer to Second Level Education', *Irish Educational Studies* 24.2–3 (2005), pp. 223–242.

119 M. Daly (2001), op. cit.; N. Folbre, 'A theory of the misallocation of time' in N. Folbre and M. Bittman, (eds), *Family Time: the Social Organisation of Care* (New York: Routledge, 2004), pp. 6–24; D. Reay, *'Doing the dirty work of social class? Mothers' work in support of their children's schooling'* in M. Glucksmann, L. Pettinger, J. Parry and R. Taylor (eds), *A New Sociology of Work* (London: Blackwell (2005), pp. 104–118; U. Barry, op. cit.; J. Tronto, 'Gender and Care' in *International Encyclopedia of the Social and Behavioral Sciences* (London: Elsevier, 2002).

120 K. Lynch, 'Love labour as a distinct and non-commodifiable form of Care Labour', *Sociological Review* 54(3) (2007), pp. 550–570.

121 R. Lister, *Citizenship: Feminist Perspectives* (London: Macmillan, 1997); S. Sevenhuijsen, *Citizenship and the Ethics of Care: Feminist Considerations on Justice, Morality and Politics* (London: Routledge, 1998) S. Duncan (2003), op. cit.

122 F. McKay, 'Women Politicians and the Ethic of Care', *Gender and Scottish Society: Polities, Policies and Participation* (Edinburgh: Unit for the Study of Government in Scotland, University of Edinburgh, 1998), p. 50.

123 J. Finch and D. Groves, *A Labour of Love: Women, Work and Caring* (London: Routledge, 1983); A. Hochschild, *The Managed Heart: Commercialization of Human Feeling* (Berkeley: University of California Press, 1989); A. Hobson (ed.), *Gender and Citizenship in Transition* (Basingstoke: Macmillan, 2000) B. Ungerson, 'The Commodification of Care: Current Policies and Future Politics' in B. Hobson (ed.), *Gender and Citizenship in Transition* (Basingstoke: Macmillan, 2000), pp. 173–200; G. Meagher, 'Is it wrong to pay for housework?' *Hypatia* 17.2 (2002), pp. 52–66.

124 J. Tronto, *Moral Boundaries: A Political Argument for an Ethic of Care* (London: Routledge, 1993); M.C. Nussbaum, 'Human Capabilties, Female Human Beings' in M.C. Nussbaum and J. Glover (eds), *Women, Culture and Development: A Study of Human Capabilities* (Oxford: Oxford University Press, 1995), pp. 61–104; M.C. Nussbaum, 'Emotions and Women's Capabilities in M.C. Nussbaum and J. Glover (eds), *Women, Culture and Development: A Study of Human Capabilities* (Oxford: Oxford University Press, 1995), pp. 360–395; M.C. Nussbaum, *Women and Human Development: The Capabilities Approach* (Cambridge: Cambridge University Press, 2000); N. Fraser and L Gordon, 'A Genealogy of "Dependency": Tracing a Keyword of the U.S. Welfare State' in N. Fraser (ed.), *Justice Interruptus* (New York: Routledge, 1997), pp. 121–149; M. Leonard, 'Women Caring and Sharing in Belfast' in A. Byrne and M. Leonard (eds), *Women and Irish Society: A Sociological Reader* (Belfast: Beyond the Pale Publications, 1997), pp. 111–126; E. Kittay, *Love's*

Labor: Essays on Women, Equality and Dependency (New York and London: Routledge, 1999).

125 B. Gray, op. cit.
126 M. Daly (2004), op. cit., p. 129.
127 Ibid., p. 34.
128 CSO, *Census of Population 2006* (Cork: Central Statistics Office, 2006).
129 CSO (2010), op. cit.
130 The term 'Celtic Tiger' first appeared in a Morgan Stanley article in 1994. The term Celtic Tiger is analogical to East Asian Tigers, a term applied to the economies of Hong Kong, Singapore, South Korea, Taiwan and other countries in Eastern Asia during the period of their phenomenal economic growth in the 1980s and 1990s.
131 R. O'Donnell, op. cit.
132 B. Hilliard, op. cit.
133 CSO (2009), op. cit.
134 CSO (2012), op. cit.
135 CSO (2012), op. cit., p.18
136 CSO (2012), op. cit.
137 Ibid.
138 CSO (2012), op. cit., p. 28.
139 Citizens Information Board, *Income Tax Bands* (online: http://www.citizensinformation.ie/en/money_and_tax/tax/income_tax/how_your_tax_is_calculated.html, 2014) [accessed 28/01/14].
140 Government of Ireland, *Budget 2009* (Dublin: Government Publications, 2009); Government of Ireland, *Budget 2010* (Dublin: Government Publications, 2010a); Government of Ireland, *Budget 2011* (Dublin: Government Publications, 2011); Government of Ireland, *Budget 2012* (Dublin: Government Publications, 2012a); Government of Ireland, *Budget 2013* (Dublin: Government Publications, 2013).
141 Government of Ireland, *Pathways to Work: Government Policy Statement on Labour Market Activation* (Dublin, Department of An Taoiseach: Government Publications, 2012).
142 Ibid.
143 Government of Ireland, Department of Social Protection, *Job Path* (online: http://www.welfare.ie/en/Pages/JobPath.aspx, 2014) [accessed 24/01/14].
144 J. Wickham, 'Technological and Organisational Choice', Policy Paper (Dublin: Employment Research Centre, University of Dublin, Trinity College, 2004), p. 36.
145 Social Justice Ireland, *Policy Briefing 2012 Poverty and Income Distribution* (online: http://www.socialjustice.ie/sites/default/files/file/Budget/2012/2011-12-07%20-%20Budget%202012%20Analysis%20and%20Critique.pdf, 2013) [accessed 19/11/13].
146 OECD, *Growing Unequal? Income Distribution and Poverty in OECD Countries* (Paris: OECD, 2008).
147 In national data, compiled by the Central Statistics Office, the at-risk-of-poverty rate shows the percentage of persons in the total population having an equivalised disposable income that is below the national 'at-risk-of-poverty threshold' which is set at sixty per cent of the national median equivalised disposable income. The OECD at-risk-of-poverty rate

is calculated by establishing the equivalised disposable income for each person, calculated as the household total net income divided by the equivalised household size. The OECD scale assigns a weight of 1.0 to the first adult, 0.5 to the other persons aged over fourteen or over who are living in the household and 0.3 to each child aged under fourteen. The purpose of the equivalence scale is to account for the size and composition of different income units and thus allows a more accurate comparison between households.

148 One Parent Family Agency, *Pre-Budget submission 2014* (online: http://www.onefamily.ie, 2014) [accessed 07/01/14].

149 Combat Poverty Agency, *Developing a Local Anti-Poverty and Social Inclusion Strategy: a guide* (Dublin: Combat Poverty Agency, 2008).

150 TASC, *The Solidarity Factor: Public Responses to Economic Inequality in Ireland* (Dublin: TASC at New Ireland, 2009). p. 2.

151 Treoir, *Babies and Bosses*, Newsletter November/December 2003 (online: www.treoir.ie, 2003) [accessed 9/6/04].

152 Family Support Unit, *Government Discussion Paper: Proposals for Supporting Lone Parents* (Dublin: Department of Social and Family Affairs, 2006).

153 Barnardos, 'Analysis of Budget 2012 from a Children and Families Perspective'(online: http://www.barnardos.ie/assets/files/Advocacy/Analysis%20of%20Budget%202012%20from%20a%20Children%20and%20Families%20Perspective.pdf, 2012) [accessed 28/01/14].

154 Government of Ireland (2010), op. cit.

155 Barnardos (2012), op. cit.

156 F. McGinnity, H. Russell and E. Smyth, 'Gender, Work-Life Balance and Quality of Life' in T. Fahey, H. Russell and C.T. Whelan (eds), *Best of Times? The Social Impact of the Celtic Tiger* (Dublin: IPA, 2005), pp. 199–216.

157 T. Inglis (2008), op. cit., p. 19.

158 S. O'Sullivan, op. cit.

159 A. Ryan, 'Contemporary discourses of working, earning and spending: acceptance, critique and the bigger picture' in C. Coulter and S. Coleman (eds), *The End of Irish History?: Critical Reflections on the Celtic Tiger* (Manchester: Manchester University Press, 2003).

160 P. Lunn and T. Fahey, *Households and Family Structures in Ireland* (Dublin: Family Support Agency, 2011), p. xiii.

161 S. O'Sullivan, op. cit., p. 281.

162 K. Lynch and E. McLaughlin, op. cit.; K. Lynch (1989), op. cit.

163 U. Barry (2008), op. cit.

164 F. McGinnity, H. Russell, J. Williams and S. Blackwell, *Time Use in Ireland 2005* (Dublin: ESRI, 2005).

165 F. McGinnity, H. Russell and E. Smyth, op. cit.

166 B. Gray, op. cit., p. 51.

167 Ibid., p. 52.

168 M. Fine Davis, 'Fathers and Mothers: Dilemmas of the Work Life Balance' Work Life Balance Conference Proceedings (University of Dublin, Trinity College, 2002), pp. 11–13.

169 S. Halford, M. Savage and A. Witz, *Gender, Careers and Organisations* (London: Macmillan, 1997); C. Cockburn, 'Resisting Equal Opportunities' in S. Jackson and S. Scott (eds), *Gender: A Sociological Reader* (London and New York: Routledge, 2002), pp. 180–191; P. Barker and K. Monks, *Career*

Progression of Chartered Accountants (Dublin: Dublin City Business School, 1994); P. O'Connor, 'Ireland: A Man's world?', *The Economic and Social Review* 31.1 (2000), pp. 81–102.

170 U. Barry (2008), op. cit., p. 2.

171 A. Hochschild (1990), op. cit., p. 11.

172 I. Bacik, op. cit., p, 97.

2. COMPLEX INEQUALITY

1 S. Walby, *Gender Transformations* (London and New York: Routledge, 1997).

2 S. Walby (2007), op. cit., pp. 449–470.

3 L. McCall (2005), op. cit., pp. 1771–1800.

4 N.K. Hayles, *Chaos and Order: Complex Dynamics in Literature and Science* (Chicago: University of Chicago Press, 1991).

5 S. Walby (2007), op. cit.

6 M. Hawkesworth, *Feminist Inquiry: From Political Conviction to Methodological Innovation* (New Jersey: Rutgers University Press, 2006).

7 M. Marx Ferree, 'Introduction' in M. Marx Ferree and A.M. Tripp (eds), *Globalization and Feminism: Opportunities and Obstacles for Activism in the Global Arena* (New York: New York University Press, 2006), pp. 4–23, p. 10.

8 K.W. Crenshaw (1989), op. cit.

9 P. Hill Collins, *Black Feminist Thought: Knowledge, Consciousness and the Politics of Empowerment*, 2nd edition (New York: Routledge, 2000), p. 42.

10 A. Brah and A. Phoenix, 'Ain't I a Woman?: Revisiting Intersectionality' *Journal of International Women's Studies* 5.3 (2004), pp. 75–87, p. 76.

11 L . McCall (2001), op. cit.

12 K. Ashcraft, 'Managing Maternity Leave: A Qualitative Analysis of Temporary Executive Succession', *Administrative Science Quarterly* 44 (June 1999), pp. 240–280, p. 240.

13 P. Buzzanell and M. Liu, 'It's "give and take": maternity leave as a conflict management process', *Human Relations* 60 (2007), pp. 383–495.

14 C.J. Gatrell (2011), op. cit.

15 C.J. Gatrell, 'Maternal Body Work: How Women Managers and Professionals Negotiate Pregnancy and New Motherhood at Work', *Human Relations* 66.5 (2013), pp. 621–664, p. 623.

16 P. Stone, op. cit.; B. Jones, op. cit.; L. McKie, I. Biese and M. Jyrkinen, op. cit.

17 E. Martinez, 'Beyond Black/White: The Racisms of Our Times', *Social Justice* 20 (1993), pp. 1–2.

18 M.L. Fellows and S. Razack, 'The Race to Innocence: Confronting Hierarchical Relations among Women', *Journal of Gender, Race and Justice* 1.2 (1998), pp. 335–352.

19 A.M. Hancock, 'When Multiplication Doesn't Equal Quick Addition: Examining Intersectionality as a Research Paradigm', *Perspectives on Politics* 5.1 (2007), pp. 63–79.

20 P. Hill Collins, *Fighting Words: Black Women and the Search for Justice* (Minneapolis: University of Minnesota Press, 1998); K.W. Crenshaw, 'Mapping the margins: intersectionality, identity politics and violence against women of colour', *Standford Law Review* 43.6 (1991), pp. 1241–1299; A. Phoenix and P. Pattynama, 'Editorial: Intersectionality', *European Journal of Women's Studies*, 13(3) (2006), pp. 186–192.

21 L. McCall (2005), op.cit.

22 L. McCall (2005), op.cit., p. 1773.
23 S. Walby (2007), op. cit.
24 A. Phoenix, 'Centring marginality? Otherness, difference and the "Psychology of Women"', British Psychological Association Conference 2006 Proceedings 14.1 (February 2006), p. 1.
25 Concepts of 'system' include 'social relations' (Emirbayer, 1997), 'regime' (Connell, 1987; Esping-Andersen, 1999), 'network' (Latour, 1987; Scott, 2000) and 'discourse' (Foucault, 1977), in S. Walby (2007), op. cit., pp. 3–50.
26 Ibid.
27 S. Walby, *Theorizing Patriarchy* (Oxford: Blackwell, 1990); S. Walby, 'The European Union and Gender Equality: Emergent Varieties of Gender Regime', *Social Politics* 11.1 (2004), pp. 4–19; S. Walby, *Globalization and Inequalities: Complexity and Contested Modernities* (London: Sage, 2009).
28 S. Walby (2007), op. cit.
29 M. Marx Ferree (2009), op. cit.
30 Ibid.
31 A. Giddens, *The Consequences of Modernity* (Cambridge: Polity Press, 1990).
32 M. Marx Ferree (2009), op. cit.
33 Ibid.
34 M. Foucault (1977), op. cit.
35 M. Foucault, *The History of Sexuality*, vol. I (Harmondsworth: Penguin, 1981).
36 A. Armstrong, *Foucault and Feminism* (online: http://www.iep.utm.edu/f/foucfem.htm, 2003) [accessed 28/04/05].
37 G. Letherby (2002), op. cit., p. 286.
38 G. Letherby (2002), op. cit.
39 R. Dhamoon, 'Considerations in Mainstreaming Intersectionality as an Analytic Approach', paper delivered at 2008 Annual Meeting of the Western Political Science Association, San Diego (20–22 March 2008).
40 I. Grewal and C. Kaplan, 'Introduction: Transnational Feminist Practices and Questions of Postmodernity' in I. Grewal and C. Kaplan (eds), *Scattered Hegemonies: Postmodernity and Transnational Feminist Perspectives* (Minneapolis: University of Minnesota Press, 1994), pp. 1–36.
41 R.W. Connell, *Masculinities* (Cambridge: Polity Press, 1995), p. 215.
42 M. Foucault, *Politics, Philosophy, Culture: Interviews and Other Writings 1976–1984* (New York: Routledge, 1990), p. 33.
43 R.W. Connell (1995), op. cit., p. 80.
44 B. Skeggs (1997), op. cit.
45 C. Hughes, *Key Concepts in Feminist Theory and Research* (London: Sage, 2002), p. 151.
46 Stanford Internet Encyclopedia of Philosophy, 'Feminist Standpoint Theory' (online: http://www.iep.utm.edu/fem-stan/, 2014) [accessed 12/12/13].
47 N. Hartsock, 'The Feminist Standpoint: developing the ground for a specifically feminist historical materialism' in S. Harding (ed.), *Feminism and Methodology* (Bloomington: University of Indiana Press, 1987), pp. 156–180.
48 N. Hartsock, 'The feminist standpoint: developing the ground for a specifically feminist historical materialism' in D. Meyers (ed.), *Feminist Social Thought: A Reader* (New York: Routledge, 1997), pp. 462–483, p. 470.
49 J. Sprague, 'Comment on Walby's "Against Epistemological chasms: the

science question in feminism revisited": structured knowledge and strategic methodology', *Signs* 26(2) (2001), pp. 526–536, p. 529.

50 C. Hughes (2002), op. cit., p. 153.

51 G. Letherby, *Feminist Research in Theory and Practice* (Buckingham: Open University Press, 2003), p. 47.

52 G. Letherby (2003), op. cit., p. 57.

53 L. Stanley and S. Wise, *Breaking Out Again: Feminist Ontology and Epistemology* (London: Routledge, 1993), p. 116.

54 Ibid., p. 114.

55 B. Temple, '"Collegiate accountability" and bias: the solution to the problem?' *Sociological Reseach Online* 2(4) (1997) (online: www/socresonline/org.uk/socresonline/2/4/8.html., 1997:5.2, 1997) [accessed 10/08/10].

56 C. Weedon, *Feminist Practice and Poststructuralist Theory*, 2nd edition (Oxford: Blackwell, 1997).

57 M. Maynard, 'Feminists' knowledge and the knowledge of feminisms: epistemology, theory, methodology and method' in T. May and M. Williams (eds), *Knowing the Social World* (Buckingham: Open University Press 1998), pp. 120–137.

58 N. Rose, *Powers of Freedom: Reframing Political Thought* (Cambridge: Cambridge University Press, 1999), p. 52.

59 B. Gray, op. cit., pp. 18–19.

60 A. Brah, *Cartographies of Diaspora: Contesting Identities* (London: Routledge, 1996).

61 R. Felski, *The Gender of Modernity* (Cambridge MA: Harvard University Press, 1995), p. 21.

62 B. Gray, op. cit., p. 19.

63 S. Walby (2007), op. cit., pp. 449–470.

64 L. Stanley and S. Wise, 'Method, methodology and epistemology in feminist research processes' in L. Stanley (ed.), *Feminist Praxis: Research, Theory and Epistemology in Feminist Sociology* (London: Routledge, 1990), pp. 20–60, pp.21–2.

65 G. Letherby (2003), op. cit., p. 49.

66 P. Hill Collins (1998), op. cit., p. 205.

67 P. Hill Collins (2000), op. cit., p. 208.

68 P. Hill Collins (2000), op. cit., p. 228.

69 D. Smith, *The Everyday World as Problematic: A Feminist Sociology* (Boston: Northeastern University Press, 1987).

70 L. Fernandes, *Producing Workers: the Politics of Gender, Class and Culture in the Calcutta Jute Mills* (Philadelphia: University of Pennsylvania Press, 1997); E. Nanako Glenn, *Unequal Labour: How Race and Gender Shaped American Citizenship and Labor* (Cambridge: Harvard University Press, 2002).

71 L. McCall (2005), op. cit.

72 B. Skeggs (2004), op.cit.; L. McCall (2005), op. cit.

73 K.W. Crenshaw, 'Mapping the margins: Intersectionality, identity politics and violence against women of color' in K. Crenshaw, N. Gotanda, G. Peller and K. Thomas (eds), *Critical Race Theory: The Key Writings That Informed the Movement* (New York: New York Press, 1995), pp. 356–383, p. 375.

74 E.R. Cole, 'Intersectionality and Research in Psychology', *American Psychologist* 64.3 (2009), pp. 170–180, p. 171.

75 D.W. Sue, 'Whiteness and ethnocentric monoculturalism: Making the "invisible" visible', *American Psychologist* 59.8 (2004), pp. 761–769.

76 b. hooks, *Killing Rage: Ending Racism* (New York: Henry Holt, 1996).

77 S.D. Farough, 'Believing is Seeing: the matrix of vision and white masculinities', *Journal of Contemporary Ethnography* 35.1 (2006), pp. 51–83; P. Kuriloff and M. Reichert, 'Boys of class: boys of colour: Negotiating the academic and social geography of an elite independent school', *Journal of Social Issues* 59.4 (2003), pp. 751–769.

78 E.V. Spelman, *Inessential Woman* (Boston: Beacon Press, 1988).

79 N. Chodorow, *The Reproduction of Mothering: Psychoanalysis and the Sociology of Gender* (Berkley and Los Angeles: University of California Press, 1978).

80 E.V. Spelman, op. cit., p. 80.

81 E. Boniolla-Silva, 'Rethinking racism: toward a structural interpretation', *American Sociological Review* 62.3 (1997), pp. 465–480; B.J. Risman, 'Gender as a social structure: Theory wrestling with activism', *Gender and Society* 18.4 (2004), pp. 429–450.

82 G.A. Knapp, 'Race, Class, Gender: Reclaiming Baggage in Fast-Travelling Theories', *European Journal of Women's Studies* 12.3 (2005), pp. 249–265; E.R. Cole, op. cit.

83 L. Weber and D. Parra-Medina, 'Intersectionality and Women's Health: Charting a path to eliminating health disparities' in V. Demos and M.T. Segal (eds), *Advances in Gender Research: Gender perspectives on Health and Medicine* (Amsterdam: Elsevier, 2003), pp. 181–230, p. 190.

84 P.T. Reid, 'Poor women in psychological research: Shut up and shut out', *Psychology of Women Quarterly* 17.2 (1993), pp. 133–150; A. Eagly and W. Wood, 'The origins of sex differences in human behaviour: Evolved dispositions versus social roles', *American Psychologist* 54.6 (1999), pp. 408–423; B. Lott, 'Cognitive and behavioural distancing from the poor', *American Psychologist* 57 (2004), pp. 100–110.

85 L. MacLean, 'Intersectionality, social locations of privilege and conceptions of women's oppression', paper prepared for the CPSA meeting, May 2009, Carleton University, Ottowa, Canada. (online: http://www.cpsa-acsp.ca/papers-2009/MacLean.pdf, 2009) [accessed 20/07/09].

86 b. hooks, op. cit., cited in Letherby (2003), op. cit. p. 50–51.

87 L. MacLean, op. cit.

88 A.M. Hancock, 'Intersectionality as a normative and empirical paradigm', *Politics and Gender* 3 (2007), pp. 248–254.

3. 'Working Mothers' Research

1 L. McCall (2005), op. cit.

2 Ibid.

3 L. Cohen, L. Manion and K. Morrison, *Research Methods in Education*, 5th edition (London: Routledge-Falmer, 2000), p. 182.

4 L. McCall (2005), op. cit.

5 G. Letherby (2003), op. cit., p. 96.

6 CSO, *Socio Economic Groupings, Census of Population 1996* (Cork: Central Statistics Office, 1996).

7 *Standard Occupational Classification*, 2nd edition (London: Her Majesty's Stationery Office, 1995).

8 CSO, *Census 2006. Volume 8: Occupations* (online: www.cso.ie, 2006) [accessed 12/08/2010].

9 S. Wilkinson, 'Focus group methodology: a review', *International Journal of Social Research Methodology* 1(3) (1998), pp. 181–203, p. 187.

10 D. Morgan, *Focus Groups as Qualitative Research* (London: Sage, 1988), p. 18

11 P. Cooper, I. Diamond and S. High, 'Choosing and using contraceptives: Integrating qualitative and quantitative methods in family planning', *Journal of the Market Research Society* 35.4 (1993), pp. 325–339.

12 S. Murray, J. Tapson, L. Turnbull, J. McCallum and A. Little, 'Listening to local voices: Adapting rapid appraisal to assess health and social needs in general practice', *British Medical Journal* 308 no. 6930 (1994), pp. 698–700.

13 G. Broom and D. Dozier, *Using Research in Public Relations: Application to Programme Management* (New Jersey: Prentice Hall, 1990).

14 D. Rose, *Revisiting Feminist Research Methodologies – A Working Paper*. Status of Women (Online: www.swc-cfc.gc/pubs, 2001) [accessed 30/07/09].

15 J. Siltanen, 'Equality, diversity and the politics of scale: The Canadian public policy experience', paper presented at ESRC seminar: 'Public Policy, Equality and Diversity in the Context of Devolution', University of Edinburgh (10 June 2005).

16 G. Letherby (1999), op. cit., pp. 359–372.

17 N. Hartsock (1987), op. cit.

18 G. Letherby (2003), op. cit., p. 140.

19 Ibid.

20 M. Foucault (1977), op. cit.; M. Foucault, *Power/Knowledge: Selected Interviews and Other Writings, 1972–1977* (Brighton: Harvester, 1980); M. Foucault, 'The subject and power', *Critical Inquiry* 8(4) (1982), pp. 776–795.

21 C. Weedon (1997), op. cit., p. 11.

22 P. Lather, *Getting Smart: Feminist Research and Pedagogy With/in the Postmodern* (New York: Routledge, 1991), p. 7.

23 B. Skeggs (1997), op. cit., p. 8.

24 B. Gray, op. cit., p. 17.

25 N. Rose (1999), op. cit., p. 31.

26 B. Gray, op. cit.

27 N. Rose, 'The death of the social? Re-figuring the territory of government', *Economy and Society* (25)3 (2006), pp. 326–356.

28 B. Gray, op. cit., p. 17.

29 Ibid., p. 18.

30 Ibid.

31 J. Scott, 'The Evidence of Experience' in H. Abelore, M. Barade and D.M. Halpenn (eds), *The Lesbian and Gay Studies Reader* (New York: Routledge, 1993), pp. 397–415, p. 401.

32 M. Foucault (1977), op. cit., p. 100.

33 N. Mauthner and A. Doucet, 'Reflections on a Voice-Centred Relational Method: Analysing Maternal and Domestic Voices' in J. Ribbens and R. Edwards (eds), *Feminist Dilemmas in Qualitative Research: Public Knowledge and Private Lives* (London: Sage, 1998), pp. 119–146.

34 Ibid., p. 126.

35 M. Marx Ferree (2009), op. cit.; L. McCall (2005), op. cit.

4. MAKING THE 'RIGHT' CHOICE

1 K. Plummer, 'Intimate Choices' in G. Browning, A. Halcli and F. Webster (eds), *Understanding Contemporary Society: Theories of the Present* (London: Sage, 2000), pp. 432–44, p. 432.

2 S. Lash, 'Foreword: Individualization in a non-linear mode' in U. Beck and E. Beck-Gernsheim, *Individualization* (London: Sage, 2002), pp. vii–xiii, p. ix.

3 Markers of tradition in Ireland like religion, nation and class are losing significance for current generations. The Church's model of a spiritual and moral life based on frugal comforts has been rejected by almost half the population, who have embraced a new lifestyle based on economic growth, the development of the European Union and the pleasures of materialism and consumerism. Ireland has experienced the second largest drop in religious belief (of fifty-seven countries surveyed in 2012), falling from sixty-nine per cent to forty-seven per cent, with forty-four per cent describing themselves as not religious and ten per cent as atheist, compared to ninety-one per cent of practicing Catholics in 1973 (Win-Gallup, 2012). The trend of young educated people going abroad to work for a year or two has replaced historic images of poor uneducated Irish economic migrants. This, together with the availability of cheap flights, internet access and social media has made the world a much smaller place and those who travel abroad can easily, cheaply and frequently stay in touch with 'home'. Traditional markers of class position such as education and comfortable lifestyle are now universal, hence class has lost some of its significance and there is now a large middle-class in Ireland, with whom most people identify, rather than the extremes of wealth or poverty. Consumption patterns and values are more indicative of class position. (WIN-Gallup International *Global Index of Religiosity and Atheism, 2012*).

4 A. Giddens (1991), op. cit.; U. Beck. *Risk Society: Towards a New Modernity* (London: Sage, 1992).

5 E. Beck-Gernsheim, op. cit., p. ix.

6 A. Giddens (1991), op. cit., p. 75.

7 G. Becker, op. cit., p. ix.

8 B. Schwartz, 'The Tyranny of Choice,.' *Scientific American* 290.4 (2004), pp. 70–75, p. 71.

9 B. Davies, 'The concept of agency: a feminist poststructuralist analysis,' *Social Analysis* 300 (1991), pp. 42–53, p. 43.

10 B. Hilliard (2007), op. cit., pp. 83–100.

11 C. Hakim (2000), op. cit., p. 273.

12 C. Hakim, *Work-Lifestyle Choices in the 21st Century* (Oxford: Oxford University Press, 2000); C. Hakim, 'A new approach to explaining fertility patterns: preference theory.' *Population and Development Review* 29.3 (2003), pp. 349–374; C. Hakim, *Key Issues in Women's Work* (London: Glasshouse Press, 2004).

13 S. Duncan (2003), op.cit.

14 C. Hakim (2003), op. cit.

15 A. Giddens, 'Foreword' in C. Hakim *Work-Lifestyle Choices in the 21st Century* (Oxford: Oxford University Press, 2000), pp. i–xiii, p. vii.

16 S. McRae, 'Choice and constraints in mothers' employment careers: McRae replies to Hakim', *British Journal of Sociology* 54.4. (2003), pp. 585–592.

17 B. Hilliard (2007), op. cit.

18 R. Crompton, op. cit., p. 175.

19 C. Hughes, op. cit., p. 100.

20 Ibid., p. 46.

21 M.C. Nussbaum (2000), op. cit., p. 114.

22 C. Hughes, op. cit.

23 R.W. Connell, 1987, op. cit.; R.W. Connell, 'Making Gendered People' in M. Marx Ferree, J. Lorber and B. Hess (eds), *Revisioning Gender* (London: Sage, 1999), pp. 449–471; S. Halford, M. Savage and A. Witz, op. cit.; P. Bourdieu, *Masculine Domination* (translated by R. Nice (Cambridge: Polity Press, 2001)).

24 M.S. Archer, *Structure, Agency and the Internal Conversation* (Cambridge: Cambridge University Press, 2004), p. 115.

25 J. Williams, op. cit.

26 B. Davies, op. cit., p. 43.

27 C. Hughes, op. cit.

28 G.K. Hadfield, op. cit., pp. 338–351.

29 NWCI, *Valuing Care Work* (online:www.ie/publications, 2003) [accessed 29/10/04]; NWCI, *Campaign for Social Welfare Reform* (online: www.nwci.ie, 2005) [accessed 28/02/05].

30 J. Williams, op. cit., p. 41.

31 A. Oakley (1974), op. cit.

32 J. Bernard, *The Future of Marriage* (London: Souvenir Press, 1973).

33 H. Hartmann, 'The family as a locus of gender, class and political struggle: the example of housework', *Signs* 6.3 (1981), pp. 366–394.

34 B. Hilliard (2007), op. cit.

35 H. Dillaway and E. Paré, op. cit., pp. 437–464.

36 A. Garey, 'Constructing motherhood on the night shift: "Working mothers" as "stay-at-home moms"' in K.V. Hansen and A.I. Garey (eds), *Families in the U.S.: Kinshop and domestic policies* (Philadelphia: Temple University Press, 1998), pp. 709–726; D. Johnston and D. Swanson, 'Moms hating moms: The internalization of mother war rhetoric, *Sex Roles* 51 (2004), pp. 496–510.

37 S. Lash (1994), op. cit.

38 R. Crompton, op. cit.

39 U. Beck (1992), op. cit.

40 C. Hughes, op. cit.

41 B. Hilliard (2007), op. cit., p. 99.

42 A. Jones, 'Teaching post-structuralist feminist theory in education: student resistances', *Gender and Education* 9.3 (1997), pp. 261–270, p. 263

43 R.P. Petchesky, 'Foetal Images: The power of visual culture in the politics of reproduction' in M. Stanworth (ed.), *Reproductive Technologies: Gender, Motherhood and Medicine* (Cambridge: Polity, 1980), pp. 59–80, p. 68

44 K. Lynch and M. Lyons, op. cit., p. 182

45 H. Russell and M. Corcoran, *The Experiences of those Claiming the One-Parent Family Payment: A Qualitative Study* (Dublin: Department of Social and Family Affairs, 2000).

46 J. Nedelsky, *Law, Autonomy and the Relational Self: A Feminist Revisioning of the Foundations of Law* (Oxford: Oxford University Press, 2005), p. 2.

47 Z. Eisenstein, *The Radical Future of Liberal Feminism* (Boston: Northeastern University Press, 1993), p. xiii.

48 S. Earle and G. Letherby, 'Conceiving Time? Women who do or do not conceive', *Sociology of Health and Illness* 29.2 (2007), pp. 233–250, p. 234.

49 P. DiQuinzio, op. cit.

50 A. Crittenden, op. cit., p. 250.

51 Tertia, *The Cutthroat World of Motherhood* (online: Parenting Issues. http://www.tertia.org, 2006) [accessed 10/10/08].

52 Hakim (2000), op. cit., p.18.

53 V. Hardie, 'The world became a more dangerous place' in K. Gieve (ed.), *Balancing Acts: On Being a Mother* (London: Virago, 1989).

54 V. White, 'Our children don't need corporate creches – all they need is love', *Irish Examiner*, Thursday, 30 May, 2013.

55 Government of Ireland, *Public Service Stability Agreement 2013–2016 'Haddington Road Agreement'* (Dublin: Government Publications, 2013).

56 C. Cockburn, op. cit., p. 185.

57 J. Williams, op. cit., p. 6.

58 J. Warner (2006), op. cit., p. 9.

59 C. Wright Mills, *The Sociological Imagination* (New York: Oxford University Press, 1959).

5. Reflexive moral reasoning

1 Z. Bauman (2000), op. cit.

2 Z. Bauman, *Thinking Sociologically* (Oxford: Blackwell, 1990).

3 Z. Bauman (2000), op. cit.

4 J. Warner, 'The Mommy Madness Generation', *Newsweek* (21 February 2005), pp. 42–49.

5 C. Gatrell (2005), op. cit.

6 H. Dillaway and E. Paré, op. cit., pp. 437–464.

7 R.T. Gill and T.G. Gill, 'A New Plan for the Family', *Public Interest*, 111 (Spring 1993), pp. 86–94, p. 89.

8 Ibid.

9 D.E. Bubeck, op. cit.; M. O'Brien (2005), op. cit., pp. 223–242.

10 D. Hoy, *Critical Resistance From Poststructuralism to Postcritique* (Massachusetts: Massachusetts Institute of Technology, 2004), p. 103.

11 V. White, 'We shouldn't make it hard for parents to stay home and care for their children', *Irish Examiner* (Thursday, 6 June 2013); A. Harris, '"I've given them the best start" Donna May, stay-at-home mother of three', *The Herald* (21 June 2013); S. Biddulph, *'Raising Babies: Why Your Love is Best: Should Under 3s go to Nursery?'* (London: Harper Thorsons, 2006); L. Schlessinger, *In Praise of Stay-at-Home-Moms* (New York: HarperCollins, 2009); B. Mooney, 'The Scientific PROOF that sending mothers out to work harms children', *Mail online/femail* [http://www.dailymail.co.uk/femail/article-2296567] 20 March 2013.

12 J. Williams, op. cit., p. 16.

13 S. Duncan (2003), op. cit.

14 Ibid.

15 P. Bourdieu (1977), op. cit., p. 77.

16 Ibid.

17 G.K. Hadfield, op. cit., p. 343.

18 OECD, *Closing the Gender Gap Act Now* (Paris: OECD Publishing, 2012), p. 160.

19 U. Beck, 'The Reinvention of Politics: Towards a Theory of Reflexive Modernization' in U. Beck, A. Giddens and S. Lash (eds), *Reflexive Modernization: Politics, Tradition and Aesthetics in the Modern Social Order* (Cambridge: Polity Press, 1994), pp. 1–55, p. 16.

20 J. Rubery, M. Smith and C. Fagan, 'National Working Time Regimes and Equal Opportunities', *Feminist Economics* 4.1 (1998), pp. 71–101.

21 S. Duncan, 'Mothering, Class and Rationality', *The Sociological Review* 53.2. (2005), pp. 50–76, p. 54.

22 J. Warner, 'The Motherhood Religion' in A. O'Reilly (ed.), *Maternal Theory: Essential Readings* (Toronto: Demeter Press, 2007), pp. 705–725, p. 713.

6. THE MYTH OF MOTHERHOOD

1 S. Hays, op. cit.; F. Williams (2000), op. cit.; F. Williams, 'Changing Families – Changing Values?' ESRC Research Group on Care, Values and the Future of Welfare (London: 22 October 2001); F. Williams, *Rethinking Families* (London: Calouste Gulbenkian Foundation, 2004).

2 A. Oakley (1974), op. cit., p. 186.

3 S. Hays (1996), op. cit., p. 54.

4 C.L. Macdonald, 'Manufacturing motherhood: the shadow work of nannies and au pairs' *Qualitative Sociology* 21(1) (1998), pp. 25–48, p. 30.

5 D. Richardson, op. cit.

6 R.W. Connell (1995), op. cit.; P. O'Connor (2002), op. cit.

7 G. Letherby, 'Other than mother and mother as others: the experience of motherhood and non-motherhood in relation to "infertility" and "involuntary childlessness"', *Women's Studies International Forum* 22.3 (1999), pp. 359–372.

8 A. Rich, *Of Woman Born: Motherhood as Experience and Institution* (USA: Virago Press, 1977).

9 G. Letherby and C. Williams, 'Non-motherhood: ambivalent autobiographies', *Feminist Studies* 25.3 (1999), pp. 719–728, p. 721.

10 L. Conner, *Wedlocked Women* (London: Feminist Books Ltd, 1974), p. 165.

11 S. Lawler, *Mothering the Self: Mothers, Daughters, Subjects* (New York: Routledge, 2000), p. 149.

12 S. Lawler, op. cit., p. 20.

13 J. Warner (2006), op. cit., p. 67.

14 U. Beck (1992), op. cit.

15 J. Buxton, op. cit.

16 D. Johnston and D. Swanton (2004), op. cit., pp. 497–510.

17 N. Folbre, *Who Pays for the Kids?: Gender and the Structures of Constraint* (London: Routledge, 1994).

18 C. Hughes, op. cit., p. 94.

19 Lobby groups that campaigned for legislative change to tax and welfare systems include the National Council for the Status of Women (now known as the National Women's Council of Ireland), Irish Women's Liberation Movement, AIM, Irishwomen United and SIPTU Trade Union.

20 V. White (2010), op. cit.

21 Government of Ireland, Paper 3: 'Child health, development and well-being in the early years in Ireland – Key messages from research', *Right from the Start: Report of the Expert Advisory Group on the Early Years Strategy* (Dublin: Government Publications, 2013), p. 77.

7. CHILDCARE

1 European Anti Poverty Network, 'Access to Affordable Childcare for Low Income Families November 2007' (online: http://www.eapn.ie/eapn/wp-content/uploads/2009/10/access-to-affordable-childcare-for-low-income-fa milies.pdf, 2007) [accessed 10/01/14].

2 Government of Ireland, *National Action Plan for Social Inclusion 2007–2016* (Dublin: Government Publications, 2007), p. 30.

3 Government of Ireland, Department of Children and Youth Affairs, *Early Childhood Care and Education Scheme* (Dublin: Government Publications, 2010).

4 Government of Ireland, Department of Children and Youth Affairs, *Right from the Start: Report of the Expert Advisory Group on the Early Years Strategy* (Dublin: Government Publications, 2013).

5 Government of Ireland, *National Development Plan 2000–2006* (Dublin: Government Publications, 2000).

6 Barnardos; Childminding Ireland; Forbairt Naíonraí Teo; IPPA The Early Childhood Organisation; Irish Steiner Waldorf Early Childhood Association; National Children's Nurseries Association and Saint Nicholas Montessori Teachers Association.

7 Government of Ireland, *Child Care Act 1991* (Dublin: Government Publications, 1991).

8 Government of Ireland, Department of Health and Children, *Childcare Regulations* (Dublin: Government Publications, 2006).

9 Government of Ireland, Department of Health and Children, *National Childcare Strategy 2006–2010: Guidelines for Childminders, revised edition* (Dublin: Government Publications, 2008).

10 The tax free income was increased from €10,000 to €15,000 in subsequent budgets. However, the limit to overall earnings remains the same at €15,000.

11 Goodbody Economic Consultants conducted an analysis of childminding in Ireland, based on CSO data for paid, non-relative childminders, drawing on data in the Quarterly National Household Survey: Special Module, Childcare, Quarter 4, 2007, p. 4. The Goodbody Report is *Children 2020: Cost-Benefit Analysis* (Dublin: Goodbody Consultants, 2011) p. 50. This analysis is cited in Start Strong, *Childminding: Regulation and Recognition. Policy Brief 12* (Dublin: Start Strong, 2012), p. 1.

12 OECD (2002), op. cit.

13 Start Strong, op. cit.

14 J. Hearne, 'Ratios and regulations: how crèches are controlled' (online: my childcare.ie, 2012) [accessed 10/01/14]

15 M. Fine Davis, *Childcare in Ireland Today*, Social Attitude and Policy Research Group (Dublin: Trinity College, 2007), p. 21.

16 G. Collins and J. Wickham, *What Childcare Crisis? Irish Mothers Entering the Labour Force*, ERC Labour Market Observatory (Dublin: Trinity College, 2001).

17 OECD, *Early Childhood Education and Care – Country Note for Ireland* (online: http://www.oecd.org/dataoecd/51/18/3445332.pdf, 2004) [accessed 13/01/14].

18 NESC, *The Developmental Welfare State. Report 113* (on line: http://nesc.ie/dynamic/docs/NRSC%20DWS_RZ%20Text+Cover.pdf., 2005) [accessed 13/01/14]

19 Though there has been increased government attention and funding to

childcare in recent years, government policy and action has consistently avoided addressing the issue of affordability, focusing instead on issues of supply, co-ordination and quality. This is despite expert recommendations to government that include:

- Extending the period of paid parental leave to one year (OECD, 2004, op. cit.);
- Provision of quality early childhood education and care services to all children under one year for parents that do not wish to stay at home and from one year up to when children are eligible for a free pre-school place (NESF, *Early Childhood and Education Report 31* (Dublin: NESF, 2005));
- A publicly subsidised early childhood care and education (ECCE) model including subsidised full day care for one- and two-year-olds, universal ECCE for all three- and four-year-olds and subsidised extended care for five- to fourteen-year-olds (NWCI, *An Accessible Childcare Model* (Dublin: NWCI, 2005));
- Linking childcare supports to the use of formal childcare (OECD, *Country Profiles: An Overview of Early Childhood Education and Care Systems in Participating Countries – Ireland* (Paris: OECD, 2006)).

20 Government of Ireland (2013), op. cit.
21 European Commission, *Rationale of Motherhood Choices: Influence of Employment Conditions and Public Policies* (Brussels: European Commission, 2004).
22 OECD, *Thematic Review of Early Childhood Education and Care Policy in Ireland* (Paris: OECD, 2004).
23 The Equal Opportunities Childcare Programme (2000); Siolta, the National Qualifications Framework for Early Childhood Education (2006); the Early Childhood Care and Education Scheme (2010).
24 OECD, *Babies and Bosses: Reconciling Work and Family Life, A Synthesis of Findings for OECD Countries* (Paris: OECD, 2007).
25 EAPN (2007), op. cit.
26 CSO (2012), op. cit.
27 J. Murphy-Lawless, op. cit., pp. 89–94.
28 OECD, *Employment Outlook Study* (Paris: OECD, 1990).
29 E. Coveney, J. Murphy-Lawless and S. Sheridan (1998), op. cit., p. 11.
30 S. O'Sullivan, op. cit., p. 279.
31 K. Lynch and M. Lyons, op. cit., p. 173.
32 M. O'Brien (2007), op. cit., pp. 139–157.
33 U. Barry (2008), op. cit., p. 2.
34 O. O'Connor and M. Murphy, 'Women and Social Welfare' in U. Barry (ed.), *Where Are We Now? New Feminist Perspectives on Women in Contemporary Ireland* (Dublin: TASC at New Island, 2008), pp. 30–52.
35 F. Williams (2000), op. cit.; F. Williams, (2001), op. cit.; NWCI (2003), op. cit.; G. Kiely, 'The Value of Unpaid Work in the Home', International Year of the Family + 10: Working for the Family Conference, University College Dublin (21 October 2004); F. Kennedy. *Cottage to Crèche: Family Change in Ireland* (Dublin: IPA, 2001); NWCI, *Campaign for Social Welfare Reform* (online: www.nwci.ie, 2005) [accessed 28/02/05]; NWCI (2009), op. cit. [accessed 23/03/10].
36 Government of Ireland, *Budget 2006* (Dublin: Department of Finance, 2006).
37 Government of Ireland, *Budget 2009* (Dublin: Department of Finance, 2009).

38 Government of Ireland (2010), op. cit.
39 U. Barry (2008), op. cit., p. 14.
40 Government of Ireland (1937), op.cit.
41 J. Bennett, 'ECEC financing in Ireland', paper presented at *A Decade of Reflection, Early Childhood Education and Care in Ireland 1996–2006* (Dublin: DIT, 2006).
42 J. Ferguson, op. cit.
43 K. Lynch (1989), op.cit
44 K. Lynch (2007), op. cit.
45 D.E. Bubeck, op. cit.
46 G. Collins and J. Wickham, op. cit., p 11.
47 Women's Health Council, *Women's Mental Health: Promoting a Gendered Approach to Policy and Service Provision* (Dublin: The Women's Health Council, 2004).
48 K. Lynch (2007), op. cit.
49 C. Vincent and S. Ball, *Childcare, Choice and Class Practices: Middle-Class Parents and Their Children* (Oxon and New York, 2006), p. 163.
50 RTE, 'Breach of Trust', *Prime Time* (Tuesday 28 May 2013).
51 C. O'Brien, 'Crèche Crisis: The Staff Speak', *Weekend Review, The Irish Times* (Saturday 1 June 2013).
52 V. White (2013), op. cit.
53 Government of Ireland, *Child & Family Agency Bill 2013* (Dublin: Department of Children and Youth Affairs, Government Publications, 2013).
54 F. McGinnity and H. Russell, op. cit.
55 C. Vincent and S. Ball, op. cit.
56 Patricia Murray quoted by C. O'Brien in 'Most childminders not declaring income', *The Irish Times* (4 July 2009).
57 O. O'Connor and M. Murphy, op. cit., pp. 30–52.
58 P. O'Connor, J. Smithson and M. des Dores Goerreiro, 'Young People's Awareness of Gendered Realities' in J. Brannen, S. Lewis and A. Nielsen (eds), *Young Europeans: Work and Family* (London: Routledge, 2002), pp. 89–115.
59 R.W. Connell, 1987, op. cit., p. 106.
60 K. Lynch and M. Lyons, op. cit., p. 181.
61 E. Mahon (1991), op. cit., pp. 2–10.
62 Pre school child @ €4.90 plus two school-going children at €6.00 each x 12 hrs = €202.80; CSO, *Quarterly National Household Survey – Childcare. Q4, 2007* (www.cso.ie).
63 K. Lynch and M. Lyons, op. cit.
64 J. Baker, K. Lynch, S. Cantillon and J. Walsh (eds), op. cit.
65 OECD (2012), op. cit., p. 15.
66 1 Physiotherapist, 1 Director of Nursing, 1 Clinic Nurse Manager, 1 Personal Carer, 3 Nurses, 2 Midwives and 1 Respite Carer = 10.
67 K. Lynch and M. Lyons, op. cit., p. 173.
68 Rollercoaster (online discussion: http://www.rollercoaster.ie/Discussions/tabid/119/ForumThread/141392186/Default.aspx, 2013).
69 Magic Mum (online discussion: http://www.magicmum.com/phpBB/vietopic.php?f=117&t=566863, 2013).
70 C. Vincent and S. Ball, op. cit., p. 163.
71 S. Holloway, 'Local Childcare Cultures: Moral geographies of mothering and the social organisation of pre-school education', *Gender, Place & Culture: A*

Journal of Feminist Geography 5.1 (1998), pp. 29–53; S. Duncan (2005) op. cit., pp. 50–76.

8. WHO CARES? – CHILDMINDERS

1 M. Daly and K. Rake, *Gender and the Welfare State: Care, Work and Welfare in Europe and the USA* (London: Polity, 2003).
2 Women's Health Council, op. cit.
3 K. Lynch and M. Lyons, op. cit., p. 176.
4 A. Oakley (2002), op. cit., p. 88.
5 G. Meagher, op. cit., pp. 52–66.
6 M. Daly (ed.) (2001), op. cit.; N. Folbre (2004), op. cit., pp. 7–24; U. Barry (2008), op. cit., pp. 1–29.
7 Government of Ireland (2006), op. cit.
8 Government of Ireland, Department of Justice Equality and Law Reform, *National Childcare Strategy Report of the Partnership 2000 Expert Working Group on Childcare* (Dublin: Government Publications, 1999).
9 C. O'Sullivan, 'Government fails to clamp down on black market childminders' *Irish Examiner* (Monday, 18 October 2010).
10 OECD, *Thematic Review of Early Childhood Education and Care: Background Report. Ireland* (online: www.oecd.org/\els\social\family\database, 2002) [accessed 14/05/05].
11 U. Barry (2008), op. cit.
12 J. Wheelock and K. Jones, 'Grandparents are the next best thing: informal childcare for working parents in urban Britain', *Journal of Social Policy* 31.3 (2002), pp. 441–463; B. Hilliard (2007), op. cit., p. 98.
13 E. Kittay, op. cit.; J. Tronto (2002), op. cit.
14 K. Lynch and M. Lyons, op. cit., p. 177.
15 Ibid.
16 E. Nanako Glenn, 'From Servitude to Service Work: Historical Continuities in the Racial Division of Paid Reproductive Labor', *Signs* 18.1 (1992), pp. 1–43, p. 22–23.
17 *Right from the start* (2013), op. cit.
18 Early Childhood Ireland, *Early Childhood Ireland Salary Survey 2012*. Available at: (online: http://www.earlychildhoodireland.ie/policy-advocacy-and-research/surveys/salary-survey-2012).
19 C. O'Brien (2013), op. cit.
20 Pobal, *Annual Survey of the Early Years Sector 2012* (Dublin: Pobal, 2013).
21 C. O'Brien, op. cit.
22 B. Ehrenreich and A. Hochschild, *Global Woman: Nannies, Maids and Sex Workers in the New Economy* (New York: Henry Holt, 2003).
23 F. McKay, op. cit.
24 R. Dhamoon, op. cit.
25 K. Lynch and M. Lyons, op. cit., p. 179.
26 K. Lynch and M. Lyons, op. cit., p. 180.
27 M. Badgett, V. Lee and N. Folbre, 'Assigning Care: Gender Norms and Economic Outcomes', *International Labour Review*, 138.3 (1999), pp. 311–326, p. 318.
28 P. Freund and M. Maguire, *Health, Illness and the Social Body: A Critical Introduction*, 3rd edition (London: Prentice Hall, 1999), pp. 89–90.

29 H. Dillaway and E. Paré, op. cit., pp. 437–464.
30 J. Tronto (1993), op. cit., J. Tronto (2002), op. cit.
31 K. Lynch (1989), op. cit., pp. 1–14; K. Lynch (2008), op. cit.
32 E. Mahon (1998), op. cit., pp. 170–181; A. Hattery, op. cit.
33 E. Mahon (1998), op. cit.
34 M.G. Dietz, 'Citizenship with a Feminist Face: The Problem with Maternal Thinking', *Political Theory* 13.1 (1985), pp. 19–39; R. Voet, *Feminism and Citizenship* (London: Sage, 1998).
35 K. Lynch and M. Lyons, op. cit., p. 179.
36 Illness benefit is paid to people who are medically unfit for work. A general practitioner signs a weekly certificate which the employee submits to the employer and to the state. Payment is made directly to the recipient by the state. The value of illness benefit at the time of the research was €160 per week.
37 C. O'Sullivan, op. cit.
38 Boards.ie, thread: 'How much to pay a childminder?' (online: http://www.boards.ie/vbulletin/showthread.php?p=61254920, 2013) [accessed 17/01/14].
39 Ask about Money, thread: 'Childminding and Social Welfare Payments' (online: http://www.askaboutmoney.com/showthread.php?t=175168, 2013) [accessed 17/01/14]; Ask about Money, thread: 'Paying somebody cash' (online: http://www.askaboutmoney.com/showthread.php?t=183663, 2013) [accessed 17/01/14].
40 C. O'Brien, op. cit.
41 TASC, op. cit.
42 Ibid.
43 OECD, *Trends in the income position of different household types* (Online: ww.oecd.org/\els\social\family\database, 2009) [accessed 23/01/09].
44 OECD (2002), op. cit.
45 Ibid.
46 K. Pitt, 'Being a New Capitalist Mother', *Discourse and Society* 13.2 (2002), pp. 251–267.

9. CHILDREN'S CAPITALS

1 Growing up in Ireland (2012), op. cit., p. 128.
2 K. Pitt, op. cit., pp. 251–267.
3 R. Quiney, op. cit., p. 20.
4 B. Ehrenreich, *Fear of Falling: The Inner Life of the Middle Class* (New York: Perennial, 1990).
5 P. Bourdieu (1984), op. cit.
6 J. Williams, op. cit., pp. 35–36.
7 S. Hays, op. cit.; A. Hochschild (1997), op. cit.; J. Warner (2006), op. cit.
8 K. Figes (1998), op. cit. and 'A Distress Not to be Borne', *The Guardian* (24 June 2002); R. Abrams, *Three Shoes, One Sock and No Hairbrush; Everything You Need to Know about Having Your Second Child* (London: Cassell, 2001); R. Cusk, op. cit.; N. Wolf, *Misconceptions: Truth, Lies and the Unexpected on the Journey to Motherhood* (London: Chatto and Windus, 2001); A. Enright, *Making Babies: Stumbling into Motherhood* (London: Jonathan Cape, 2004); F. Looney, *Misadventures in Motherhood: Life with The Small Girl, The Boy and The Toddler* (Dublin: O'Brien Press, 2005).
9 K. Pitt, op. cit.

10 R. Quiney, op. cit.
11 I. Knight, 'Who are they trying to Kid?', *Sunday Times* (9 September 2001); T. Macleod, 'The Truth about Motherhood – If You're an Angst Ridden Novelist, That Is', *Evening Standard* (2 September 2001); S. Herbert, 'I've had a baby too', *Sunday Telegraph* (9 September 2001).
12 A. Enright, op. cit.
13 F. Looney, op. cit.
14 A. Enright. op. cit. p. 1.
15 A. Pearson. *I don't Know How She Does It* (London: Anchor Books, 2003).
16 K. Keohane and C. Kuhling, *Collision Culture: Transformations of Everyday Life in Ireland* (Dublin: Liffey Press, 2004).
17 P. Bourdieu (1984), op. cit.
18 M. Benn, op. cit.
19 L. Berlant, *The Queen of America Goes to Washington City: Essays on Sex and Citizenship* (Durham NC: Duke University Press, 1997).
20 B. Ehrenreich, op. cit.
21 R. Quiney, op. cit., p. 31
22 S. Hays, op. cit.; A. Lareau, op. cit., pp. 747–776.
23 A. Giddens, *The Constitution of Society: Outline of the Theory of Structuration* (Cambridge: Polity Press, 1984).
24 I. Dyck, 'Integrating Home and Wage Workplace: Women's Daily Lives in a Canadian suburb', *The Canadian Geographer* 33 Winter (1989), pp. 329–341.
25 S. Holloway, 'Reproducing Motherhood' in N. Laurie, C. Dwyer, S. Holloway and F. Smith (eds), *Geographies of New Femininities* (London: Longman, 1999), pp. 91–112.
26 C. Vincent and S. Ball, op. cit., p. 164.
27 Dillaway and Paré, op. cit.
28 A.M. Halpenny, E. Nixon and D. Watson, *Parent's Perspectives on Parenting Styles and Disciplining Children* (Dublin: Office of the Minister for Children and Youth Affairs, 2010).
29 Growing Up in Ireland, *Child Cohort, Key findings: 9 year olds, No. 3: The Education of Nine-Year Olds, November 2009* (online: http://www.growingup.ie/fileadmin/user_upload/documents/Update_Key_Findings/Key_Findings_3.pdf, 2009) [accessed 13/01/14].
30 CSO, *Quarterly National Household Survey, Parental Involvement in Children's Education Q2 2012* (Cork: Central Statistics Office, 2014).
31 J. Williams. op. cit.
32 J. Warner (2006), op. cit.
33 R. Quiney, op. cit., p. 34.
34 L. Rubin, *Families on the Fault Line* (New York: Harper Collins, 1994), p. 70.
35 CSO (2014), op.cit.
36 D. Reay (1998), op. cit.
37 P. Duncan, 'Most Primary Pupils get homework help', *The Irish Times* (Friday 3 January 2014).
38 TV3, 'Back To School: Homework' (online: //www.tv3.ie/ireland_am_article.php?locID=1.901.983&article=111668, 2013) [accessed 11/01/14]; Schooldays.ie. Homework: how much time should your child spend on it? (online: http://www.schooldays.ie/articles/Homework-how-much-time, 2013) [accessed 13/01/14].
39 A.M. Halpenny, E. Nixon and D. Watson, op. cit.

40 Growing up in Ireland (2012), op. cit.
41 OECD, *Education at a Glance 2013. OECD Indicators – A Country Profile for Ireland June 2013* (Paris: OECD, 2014).
42 Irish National Teachers Organisation, 'Overcrowded Classes: The Facts' in *Touch September 2013* (online: http://www.into.ie/ROI/ProtectingPrimary Education/ClassSizeSupplement.pdf, 2013) [accessed 22/01/14].
43 Irish National Teachers Organisation 'Irish Spending on Education Falls Sharply', Press Release (Tuesday 25 June 2013).
44 G. Mooney-Simmie, 'The Pied Piper of Neo-liberalism Calls the Tune in the Republic of Ireland: An Analysis of Education Policy Text from 2000–2012', *Journal for Critical Education Policy Studies* 10.2 (2012), pp. 485–514.
45 DES Circular 0016/2014. 'Standardisation of the school year in respect of primary and postprimary schools for the years 2014/15; 2015/16 and 2016/17.
46 CSO, *Quarterly National Household Survey Childcare Fourth Quarter 2002* (online: http://www.cso.ie/en/media/csoie/releasespublications/documents/labourmarket/2002/qnhs_moduleonchildcareqtr42002.pdf, 2003) [accessed 11/01/14].
47 CSO, *Quarterly National Household Survey Childcare Quarter 4 2007. Types of Childcare Used by Children Aged 0–12 years, by School Going Status and Region, Quarter 4 2007* (online: http://www.cso.ie/en/media/csoie/releasespublications/documents/labourmarket/2007/childcareq42007.pdf, 2009) [accessed 11/01/14].
48 Department of Social Protection, *Subsidised after-school child care scheme* (online: http://www.welfare.ie/en/pressoffice/pdf/SW135, 2013) [accessed 23/12/13].
49 The Suzuki Method is based on the principle that all children possess ability and that this ability can be developed and enhanced through a nurturing environment. Essential elements include an early start (aged 3–4 is normal in most countries); the importance of listening to music; learning to play before learning to read; the involvement of the parent; a nurturing and positive learning environment and a high standard of teaching by trained teachers.
50 M. Benn, op. cit.
51 S. Hays, op. cit.; J. Warner (2006), op. cit.
52 L. Conner, op. cit.; S. Walby (1990) op. cit.
53 J. Warner (2006), op. cit.
54 A. Bennett, *Popular Music and Youth Culture* (Basingstoke: Macmillan, 2000), p. 63.
55 L. McKie, S. Gregory and S. Bowlby, op. cit., p. 918.
56 D.H.J. Morgan, *Family Connections* (Cambridge: Polity Press, 1996), p. 138.
57 P. Buchner, 'Growing up in the 1980s: Changes in the Social Biography of Childhood in the FRG' in L. Chisholm, P. Buchner, H.H. Kruger and P. Brown (eds), *Childhood, Youth and Social Change: A Comparative Perspective* (London: Falmer Press, 1990), pp. 941–958.
58 D. Devine, M. Nic Ghiolla Phádraig and J. Deegan, *Time for Children – Time for Change? Children's Rights and Welfare in Ireland during a Period of Economic Growth* (Dublin: Report to The COST Network, 2004).
59 C. O'Hagan, 'Working and mothering: interlocking locations in the caringscape', *Families Relationships and Societies* 3.2 (2014), pp. 201–218.
60 J.B. Thompson, *Ideology and Modern Culture* (Oxford: Polity Press, 1990).

61 McGinnity, Russell et al (2005), op. cit.
62 J. Warner (2006), op. cit.
63 C. Vincent and S. Ball, op. cit., p. 164.
64 S. Walby (1997), op. cit., p. 15.

10. 'TIME FOR ME IS TIME FOR EVERYBODY'

1 F. McGinnity, H. Russell and E. Smyth, op. cit., pp. 199–216
2 B. Adam, *Timescapes of Modernity. The Environment and Invisible Hazards* (London and New York: Routledge, 1998).
3 E. Ermath, 'The solitude of women and social time' in E. Forman and C. Sowton (eds), *Taking our Time: Feminist Perspectives on Temporality* (Oxford: Pergamon Press, 1989), pp. 36–46.
4 A. Knights and P. Odih, op. cit., pp. 205–231.
5 K. Davies, op. cit.
6 D.H.J. Morgan, op. cit., p. 149.
7 B. Adam, 'The Temporal Gaze: The Challenge for Social Theory in the Context of GM Food', *British Journal of Sociology* 51.1 (2000), pp. 125–142, p. 125.
8 L. McKie, S. Gregory and S. Bowlby, 'Caringscapes: Experiences of Caring and Working', Centre for research on Families and Relationships. The University of Edinburgh. Research Briefing No. 13 (February, 2004), p. 2.
9 B. Adam, *Timewatch: The Social Analysis of Time* (Cambridge: Polity Press, 1995) and *Time* (Cambridge, UK and Malden, MA: Polity, 2004).
10 B. Adam (1995), op. cit., p. 94.
11 B. Adam (1995), op. cit., p. 89.
12 E.T. Hall, *The Dance of Life: The Other Dimension of Time* (Garden City, NY: Anchor Press/Doubleday, 1983); R. Whipp, 'A time to be concerned: a position paper on time and management', *Time and Society* 3 (1994), pp. 99–116; M.A. Glucksman, '"What a difference a day makes": A theoretical and historical exploration of temporality and gender', *Sociology* 32.2 (1998), pp. 239–258; K. Jurczyk, 'Time in women's everyday lives: Between self-determination and conflicting demands', *Time and Society* 7.2–3 (1998), pp. 283–308.
13 L. McKie, S. Gregory and S. Bowlby, op. cit.
14 B. Adam (1995), op. cit., p. 91.
15 P. Treanor, op. cit.
16 V. Sarantinos, 'Flexibility in the workplace: What happens to commitment? *Business and Public Affairs*, vol. 1.2, pp. 1–10.
17 A. Hochschild (1997), op. cit.
18 S. Halford, M. Savage and A. Witz, op. cit.
19 Ibid., p. 15.
20 E. Mahon (1991), op. cit.; P. Barker and K. Monks, op. cit.; P. O'Connor (2000), op. cit.
21 J. Williams, op. cit.
22 S. Bordo, *Unbearable Weight: Feminism, Western Culture and the Body* (Berkeley: University of California Press, 1993).
23 C. O'Hagan, 'Broadening the intersectional path: revealing organizational practices through "working mothers" narratives about time', *Gender Work and Organisation*, 23 JUN 2014 | DOI: 10.1111/gwao.12056 (2014).
24 Best Place to Work Institute, *Mission and Values* (online: www.greatplace

towork.ie/gptw/mission.php, 2008) [accessed 14/06/08]; Chartered Institute of Personnel and Development. *Flexibility Vital for Workplace Productivity* (online: www.cipd.co.uk/ireland, 2009) [accessed 7 September 2009].

25 C. Delphy and D. Leonard, *Familiar Exploitation: A New Analysis of Marriage in Contemporary Western Societies* (Oxford: Polity Press and Blackwell Publishers, 1992); L.C. Sayer, P.N. Cohen and L.M. Casper, *Women, Men and Work* (Washington, DC: Russell Sage Foundation and Population Reference Bureau, 2004); B. Hilliard (2007), op. cit., pp. 83–100.

26 R. Gelles, *Contemporary Families: A Sociological Review* (Thousand Oaks, California: Sage, 1995).

27 L. Thompson and A.J. Walker, 'The Place of Feminism in Family Studies', *Journal of Marriage and the Family* 57.4 (1995), pp. 846–865; J.M. Riggs, 'Mandates for Mothers and Fathers: Perceptions of Breadwinners and Care Givers', *Sex Roles* 37 (October 1997), pp. 565–580.

28 K. Lynch and M. Lyons, op. cit., p. 175

29 S. Coltrane, 'Research on Household Labor: Modeling and Measuring the Social Embeddedness of Routine Family Work', *Journal of Marriage and the Family* 62.4 (2000), pp. 1208–1233.

30 O. Sullivan, 'The Division of Domestic Labour: Twenty Years of Change?' *Sociology* 34.3 (2000), pp. 436–456.

31 S. Coltrane, op. cit., p. 1226.

32 F. McGinnity and H. Russell, op. cit., p. 4.

33 B. Hilliard, 'Changing gender roles in initimate relationships' in J. Garry, N. Hardiman and D. Payne (eds), *Irish Social and Political Attidudes* (Liverpool: University of Liverpool Press, 2006), pp. 33–42, p. 38.

34 F. McGinnity and H. Russell, op. cit.

35 U. Beck and E. Beck-Gernsheim, *Individualization* (London: Sage, 2001).

36 A. Oakley (2002), op. cit., p. 121.

37 K. Davies, op. cit., p. 131.

38 H. Land, 'The changing worlds of work and families' in S. Watson and L. Doyal (eds), *Engendering Social Policy* (Buckingham: Open University Press, 1999), pp. vii – xii.

39 C. Sirianni and C. Negrey, 'Working Time as Gendered Time', *Feminist Economics* 6.1 (2000), pp. 59–76, p. 64.

40 J. Scott, 'Family change: revolution or backlash?' in S. McRae (ed.), *Changing Britain, Families and Households in the 1990s* (Oxford: Oxford University Press, 1999), pp. 98–119.

41 C. Delphy and D. Leonard, op. cit.

42 O. Sullivan, op. cit., 2000.

43 F. McGinnity and H. Russell, op. cit.

44 S. Jackson and S. Scott, 'Paid and Unpaid Work Introduction' in S. Jackson and S. Scott (eds), *Gender: A Sociological Reader* (London and New York: Routledge, 2002), pp. 151–153, p. 151.

45 C. Delphy and D. Leonard, op. cit., p. 240.

46 S. Chira, *A Mother's Place: Choosing Work and Family without Guilt or Blame* (New York: Harper Perennial, 1998).

47 F. McKay, op. cit.

48 K. Davies, op. cit., p. 41.

49 R. Gelles, op. cit.

50 K. Davies, op. cit.; S.F. Berk, *The Gender Factory: the Apportionment of Work in*

American Households (New York: Plenum Press, 1985); A. Hochschild (1989), op. cit.

51 B. Adam (1990), op. cit.

52 L.C. Sayer, 'Gender differences in the relationships between long employee hours and multitasking' in T. Van der Lippe and P. Peters (eds), *Time Competition: Disturbed Balances and New Options in Work and Care* (New York: Edward Elgar, 2007), pp. 403–435.

53 L.C. Sayer, P.N. Cohen and L.M. Casper, op. cit.

54 C. West and D.H. Zimmerman, 'Doing Gender', *Gender & Society* 1.2 (1987), pp. 125–151; J. Brines, 'Economic Dependency, Gender and the Division of Labor at Home', *American Journal of Sociology* 100.3 (1994), pp. 652–688; N. Folbre and J.A. Nelson, 'For love or money – or both?', *Journal of Economic Perspectives* 14.4 (2000), pp. 123–140.

55 F. McGinnity and H. Russell, op. cit.

56 S. Bianchi, M. Milkie, L. Sayer and J. Robinson, 'Is Anyone Doing the Housework? Trends in the Gender Division of Household Labour', *Social Forces* 79 (2000), pp. 191–228; S. Pacholok and A.H. Gauthier, 'A Tale of Dual-Earner Families in Four Countries' in N. Folbre and M. Bittman (eds), *Family Time: The Social Organisation of Care* (London: Routledge, 2004), pp. 196–223.

57 F. McGinnity and H. Russell, op. cit., p. 72.

58 F. McGinnity and H. Russell found women do thirty-nine extra minutes paid/unpaid work per average day, which amounts to 14,235 minutes per year, or 237 more hours committed time than men per year (F. McGinnity and H. Russell, op. cit., p. 71).

59 F. Forman, 'Feminizing Time: An Introduction' in In E. Forman and C. Sowton (eds), *Taking our Time: Feminist Perspectives on Temporality* (Oxford: Pergamon Press, 1989), pp. 1–9, p. 7.

60 Delphy and Leonard, op. cit.

61 S. Maushart, *Wifework* (New York: Bloomsbury, 2001).

62 J. Duncombe and D. Marsden, 'Whose Orgasm is this Anwyay? "Sex Work" in Long-term heterosexual couple relationships' in S. Jackson and S. Scott (eds), *Gender: a Sociological Reader* (London: Routledge, 2002), pp. 231–237.

63 C. Gatrell (2005), op. cit.

64 M.C. Bateson (op. cit.), p. 166–8.

65 A. Hochschild (1990), op. cit.

66 F. McGinnity and H. Russell, op. cit. p. 4.

67 M. Benn, op. cit.

68 A. Nilsen and J. Brannen, 'Theorising the individual-structure dynamic' in J. Brannen, S. Lewis, A. Nilsen and J. Smithson (eds), *Young Europeans, Work and Family: Futures in Transition* (London: Routledge, 2002), pp. 30–48.

69 H. Nowotny, op. cit., pp. 421–454.

11. A NEW GENDER REGIME

1 M. Wetherell, 'Positioning and interpretative repertoires: conversation analysis and poststructuralism in dialogue', *Discourse & Society* 9.3 (1998), pp. 386–412.

2 A. Oakley (2002), op. cit.

3 A. Jaggar, *Feminist Politics and Human Nature* (UK: Harvester Press, 1983), p. 56.

4 N. Rose (1999), op. cit., p. 52

5 S. Cantillon, C.Corrigan, P. Kirby and J. O'Flynn (eds), op. cit., p. 304.
6 P. Kirby 'Introduction' in D. Jacobsen, P. Kirby and D. O'Broin (eds) *Taming the Tiger: Social Exclusion in a Globalised Ireland* (Dublin: New Ireland Press, 2006), pp. 13–23.
7 M.D. Higgins, *Renewing the Republic* (Dublin: Liberties Press, 2011), p. 78.
8 N. Fairclough, op. cit., p. 80.
9 G. Pascall and J. Lewis, op. cit., p. 380.
10 G. Pascall and J. Lewis, op. cit, p. 373.
11 The gender pay gap stands at less than seventeen per cent before women have children, but after at least one child the gap moves to fourteen per cent. OECD, *Closing the Gender Gap: Act Now* (Paris: OECD Publishing, 2012).
12 P. Lunn and T. Fahey, op. cit., p. xiii.
13 Ibid.
14 Government of Ireland, *Organisation of Working Time Act (1997)* (Dublin: Government Publications, 1997).
15 Robert Walters, Ireland Employee Insights Survey (online: http://www.robertwalters.ie/wwwmedialibrary/files/Ire%20Content/employee-insight-survey-ireland-2012.pdf, 2013) [accessed 31/01/14].
16 Pascall and Lewis, op. cit.
17 J.C. Gornick and M.K. Meyers, *Families that Work: Policies for Reconciling Parenthood and Employment* (New York: Russell Sage Foundation, 2003).
18 Government of Ireland (2013), op. cit.
19 European Platform for Investing in Children, Denmark: Towards ideal conditions for balancing family and work. (online:http://europa.eu/epic/countries/Denmark/index_en.htm , 2013) [accessed 30/1/2014].
20 Government of Ireland (2013), op. cit.
21 M. Raftery and E. O'Sullivan, *'Suffer the Little Children'* (Dublin: New Island Books, 1999). This book documents the treatment of children in the care of state institutions and religious-run schools. The book details the systematic physical, emotional, sexual and psychological abuse suffered by generations of Irish children in the institutions purported to protect them. This book was published in 1999 and a three-part TV documentary made by Mary Raftery (*States of Fear*) was broadcast in 1999. Following the broadcast there was a national outcry, which led to the setting up of the Commission to Inquire into Child Abuse. The Irish Taoiseach issued a public apology on behalf of the government and many subsequent enquiries and reports were published on the abuse of children in the care of the state and by religious in Ireland.
22 T. McGibney, McGibney & Co., Virginia, Co. Cavan, cited in S. Ryan 'Can't really afford to quit work to look after your child? . . . think again', *Herald.ie* (19 June, 2013).
23 J. Geraghty, chief executive of LA Brokers, cited in J. Cradden, 'Raising children can be extremely expensive', *Independent.ie.* (10 February 2009).
24 E. Garvey, E. Murphy and P. Osikoya, *Estimates of the Cost of a Child in Ireland* (Dublin: Combat Poverty Agency, 2011).
25 A. MacEwan, 'Early childhood education as an essential component of economic development', Political Economy Research Institute, University of Massachusetts, Amherst, January 2013 (online: http://www.peri.umass.edu/fileadmin/pdf/published_study/ECE_MacEwan_PERI_Jan8.pdf) [accessed 31/07/14].
26 Start Strong, *The Economics of Children's Early Years Early Care and Education in*

Ireland: Costs and Benefits (online: http://www.startstrong.ie/files/ Economics_of_Childrens_Early_Years.pdf.) [accessed 31/07/14]

27 Many social and voluntary organisations have called for universalism in childcare, including the National Women's Council *An Assessible Childcare Model* (Dublin: NWCI, 2005), the European Anti-Poverty Network Ireland, *Ireland Benchmarking Paper on Childcare* (Dublin: EAPN, 2007); Combat Poverty Agency, *Submission to the NESF on Improving the Delivery of Quality Public Services* (Dublin: CPA, 2006); Start Strong, *Children 2020 Planning Now, for the Future, Children's Early Care and Education in Ireland, November 2010* (Dublin: Start Strong, 2010).

28 According to the OECD, childcare supports are a key factor in the determination of maternal employment behaviour during the early years. OECD, *Doing Better for Families* (Paris: OECD, 2011), p. 141.

The OECD highlights that, in Ireland, women's labour market participation rates are well below those of best-performing OECD economies, especially for mothers and high childcare costs and limited supply are major obstacles to participation. OECD *Going for Growth: Economic Policy Reforms* (Paris: OECD, 2012b).

The European Pact for Gender Equality 2011–2020 reaffirms the importance of integrating a gender perspective into all policies and urges member states to improve the supply of affordable and high-quality childcare services and promote flexible working arrangements. Council of the European Union, *Council Conclusions on the European Pact for Gender Equality for the period 2011–2020*. Employment, Social Policy, Health and Consumer Affairs Council meeting Brussels (7 March 2011) cited in NWCI, *Budget 2014: Submission* (Dublin: NWCI, August 2013).

29 The average is approximately 0.7 per cent of GDP with some countries, such as Iceland, Denmark and Sweden as high as 1.4 per cent. In Ireland we spend approximately 0.4 per cent. OECD, Family database www.oecd.org/social/ family/database, updated 18/10/2012. PF3.1: *Public spending on childcare and early education*; NWCI, *Budget 2014: Submission* (Dublin: NWCI, August 2013).

30 OECD, *Gender Brief*. Prepared by the OECD Social Policy Division (online www.oecd.org/els/social Version, March 2010).

31 NESC, op. cit.

32 National Foundation for Education Research, 'Compulsory age of starting school in European countries'. (online: http://www.nfer.ac.uk/nfer/index. cfm?9B1C0068–C29E-AD4D-0AEC-8B4F43F54A28) [accessed 31/07/14].

33 Ibid.

34 OECD (2010), op. cit.

35 Barnardos, *Childrens' Budget 2013* (online: http://www.barnardos.ie/assets/ files/Advocacy/2013ChildrensBudget.pdf.) [accessed 31/07/14].

36 TASC, op. cit., p. 2.

37 CORI, op. cit.

38 C. Ryan, 'Women disproportionately hit by contributory pension scheme cuts', *Irish Examiner* (22 April, 2014).

39 M. Daly, *An Evaluation of the Impact of the National Childminding Initiative on the Quality of Childminding in Waterford City and County* (Waterford City and County Childcare Committees and HSE South, 2010).

40 In nursing, programmes designed to prepare nurses for entry to the profession have been offered by third-level colleges in Ireland since 1994. M.

McCarthy and A. Higgins, 'Moving to an all graduate profession: preparing preceptors for their role', *Nurse Education Today* 23(2) (2003) pp. 89–95.

41 Scottish Commission for the Regulation of Care, *Improving the Quality of Care in Scotland: An Overview of Care Commission findings, 2002 to 2010* (Scotland: SCRC, 2011).

42 Lynch and Lyons, op. cit., p. 173.

43 Social Justice Ireland, op. cit.

44 Government of Iceland, Althingi (n.d.) Pingskjol — Parliamentary documents. (online:www.althingi.is, 2014) [accessed 30/01/14].

45 Government of Ireland (2013), op. cit.

46 Government of Ireland, *Circular 14 of 2009 Shorter Working Year Scheme* (online: http://hr.per.gov.ie/family-friendly-policies) [accessed 31/07/14].

47 Rollercoaster is described as Ireland's No. 1 website for pregnancy and parenting. Discussions, fora and articles include pregnancy, parenting, baby, family life, nutrition, childcare, childminders, money and work.

   MagicMum is described as a website for Irish mums and mums-to-be. Discussions and articles include health, fertility, parenting, toddlers, teen years, family life.

48 Irish organisations which campaign for justice and equality include: Social Justice Ireland, TASC, GLEN, Society of St Vincent de Paul, One Family, Age Action Ireland, Forum of People with Disabilities, Immigrant Council of Ireland, Irish National Organisation of the Unemployed, Irish Traveller Movement, OPEN – One Parent Network, Migrant Rights Centre Ireland, Threshold, AIM Family Services, Barnardos, National Women's Council of Ireland, Irish Congress of Trades Unions, Irish Council for Civil Liberties.

49 R. Lister, op. cit.; B. Siim, *Gender and Citizenship* (Cambridge: Cambridge University Press, 2000).

50 J. Blackmore, *Troubling Women: Feminism, Leadership and Educational Change* (UK: Open University Press, 1999).

Index